TIGHTROPE

TIGHTROPE

A Racial Journey to the Age of Obama

Gail Garfield

ROWMAN & LITTLEFIELD
Lanham • Boulder • New York • London

Published by Rowman & Littlefield
A wholly owned subsidiary of
The Rowman & Littlefield Publishing Group, Inc.
4501 Forbes Boulevard, Suite 200, Lanham, Maryland 20706
www.rowman.com

16 Carlisle Street, London W1D 3BT, United Kingdom

British Library Cataloguing in Publication Information Available

Library of Congress Cataloging-in-Publication Data
Garfield, Gail, 1954–
Tightrope : a racial journey to the age of Obama / Gail Garfield.
pages cm
Includes bibliographical references and index.
ISBN 978-1-4422-2423-0 (cloth : alk. paper) — ISBN 978-1-4422-2424-7
(electronic)
1. United States—Race relations—History. 2. Racism—United States—History. 3. Families—United States—History. 4. Group identity—United States—
History. I. Title.
E185.615.G33 2014
305.800973—dc23
2014008855

∞™ The paper used in this publication meets the minimum requirements of
American National Standard for Information Sciences Permanence of Paper
for Printed Library Materials, ANSI/NISO Z39.48-1992.

Printed in the United States of America

In memory of my ancestors, whose wisdom, courage, and creative footprints provided lessons that continue to guide my steps along the racial tightrope.

CONTENTS

ACKNOWLEDGMENTS

My family has taught me what it truly means to be human: how to love when overwhelmed by hate; how to cry out in despair and laugh uncontrollably at the absurdity of it all; how to be cruel, unforgiving, and compassionate; how to be selfish and generous of spirit; and how to accept defeat and struggle against fear. Family is both my source of strength and my weakness, and I thank my family for its many gifts in making this book possible.

Among my friends and colleagues, there are those who simply believed in me. I thank Sandra Morales DeLeon, Barbara Katz-Rothman, Pauline Daniels, Rosemary Barberet, Janice Johnson-Diaz, Antonio (Jay) Pastrana Jr., Janice Holland, Priscilla Simon, and Keith Jackson for reading drafts or lending a critical ear as I tried to figure out how to put the important pieces of my life back together again. Also, words cannot adequately express my gratitude to the staff of the Lloyd Sealy Library at John Jay College of Criminal Justice and, in particular, Karen Okamoto, Janice Dunham, and Nancy Egan.

I am deeply grateful to Kathryn Knigge at Rowman & Littlefield for her guidance and patience and to all of the staff who ushered *Tightrope* through the process of publication.

INTRODUCTION

With the wisdom of maturity and the lessons learned along the way, it is still difficult to predict with any degree of certainty what will unfold in the next moments, days, and years that lie ahead.

We can make detailed plans of how we would like to live our lives, and sometimes everything goes according to those plans; other times, we must adjust them and proceed accordingly. Inevitably, even with the best-laid plans, the unexpected occurs, due largely to conditions created by the plans and actions of others. We cannot control all of the circumstances that life presents to us. Therefore, on our journey we may stumble, or even fall, and fail to reach our chosen destination. Somehow, we usually manage to find a way to pick ourselves up, maybe with help from family or friends, and with a little of our courage restored but our confidence shaken, we continue on, following the dubious path of a well-thought-out plan. After all, we must and do survive even in ungodly situations and outrageous circumstances that threaten our very being.

With frustration built upon these disappointments, we gradually begin to shy away from further planning our life and instead rely more on a known quantity: experience. It says, "Remember, it's better to do this and not that, while hoping for the best." The unpredictability and nuances of life can and do confront us, often in ever-so-subtle ways, dramatically altering our chosen course: more often it is precisely that unpredictability and its nuances that intrude on a life well lived. The unexpected becomes the substance by which history is often made.

This happened on a cold and blustery winter morning, as I watched a solemn Barack Hussein Obama, weighed down by expectations, place his left hand on the Bible, raise his right hand toward heaven, and swear to our nation that he would "faithfully execute the office of President of the United States, and will to the best of my ability, preserve, protect, and defend the Constitution of the United States. So help me God."

Multitudes gathered around the Capitol steps in Washington, D.C., and around televisions across the country to witness this momentous recasting of history. Never before had the United States witnessed such a sight. On January 20, 2009, Obama became the first African American to hold the most powerful executive office in the world. Like many African Americans of my generation, I called my mother on this noteworthy occasion to see whether she, too, was watching what was long thought to be, especially by many in the black community, an improbable historic moment.

Given my life's experiences and its unpredictability, I am better able to brace myself for the worst now, but concurrently, I am thoroughly amazed when the improbable happens. From seemingly out of nowhere on the political landscape the improbable has indeed happened: Barack Hussein Obama has become the forty-fourth president of the United States.

Prior to his meteoric rise on the national political stage, I had no idea he existed. I vaguely recalled a friend, a voracious reader, once suggesting that I read *Dreams from My Father*; of course, at the time I did not. It was not until I was watching the 2004 Democratic National Convention on television that Obama made his presence known to me with his delivery of the keynote address. [1]

As an activist who has lived a life committed to racial and social justice, I wanted to know what this rising political star in the Democratic Party had to say to me. I listened intently as Obama began by talking about his past and how his grandfather had been a cook, a domestic servant in Kenya. This resonated: my mother had also toiled for most of her life as a servant—a maid, cooking in kitchens, cleaning bathrooms, and caring for children in white peoples' homes. However, like slavery, this was by no means a unique aspect of the black experience. So what did Obama have to offer that was new or different in some way from other—particularly black—politicians?

He captured my full attention with something that I had not heard a black public person talk about with such passion since the days of Dr. Martin Luther King—his dream of a better tomorrow where all could flourish regardless of differences. Many black politicians have mastered the art of oratory that is firmly rooted in the oratorical traditions of the black church. But few, even in their eloquence, have openly embraced and reaffirmed the virtues of the United States itself. I suspect it is because of their recognition that generation after generation of African Americans have been systematically excluded from, or not shared equally in, this nation's political and economic greatness, even though we have rendered great and small sacrifices to whatever lies within that greatness. Obama's words on that late summer evening in 2004 painted a striking picture—one in which inclusion overshadowed any exclusion.

Elegant yet complex with masterstrokes, the picture Obama painted was that of the quintessential American dream—the can-do spirit and the "anything is possible here" belief—built largely out of the myths, as well as realities, embodied in the immigrant experience rather than the African American experience. This allowed him to place his own personal journey firmly within that political frame. African Americans were not centrally positioned in his portrayal, but neither were they forgotten—we were, as usual, lingering in the background in his vision of the nation. Obama acknowledged, albeit in ever-so-slight brushstrokes, the fine art of human destruction and the myriad numbers of cruel and brutal acts that can destroy the human spirit, if not life itself; the African American experience was mildly alluded to in those faint hues and tones. Finalizing his artistic masterpiece, he returned to the main theme portrayed on his political canvas: the power of dreams and hopes, even amid the backdrop of human despair and destruction.

All of this was artfully delivered with an absence of anger or recrimination. There was no shame, guilt, or blame meted out, just dreams accompanied by the hope of a better tomorrow for all. In one masterful brushstroke, Obama became the embodiment of an artfully shifted racial drama that has dogged our nation since its founding. Race and race relations are the foundations on which this country's greatness has been crafted, but in Obama's portrait of the country, they are no longer barriers or impediments that inhibit one from realizing his or her full potential. On that summer evening in July, he gave many white Americans exactly what I believe they had so long awaited: in their imaginations, they saw a vibrant picture of a racially neutral society that could celebrate its multicultural inheritance and feel good about it. After all, as tangible proof, there before a national audience was a black man, an African American by choice, who enjoyed the privileges of America's greatness and stood as a true testament to the can-do and "anything is possible" attitude of our nation. The "audacity of hope" indeed. Many Americans could relate to this postracial oratorical picture. Obama's masterpiece received rousing applause.

"Well, now," I thought after watching Obama's speech, "there was nothing particularly new there." I was wrong.

Because I am a sociologist, the framing of this portrayal was not unfamiliar to me, yet something seemed a bit different. I could not readily put my finger on what it was. There was ambiguity. Here was a black man and, more important, an African American by choice, extolling the virtues of America's greatness, based largely on the immigrant rather than the black experience in the United States. I could easily position Obama's speech within the rising political trend, among both political liberals and conservatives alike, which sought to rearticulate and reframe race and race relations in a way that diminished long-standing racial disparities and grievances. Its content reminded me of what Michael Brown and others called the "whitewashing of race"—concomitantly, the whitewashing of racial inequalities and injustices—an attempt to make our thorny, complex, and ugly racial history more palatable to white audiences.[2] So for me, there was nothing particularly new about the content of his address; it was just a slightly different approach to dealing with the complexities of race and race relations in the United States.

Obama seemed well aware of the powerful reaction his portrait would elicit and the potential resonance it would have, particularly among white audiences. His portrayal of the country and his whitewashing of racial disparities and grievances seemed to be a thoroughly crafty and calculated political move. This became clear to me after I finally read *Dreams from My Father: A Story of Race and Inheritance*, in which race and race relations occupy a central theme rather than lingering somewhere in the background, as the subtitle of the book strongly suggests. When he wrote this book, Obama knew that he could not tell his own personal story in the absence of placing America's racial politics fully at the front and center of that telling. As he said in the first lines of the book's preface:

> The story of my family, and my efforts to understand that story, might speak in some way to the fissures of race that have character- ized the American experience, as well as the fluid state of identity— the leaps through time, the collision of cultures—that mark our mod- ern life. [3]

Unlike many black conservative politicians—especially those aligned with the Republican Party, who often placed the legacy and burdens of racial inequality and injustice squarely on the shoulders of African Americans themselves or denied their existence altogether in an at- tempt to garner political and financial support from whites—Obama offered a more temperate and cautious approach to racial politics. As a politician, he neither publicly denies the significance of race, nor does he affirm the importance of race relations in the shaping of American society.

This ambiguous, nonavoiding, and nonaffirming posturing provides a useful disguise that allows a seemingly broader political inclusion. By not focusing directly on the importance of race and race relations, Oba- ma gains greater latitude in order to speak to more universal interests that embrace the dreams and hopes of all. But that ambiguity allows others to impose their particular interpretation on what he seems to symbolize. As he said, "I serve as a blank screen on which people of vastly different political stripes project their own views."[4] Many Americans are becoming increasingly comfortable ignoring the signifi- cance of race in shaping others' social conditions and life opportunities. On his blank screen, racial disparities—and the social injustices that create them—become a dark secret. These blatant contradictions that everybody knows of but nobody openly talks about lurk in the shadows, but in times of trouble they raise their ugly heads to undermine Ameri- ca's greatness. Obama has chosen to walk on a delicate racial tightrope: his dreams, overshadowed by the unpredictability and nuance of race, are balancing on the hope that he will not stumble or fall as the first African American president in history.

I still wonder whether Obama's temperate stance on race and race relations is something more substantial than just a political ploy fitted to the demands and convenience of his political campaign and presidency.

When it is all said and done, maybe partial answers to this question rest in a historical assessment of his effectiveness as president based on his political decisions, agenda, and strategies he pursued. This I leave for other scholars and political pundits to analyze.

Although Obama's political maneuverings intrigue me, I am not merely interested in his political gambits and performance. I am more interested in how we, as a nation, arrived at this improbable and momentous decision to elect the first African American president, given our nation's continuous and turbulent history of race and race relations. Specifically, what interests me are the profound sociopolitical shifts in our national attitudes and behaviors toward race and race relations over the past fifty years. These have introduced important shifts in our social institutions, which in turn have influenced the ways that we engage one another. Whether those shifts are substantial and meaningful or simply a guise cloaked in new wrapping of the "age of Obama" remains to be seen.

Let us be clear: Obama is by no means the first African American to run for the office of president of the United States of America. In 1872, Victoria Woodhull's vice-presidential nominee on the Equal Rights Party ticket was Frederick Douglass, although he did not accept the nomination or campaign on behalf of the party. In 1888, at the Republican National Convention, Douglass received one vote during the roll call for the presidential nomination; again, he was not a serious candidate. Since the late 1800s, there have been too many African American men and women to name here who have sought the nomination of their parties and campaigned for the office of president, but they ran largely on third- or minor-party tickets. Obama is the first black person to actually receive the nomination of a major political party and then win the election for president of the United States. Given our contentious history of race and race relations, why has this occurred?

Some may point to Obama's distinctive family background, intelligence, and political savvy as attributes that set him apart and make him very different from other African Americans who have sought the office of president. Perhaps in the eyes of many—especially white Americans—he is perceived as a special black person, different from the rest; but he is not. While I agree that Obama possesses personal and political attributes that make him well suited to be president, through my eyes, so did Frederick Douglass. Obama's attributes are not unique qualities that other similarly positioned African Americans did not possess. I refuse to believe that his presidential election was based solely on personal attributes, political positions on issues, or simply the fact that he had the wherewithal to strategically and financially outmaneuver his political opponents. While all of these factors surely played a critical role in his election, they are not enough to fully explain why his ascendance to the highest political office in the land occurred at this particular moment in our nation's history.

Furthermore, there will be those who may argue that Obama's election was due to eventuality: it was only a matter of time before an African American would become president. Since all of our prior presidents have been white, middle-aged men, usually arising from the economically and politically elite strata of our society (of which Obama was not a part), on what premises is that eventuality based—timing, luck, fate, or a combination?

As I think back over my life and my relationship to this moment in our history, the questions that interest me have little to do with Obama the person or the charismatic political persona that is Obama and more to do with the sociopolitical shifts in race and race relations that have transpired to make this moment in our nation's history a reality. After all, usually, every four years politicians come and go; but historic moments, as improbable as they may seem, do not just happen. They do not simply pop up on the sociopolitical landscape; rather, they are born out of layers of concerted ideas and actions of the past. The question becomes, then: "What has changed in the nature of race and race relations in our society that has allowed many Americans to move beyond the improbable and claim the possible?" To do as Obama's 2008 political campaign slogan proudly proclaimed—"Yes We Can"—and elect a black man, an African American president, at this particular time in our nation's history? In other words, what has shifted in US racial attitudes and actions, especially over the past fifty years, that has enabled blacks—once the ultimate outcasts—to move, albeit begrudgingly, to a more inclusive and participatory engagement with the social and political formalities of a democratic society?

Tightrope is about race and politics and the precarious steps we have taken to address racial inequalities and injustices on our journey to this age of Obama. Whether acknowledged or not, as Americans, we all take steps on the racial tightrope: it is our unique legacy as a multiracial

nation. This book retraces some of our most significant steps along this
wavering rope: our halting, swaying missteps created by racial fears,
hatred, and anger, which reveal the important imprints of separation
and difference, and the bold, assured, and firm steps, which opened up
possibilities for connection, acceptance, and inclusion. These divergent
steps—teetering between progressive and regressive racial politics, between stifling continuity and meaningful change—have led us to where
we now tread: the age of Obama. It is an ambiguous new age steeped in
contradictions, in which our steps along the racial tightrope are a work
in progress, a history in the making, that will influence who we are and
who we hope to become as a nation.

As a part of this history, this book also retraces some of the delicate
steps that I have taken to balance on this precarious and ever-shifting
racial rope. My particular experience as an African American woman is
retraced through the steps of the black experience: growing up under
the restricted blackness of Jim Crow segregation in the rural South;
becoming a young adult in the cold whiteness of urban Minnesota; and
then moving on to the neither black nor white, but gray racial space of
the multicultural metropolis of New York City.

Tightrope speaks to this nation's attempts to maintain, negotiate,
reconcile, and even transform many of the deeply troubling contradictions of racial inequality and injustice. In entering the age of Obama,
we, as a nation, are seeking to move beyond our deeply embedded
racial history, but racial contradictions in this transformation continue
to foreshadow each step we take. Even though my steps are particular
to me, they follow the larger balancing act in attitudes and behaviors of
the past fifty years that have forced us as a nation to confront fundamental questions of racial identity—"Who am I? Who are you? Are you
a part of us? Are we a part of each other? And are we the same yet
different?" In posing these questions, I posit that they are the keys to
guiding our understanding of how we, as a nation, have stepped into
this racially ambiguous age of Obama.

On its pages, *Tightrope* pursues these questions of individual, collective, and national identity. In claiming those contradictory spaces of
identity that simultaneously separate and unite us as a nation, the meaning of race and race relations is shifting, ever so slightly, before our
eyes. The majority of the American electorate has decided to reelect a
black man, an African American, Barack Hussein Obama, as president

of the United States. The question of identity looms large over the current sociopolitical landscape, where issues of race and race relations played a critical role in the 2012 presidential election. Who governs our nation continues to influence the steps we take along the racial tightrope. Intricately linked to those large steps is my own particular journey, which is presented in this book.

I

WHO AM I?

Race and Family Relations

Who am I?" is a question that I have thought about for most of my life. The answer seemed to vary at any given moment in time and at any particular place; it always depended on my relationship with others and the circumstances surrounding my life at that time. This response, however, is clearly an intellectual abstraction, a guise that reveals very little about who I am and the nature of my life. It is a sociological construct that is partially true: how we see ourselves at any particular moment is largely fashioned out of the various identities we inherit, freely choose, and/or are forced to assume by others. Our self-image is wrapped in the sociopolitical packaging of race, gender, and class. This is largely a theoretical response to a complicated question, made by a trained sociologist but devoid of the texture that is woven with the fine threads of unpredictability and nuance.

I recognize that such a seemingly reasonable response is grossly inadequate for someone searching for answers. It masks, rather than reveals, the nature of my life and how I see myself within it. I think—no, I know—that this intellectual guise, this mask has been carefully created to hide the deeply rooted shame and guilt born out of the lies and humiliation that often accompanied my existence. Therein lies the story of my childhood.

I was born into a large Negro family of hardworking and God-fearing people. Measured by my family's Christian standards of right and wrong, I was born into guilt and shame and the lies and humiliation that came with them. I stepped into a world filled with damning whispers, accusatory looks, and finger-pointing. I entered the world as the embodiment of a moral transgression, a sin. I was born illegitimate, and my birth was yet another disgrace that my mother brought onto the family.

My mother and father were never married, yet I was not necessarily born out of wedlock. It depends on how you interpret the circumstances of my birth. My mother was legally married at the time—to the father of my sister and two older brothers but not to my biological father. On my birth certificate, I was given my mother's legally married surname. Her husband, an alcoholic veteran damaged by the ravages of World War II, walked away—no one knew in what direction—leaving behind my mother to care for five young children: my three older siblings and another brother who was a year younger than I. His biological father was, again, a different man from mine.

All of these relationships made her a black sheep, in a black family, in a rural southern community, where the very existence of black skin was deemed illegitimate under Jim Crow laws and detestable through racial customs of the rural South. Most of my mother's seven siblings were married, and hence, their children occupied the more privileged status of legitimacy under codified, customary, and Christian law.

My mother was young and attractive according to the standards of beauty in the black community at the time—long, straight hair, light complexion, and finely chiseled facial features. Given the nature of her unpredictable relationships with men in her life and the complications this brought, she was left to provide food, clothing, shelter, and care for us as a domestic worker on a maid's salary. Desperate, our very survival hanging in the balance, in the late 1950s my mother made a fateful decision that would forever recast our small family's history. She decided to give up her children, whom she called "the best that I had to give to the world." Immediately after doing so, she went to live with her sister in Miami, to work as a maid in various hotels and homes lining Miami Beach, leaving us behind but by no means forgotten.

Throughout my life, I have felt my mother's abiding presence and have always known the indisputable fact that she loved me. Ever since I can remember, she has never failed to say to me, "I want you to always know that I am your mother and I love you." This known fact, however, was not enough to sustain me. Her declarations of love did not lessen the challenges that threatened my very sense of being, nor did it help me, as a child, answer the ever-lingering question, "Who am I?"

Even though I have no doubts about my mother's love while growing up, I did have grave doubts about whether or not she really cared about me. As a child, early on, I was forced to make a distinction between love and caring. My mother gave off confusing signals by exemplifying sincere words that were followed by meaningless actions; heartfelt promises with the failure to follow through on them. Once, on the way to visit my sister, who had been adopted, while sitting in the back of a smelly Trailways bus, meandering through the back roads of rural Georgia, my mother looked over at me and said in an ever-so-casual voice, "You weren't supposed to be." She did not mean that I was unloved, but rather that she had not planned on having me. At the time, however, what my childish ears heard her say was, "You were unwanted." And my childhood experience seemed to validate what I thought I heard my mother say, regardless of her actual words.

Of course, I have no memories of when my mother moved to Miami or the particular circumstances that led her there because I was only an infant when she left. My early life experiences are pieced together from the memories of other family members, but strangely, their memories have now become my own.

Even though I was born into a large family of aunts, uncles, and cousins, with my grandfather as the patriarch, it appears that they were all hesitant to take on my mother's responsibility, to raise her five children. So she decided to place us individually in adoptive families, and in my mother's reasoning, the best people to offer a loving and caring home were schoolteachers. But everything did not necessarily go according to her plan.

There was no teacher to take my eldest brother, who saw himself as the man of the family and was extremely protective of us younger children. He was old enough to be angry at and resentful of my mother's decision to break up the family. Since no adoptive home could be found for him, my mother's youngest sister agreed to keep my brother temporarily, until my mother resettled and he could be sent to live with her. A married couple, both teachers, adopted my second-eldest brother, who recalls fond memories of sitting in a rocking chair and holding me for hours. A teacher and her husband who lived in nearby Albany, Georgia, adopted my sister. My younger brother's paternal grandmother agreed to raise him. Then, the only one left for adoption was me. But it appears that there was no teacher willing to provide a loving and caring home for me; again, I was unwanted. Another aunt agreed to take me. I do not know what the terms of that arrangement were—whether I stayed with her for a few days, months, or even a couple of years. Whatever the arrangement was, it was not permanent, and eventually I was sent to live with my maternal grandparents.

❃ ❃ ❃

My grandparents moved from Bexar, Alabama, with their seven children, to southwest Georgia in 1926. This was a period when black people in the rural South were on the move; they were searching for lives beyond the appalling racial restrictions of Jim Crow segregation and the violence it wrought. Many headed north, but not my family; they journeyed deeper into the belly of the segregated beast of rural Georgia. The exact reasons they decided to move depend largely on who is telling the story and what they wish to reveal, or, more important, what they want to conceal.

Bexar is an unincorporated rural community that consists largely of a main street with a post office and grocery store. It is an isolated agricultural community located in Marion County, Alabama, in the extreme northwestern part of the state, about three miles from the Mississippi border. My family's origins in Bexar largely evolved from a dispute between two slave-owning brothers, John and Andrew Spearman. The exact nature of that dispute is unknown; however, it resulted in a change of one brother's family name and a division of plantation property. Originally, both brothers lived on the Spearman Plantation, but with the dispute, Andrew decided to drop the suffix "-man" from his surname and became simply Spears while John retained the full name of Spearman. The brothers divided their land as well. A creek that flowed from the Mississippi became the boundary, separating what would become two plantations. On one side of the Sippi Creek, as it was called, was Andrew's property, and on the other side was John's land.

Their property did not include only land. It also included human beings—slaves—who were divided between them as well, regardless of close kin relations. Mothers were taken from fathers, children were torn from parents, and siblings were separated from their sisters and brothers. Following the abolishment of slavery, two interconnected branches of my family appeared: the Spearman branch and the Spears branch. As freed people, neither branch of my family lived in town but rather occupied the outlying areas surrounding Bexar. Most of the people in those outlying areas were related by blood; they were my kinfolk.

When I attempted to piece together the early history of the Spearman side of the family tree, my great uncle said Elvie and Caroline started that branch.[1] Elvie, whom many family members refer to as Elvis, appears to have a history, even though spotty; but the particulars of Caroline's life are largely lost to time.

Elvie, my great uncle said, "was shipped over from the old country by whites and bought by an old white man named Johnny Spearman" at nine years old. Elvie's job on the plantation was to take care of the younger slave children while their parents worked in the fields. My great uncle said:

> The slave master had a big cattle barn with stalls in it. He covered the floor with wheat straw for beds. When the children got hungry, his wife, Mrs. Nancy, would bring a gallon of milk with cornbread crumbled in it. She would pour it in the trough and give the children (that were big enough to feed themselves) wooden spoons to eat with. The ones that were unable to feed themselves, my dad, Elvie, fed them. When one got sleepy, he would lay him down on the hay and cover him up with old bale sacks to keep the flies off or keep him warm while he slept. The mothers came for them at noon to eat dinner and they would bring them back after dinner. He did this job until he was old enough to go to the field. He would do like the rest, hoe and pick cotton and work like a man.

An old, faded, and rumpled picture of Elvie shows that he grew into a tall, thin, dark-complexioned man with finely chiseled facial features. His penetrating eyes look beyond the immediate frame of the picture. What did this old ex-slave see? Could he see or even imagine the faces of future generations of his offspring living as doctors, lawyers, and ministers, as well as crooks and criminals? What about those in between who were just trying to make it through another day toiling for their living? Could he see me and wonder at my possibilities as I looked back into his staring eyes and wondered about his life as human chattel? All I know for sure is that he saw Caroline, a short, plump, fair-skinned slave woman who had been purchased from someone named Johnson in South Carolina. She, too, was now an ex-slave standing beside Elvie, holding tightly to her purse. With the slave owner's permission, they married or at least made a life with each other.

Sometime during their union, the slave master told Elvie that "he could have three acres of land if he would clean it for a cotton patch," so he could make a little money on the side. He continued to work in the master's cotton field from dawn to dusk, but on his free day, Sunday, he worked his own patch of land. Following slavery, "old man Johnny Spearman sold him 400 acres of land for $40.00. He told him that he could pay $1.00 a year until it was paid for." The first year Elvie paid him $5.00, and he kept paying until the debt was paid off.

Meanwhile, Elvie and Caroline started a family; they had twelve children, five boys and seven girls. Elvie made good use of his land, and being industrious, he was able to purchase additional property from his old slave master. He was so successful that he "gave each boy 40 acres of land and a horse and saddle. He gave the girls 40 acres each and a cow and pig." Elvie and Caroline also donated the land on which the family church was built and where the family cemetery is located. Before he passed, Elvie gave the remainder of his land to his grandchildren. Today, some of my relatives still own and live on the land that Elvie and Caroline purchased from John Spearman, but many have moved away from Bexar, Alabama.

Not much is known about the Spears side of the family, except for the fact that Isaac was once a slave on the Spears plantation, and his wife, Ellen, was a Cherokee who joined him there. Together they had four children. The details of their lives are lost on the unwritten pages of history.

But what is known is that both Spearman and Spears blood run throughout my family's veins.

In 1926, my grandparents decided to leave the land that Elvie and Caroline bequeathed to the family and moved to Beachton, a hamlet about ten miles outside of Thomasville, Georgia. The way my mother told me the story is that the family left Bexar because of "religious persecution." She said there was tension in the family church, and "my father thought it would be better to move to Georgia." "Religious persecution" suggests that my grandparents and their children were forced to flee because their safety was threatened because of some violation of the deeply held religious beliefs and practices in Bexar. To me, this sounded like an extremely vague and suspicious reason for their packing up and moving to another state, leaving all they knew behind. My mother never provided specific details to back up her account. Maybe that was because her explanation was largely a guise, a revision of our family's history in an attempt to put it into a more favorable light. But I cannot recall a time when my mother blatantly lied to me, so I suspect there might be a grain of truth in her account.

My family's religious beliefs are rooted in the Congregational Church, which is affiliated with the American Missionary Association (AMA). The AMA was founded to prepare ministers and teachers to serve the newly freed slave community, so schools associated with Congregational churches were established toward that endeavor. When my immediate family moved farther southward, they were not the first group of relatives to pick up and leave Bexar; rather, they were following a path that other family members had already made. The first group of family members followed Reverend Hanna from Bexar to Beachton in 1911. This first wave of relatives helped to organized the Evergreen Congregational Church.

In 1955, a twenty-three-year-old pastor—fresh out of divinity school and a newly ordained minister—became head minister of the Bethany Congregational Church in Thomasville, Georgia, and Evergreen Congregational Church in Beachton, Florida. He was Andrew Young, the future civil rights leader and the first black representative from Georgia in Congress since the Reconstruction era. Young would go on to be the mayor of Atlanta, Georgia, and later, United Nations ambassador from the United States. Recalling his time spent as the spiritual head of Evergreen in his book *An Easy Burden*, Young said:

> The history of Evergreen Church fascinated me. The Evergreen congregation had moved to south Georgia en masse from Alabama. They were forced to flee in 1911 when their minister, who was trained in an AMA school, was discovered teaching his members to read, write, and count. The local whites terrorized the minister and gave him twenty-four hours to leave the county. He left, but only to find a new home for the entire congregation. He came back, and one amazing night the entire congregation packed their belongings and left Alabama forever, settling in Beachton, Florida, not far from the Florida state line. I learned from Mrs. Flipper [the mother of Henry Ossian

Flipper, the first black cadet to graduate from the US Military Academy at West Point in 1877] that they chose Beachton because Allen Normal School was there. They wanted the children to be educated even though then, as now, the only employment in the Thomasville area was work on plantations.

Evergreen congregation was so loving and accepting that I quickly became comfortable. . . . No matter what I said, Deacon Spearman [my grandfather] hummed "True," or "Well, praise the Lord!"[2]

On reading Young's narrative, I wondered how far off target my mother's account of my family's history really was. Did she confuse religious persecution with that of racial persecution? Or, through her eyes, were they one and the same? If Young is correct, which migratory path did my mother choose to embrace as her own family lore—the first wave, in 1911, when family members followed Reverend Hanna to Beachton? Or the second wave of migrants, led by my grandparents, in 1926?

My mother's nobler telling of my family's journey from Alabama to Georgia differs from the tales told by other family members. I tend to believe their stories are a bit closer to the truth of why my grandparents and their children ended up in southwest Georgia. They say that my family migrated because of the extent that intermarriage occurred between family members. Given the rural isolation of Bexar, inhabited mainly by genetically related kinfolk, it is by no means surprising, at least not to me, that family members married each other. To outsiders, this might appear shameful, especially for those who uphold Christian values, but it may have been those same values that led to my family's journey farther southward.

My grandparents broke with the cultural norms of their community by refusing to allow their children to continue the tradition of marrying kinfolk, even though my grandparents, too, were the product of intermarrying. There are differing opinions within the family as to whether my grandparents were first or second cousins, both, or some form of double kin. Because of the extent of intermarrying, it is hard to determine how older family members fit into our family tree and exactly how they were related. (Added to this issue, there is extensive use of recycled names within my family.) Consequently, there are many double kin relationships as a result of the blending of the Spearses and Spearmans—for instance, I spoke with an older cousin whose mother was my

grandmother's sister, and they were Spearses; her father was my grandfather's brother, and they were Spearmans; thus, my cousin's parents
through lineage and marriage were my great aunt and uncle on both the
Spears and Spearman branches of the family. My grandfather's surname was Spearman, and my grandmother's maiden name Spears, but
there is no dispute that both Elvie and Caroline's, as well as Isaac and
Ellen's, blood pulsated through each of their veins and that they were
indeed closely related.

My brother once told me he heard that all of the people in Bexar
looked the same, and they looked just like us. I asked whether they all
had six fingers and six toes, and we had a good laugh. However, this was
no laughing matter to my mother; in matters such as this, she was
extremely protective of our family's reputation, to a fault.

❂ ❂ ❂

Arriving in rural southwest Georgia, about thirty miles from the Florida
border, my grandparents and their family took any kind of housing and
work they could find. They immediately became sharecroppers, living
and working on a piece of land belonging to a white man named Anderson. As landless tenant farmers, they tilled the land for a share of the
profit from the crops they grew. This was a legal arrangement; during
the 1920s, about three million black farmers worked under such an
agreement. Their labor was exploited, and they were cheated out of
their share of the crops. Sharecropping was a way of maintaining the
racial status quo between blacks and whites through legal means; it was
extremely difficult for sharecroppers to provide for their families, let
alone escape their indentured servitude, through subsistence farming.

Somehow, my family managed to break free of the legal entangle-
ments of this system. My mother said the family "couldn't stay because
the white man my father was renting from wanted all of the crop and
gave my father little after he had raised all of the crop." Managing to get
away, my family ended up at Pebble Hill Plantation.

Surrounding my hometown of Thomasville, nestled among the thick
Georgia pines, aromatic magnolias, and oaks draped in moss, are more
than seventy antebellum plantations. They are no longer working agri-
culture farms but largely tourist attractions or winter vacation homes.
Many are owned by wealthy white northerners who bought the man-

sions during the Reconstruction era. During the 1930s, several family members went to work at one of the largest plantations, Pebble Hill, owned by Kate Benedict Hanna Ireland. Her father had given her the three thousand acre farm as a gift in 1901.

When my family arrived, Pebble Hill was a sprawling and seemingly all-encompassing farm that had been turned into a hunting plantation: quail, pheasants, and wild turkeys were valued game and abounded in the area. A large gatehouse guarded the entrance to the estate, and the centerpiece of the plantation was the grand mansion, which was surrounded by guest cottages, a tennis court, and a swimming pool. The kitchen and laundry facilities were located in a separate building, with a full staff of cooks and washerwomen. A carriage house and garage, nurse's office, small firehouse with a fire engine, carpenter's shop, and pump house dotted the landscape. But the prize facilities were the horse stables, dog kennels, a veterinary hospital, and a cow barn that was patterned after the architecture of the University of Virginia, which was designed by Thomas Jefferson.

Even though this was not the antebellum plantation of old, the cultural remnants of that past clearly had a haunting presence. This self-contained hunting farm required cheap labor in order to function.[3] Around a hundred people worked at Pebble Hill in various capacities during the 1930s, and most of the employees were black, working menial jobs. Because Pebble Hill is located outside of town, most of the black workers and their families lived on the plantation—not on the sprawling estate itself but in the surrounding woods. About forty families lived in plantation housing, interspersed throughout the dense woods, and a small elementary school and church were located there as well. Not only were families' working lives structured by their jobs on the plantation, but also their leisure time. There was a baseball team, weddings, funerals, Easter egg hunts, and picnics for black workers at Pebble Hill. My mother felt that Mrs. Hanna was a benevolent manager toward her black workers.

My grandfather's job at Pebble Hill was to tend to the needs of the hunting dogs. He worked from morning till night; this was his job until he retired. Like others who worked there, my family initially lived on plantation property. When my grandfather's oldest daughter and her husband managed to acquire ten acres of land from Pebble Hill and gave my grandparents an acre, they built a family home in the country.

Still working at Pebble Hill, my grandfather settled into life as a small landowner, raising chickens and growing corn and other vegetables in his garden. My grandmother cooked on an old, cast-iron, wood-burning stove; hand washed clothes on a scrub board on the back porch; and made quilts in the dim light of kerosene lamps.

By the late 1950s, my grandparents were advancing in age and exhausted from their well-lived lives. They were too old and tired to raise me, a baby. When my aunt, who cooked at Pebble Hill, decided for whatever reasons that she could no longer take care of me, my grandparents temporarily assumed this responsibility. I do not know how long I actually lived with them since, as I was a baby, I have no memory of this period of my life; but suffice it to say, I did not stay. Once again in my brief life, I was shuffled off to another home.

Returning from Florida and desperate to find a home for me, my mother, along with my grandfather, asked another teacher whether she would be willing to adopt me. Her name was Madea. It was while living with Madea's family, my other family, that the question of "Who am I?" began to crystallize and take on importance.

∘ ∘ ∘

Like all children, I had no say in what kind of family I was born and raised in. I made do, accepted what was offered, learned to adjust, and the routine of family life—whether adequate or inadequate for my needs—became normal. Even though constrained by immaturity, in fundamental ways I gradually learned to express my likes and dislikes. Most often I acquiesced and obeyed the demands placed on me; sometimes I made attempts to manipulate the situation; and other times I resisted or rebelled in the face of overpowering rules and expectations. Vulnerable and susceptible to the will of adults around me, my very survival depended on the decisions and actions of those who assumed responsibility for my livelihood.

As an adult, I have come to accept that Madea was neither a "good" nor a "bad" substitute mother. She made good and bad decisions and raised me within the tremendous racial limitations placed on her own life.

Clearly, she was a giving woman, especially when there was no one else. Madea provided me a home. She was ever confronted with the challenges that come with a lack of resources and professional opportunities, which limited her ability, as head of the family, to be an effective provider. She gave what she had to give, but that does not imply that her giving was always sufficient or acceptable. At times she was self-sacrificing, indulgent, and protective of me; at other times she was cruel, selfish, unforgiving, and insensitive to my needs. These glaring contradictions made Madea both an adequate as well as inadequate parent.

Contrary to my mother's intent and dissimilar from my sister's and brothers' experiences, I was never legally adopted. My siblings were the only children in their respective households and were adopted by families that were quite small and, very important, financially secure. Madea's household was completely the opposite. It was filled with females: her mother, two sisters—her third sister was married and living with her husband—and another girl who would become an important part of my life, my adopted sister.

Like all of the other black teachers in town, Madea taught elementary school—second grade—in a racially segregated school, Douglass Elementary. She garnered the respect and esteem of the black community for being a college-trained professional, able to practice her craft yet limited by racial inequality. On a small teacher's salary, dispensed on a monthly basis, Madea was the breadwinner of the family. She constantly struggled to make ends meet, especially when it came to providing food around the end of each month. My grandmother was crippled from a stroke, one aunt did washing and ironing for white people, and the other did whatever seemed right to her at any given moment because she was mentally disabled. Their lives and the constantly struggle to make ends meet created a stressful dynamic that had an indelible impact on my life and self-image.

Madea, a short, brown-skinned woman, was the oldest of her siblings. She had married, but her husband died years before my sister and I were taken in, and she never had a child of her own. Her three sisters were childless as well. My sister and I were Madea's children. In parenting, she was strict. We had to adhere to her rules, and she took the old cliché "Spare the rod and spoil the child" to heart. It seems that the rod was never spared, and we certainly were not spoiled. We were beaten, and we were beaten often. Obstinacy, willfulness, defiance, and of course blatant disobedience of any kind to Madea's rules simply were not tolerated in her house, regardless of the situation.

I stepped into Madea's world as a toddler. My sister, who is three years older than I, says that I was about three years old when I came to live with Madea. What she remembers most about my arrival is that I was constantly eating crumbs off the floor, whether out of habit or because I was hungry. Based on her memories, my arrival at Madea's was not pleasant. I was a sickly child with whooping cough, and it seems that whenever I ate off the floor, Madea would yell at me to stop, and in response, I would go into fits of coughing. Apparently, Madea grew tired of my coughing and started to spank me when I had a fit. My sister said that she "felt sorry for [me]," and once told Madea to beat her instead. Madea did exactly that, and she learned an important lesson— after that beating, she "didn't take up for [me] anymore." Maybe it was partly because she had her own beatings to contend with.

We lived in a house that Madea's father had built, the last house at the end of a clay-packed dirt road. When it rained, the soft red clay became muddy and stuck to the soles of your shoes and, if you were barefoot, oozed between your toes. The street was lined on one side with houses, and on the other side was a large pecan orchard. During pecan season, in the winter months of October, November, and December, the tall trees, with their spreading, leafless limbs, were heavy with the weight of the ripening nuts, and then the pecans would fall. During pecan season, my sister and I were required to slip through a small hole in the fence, put the falling pecans in a burlap sack, and then bring our stolen goods home to be taken to the pecan market. Usually our booty would fetch about three or four dollars, of which most would be given to Madea to buy food. My memories of those times linger vividly in my hands and fingers, because with no gloves for protection, they became frostbitten. Even now, they cannot tolerate cold without becoming extremely swollen and paralyzed.

This was not the only work that we were required to do outside of the home in order to contribute to the well-being of the household and to help make ends meet for the family. I also swept the floors of a black-owned insurance office, my sister babysat white children, and we did any other odd job for a quarter or fifty cents. Stealing pecans was simply one of the more dramatic areas of work—but it was nothing compared to the work Madea did, whether legal, illegal, or quasi-legal.

Besides teaching, during school events she would often sell candy apples to make a little money. When school was out for the summer months, she was not too proud to find a temporary job cleaning white people's houses. She was an avid numbers player, an illegal lottery of sorts played in the black community. This was nothing particularly unusual in our community; the numbers man could be seen darting in and out of everybody's house. Madea kept a copy of a dream book to readily find the number that was associated with a particular dream on her nightstand, and we got the *Pittsburgh Courier* newspaper to see what numbers would be hidden in Sonny Boy's cartoon. She would recall her nighttime dreams and check the numbers that were assigned to them, check Sonny Boy's pick of the day, and then place a bet, usually no more than a quarter or fifty cents unless she felt sure or lucky, when she would place a dollar bet. My sister and I were also encouraged to remember our dreams for checking, and if Madea played a number based on our dreams, she would often give us a nickel or dime if it worked out, and we would immediately head to the store to buy penny candy.

Out of all of Madea's extra jobs, it was her gambling at the racetrack that created the most tension in our household, mainly because of the gossip it caused. With her other friends—not those who were teachers—Madea would trek several times a week to bet on the races at the dog track, which was located in northern Florida, about an hour's drive from our hometown. There she would bet on the races. Most times she would only break even, but sometimes she was lucky—those were good family times and major grocery-shopping occasions, and my sister and I would always get a sweet of some kind.

Playing the numbers was okay, but a woman, a teacher no less, going to the racetrack and betting on dogs was viewed as unacceptable, particularly by churchgoing people. The word got around, and it created confusion and chaos in the household. My grandmother and aunts were not necessarily against gambling—on occasion they, too, would place a bet on a number—but rather objected to Madea risking the little money we had on a bet. They also felt that going up and down the highway to the dog track was not suitable for a woman of her position. My aunt, especially, would have violent arguments with Madea about this; sometimes she would take Madea's keys from her or hide them to prevent her from leaving. During those times, my heart would break as Madea cried in defeat. In addition to the possibility of bringing home winnings, I think Madea's going to the races and socializing with her friends was probably her only real pleasure and joy in life.

Meanwhile, I was developing into an extremely shy and introverted child; my sister called me "strange." Forced to do things that I did not want to do, I began to gradually resent the demands Madea placed on me. One of my most humiliating experiences as a child was when Madea forced me to visit my father every Friday afternoon.

Yes, I knew who my father was and was well aware of him.

Whenever my mother had a week off from work, she would come back home for a visit, ostensibly to see how her children were doing. On these visits, she would come and get me, and we would stay at my grandparents' house in the country. My mother was different from the other women in my life: she possessed a flamboyant air and was stylishly dressed; she doted on me and gave me kisses; and in her presence, I felt truly special. When she came into town, one of the things that we would always do together was visit my father. A tall, brown-skinned, handsome man with stooped shoulders, he cut an imposing presence. He lived in a large house with his companion, a dark-complexioned woman, who was also a teacher at my elementary school. She hated my mother and resented my very being. Even so, my mother was sometimes bold enough to visit my father at home, but usually we would go to the pool hall instead.

My father owned the pool hall—a dark, smoky place filled with men standing around smoking cigarettes or shooting pool. He sat in a large chair on a small platform in the corner, keeping a watchful eye over the establishment. Next door was a small greasy spoon that he also owned. Both establishments were located in a neighborhood known as the Bottom, the black part of town. Whenever we appeared, my father always smiled and was cordial and solicitous of my mother. He would take her to his restaurant to sit and talk, and I trudged along. Eventually, the conversation would turn to me, and my mother would always tell my father what I needed and ask him to give me some money. He never failed to do so in her presence, but he would express his reservations, believing that his money would go only toward Madea's betting and gambling on dogs. When I returned home from my stay with my mother, I would promptly give Madea the money that my father had given me.

In the rare moments when my father and I would have a conversation, he would tell me that my mother was the prettiest woman he had ever seen. For her part, my mother said he was always asking her to marry him. She refused because, as she said, "he was too smart for me and he would try to run my life." Instead she wanted to marry a "stupid man so I could tell him what to do." Everyone knew that my father was smart, with a master's degree in business; but only my mother and father knew the true nature of their relationship. Everyone else also seemed to know that he had a terrible temper and that he was not a man to be messed with; people were fearful of what he might do. My mother would tell me that she "could handle my father," and I believed her. I could not handle him, but I was not afraid of him either. As a child, I loved my father because I was supposed to love him, not because he merited or earned my affection.

In fact, he was often mean and cruel to me. He resented Madea sending me to the pool hall every Friday to ask for lunch money, thinking that she wanted the money only for gambling. Sometimes, as I approached the door of his pool hall, he would yell and tell me to go away. If I made it through the door, he would often talk harshly to me and send me away empty-handed. But there were other times when I think he simply felt sorry for me and out of pity would give me a dollar or two. I do not know whether he was embarrassed or ashamed that his illegitimate daughter would turn up at his place of business asking for money, or whether he simply thought the pool hall was an inappropriate place for a child. My visits were a public spectacle; the men playing pool would pretend not to see or hear me, a small child, beg my father for lunch money and then often be yelled at in return. I dreaded going to the pool hall but went obediently every Friday. Afterwards, I would hate myself for actively participating in my own humiliation, but I began to hate Madea even more for making me do so.

Madea knew how my father felt about her and how he treated me in retaliation. Male friends who frequented the pool hall told her each week what was happening, but Madea insisted on my going anyway. My mother also knew what was going on, but to my knowledge said nothing to Madea about it. To help out, my mother would occasionally send money to Madea or send me clothes for the start of the school year.

As my resentment gradually turned into anger toward Madea, I began to rebel. I do not recall how old I was, but I stopped visiting my father. This meant that there might not be money available to buy school lunch for my sister and me, though often Madea would find money from somewhere to pay for our lunches, because she did not want the other teachers gossiping.

As a result of my growing anger and rebellion, the beatings grew more intense and crueler. I remember one time, when I was eight years old, that Madea beat me until my arms and legs were covered with welts that were full of blood. I cannot seem to recall the precipitating incident—it might have been the first time that I talked back to her—but it was the worst beating that I had ever received from her up until that point. Usually she used a belt or a switch from a tree to do the whipping. That time it was a switch, but I was determined not to cry, while she was equally determined to make my tears flow. They did, and when she finished, the blood was ready to burst forth from the marks on my body. My grandmother tried to come to my defense by saying to Madea, "You shouldn't beat that child like that," but Madea dismissed her appeal. She believed that her mother was intervening only because I was fair complexioned, not because of the harm that beating causes to a child.

Not only was my body seriously scarred from this beating, but also my very sense of being. My self-esteem had been thoroughly violated, and I was deeply embarrassed by the welts on my body. What wrong could a child commit to deserve such treatment?

Madea beat me into silence. Following this and subsequent beatings, I would go for weeks without uttering a word to anyone in the household. When this happened, ironically, it was Madea's younger, mentally disabled sister who would always taunt me, saying, "You are crazy, just like my mother." It was my sister who often helped me find my voice again. Whenever there was a dispute between us, she was always the first one to make amends. She simply hated for me to be mad at her or not talk to her, for any reason. During my silences, those periods of time when my sense of personal violation was so overwhelming, my sister was more determined than ever to make me laugh. Her silliness and laughter helped me to survive. I give her full credit and my sincerest appreciation for her help during this difficult time.

I was miserable! I would write to my mother, pleading for her to come and get me; or when she visited, I begged her to please take me back to Florida with her. I needed her to take me out of that situation.

The best she could do was offer a temporary respite—as I grew older, during the summers my mother started to send for me. I would stay with her for several weeks or for the whole summer, and sometimes my brothers and sister who had been adopted would join us. My mother, by then married to my stepfather, had to get up at around 4:00 a.m. in order to get to her job as a maid. Usually, her husband would drive her to work on Miami Beach before he went to his job as a janitor at the post office.

Until they returned home, there were no rules. I could eat anything I wanted for breakfast, watch television, read, have lunch, and visit with other children. I had the whole day to myself. My mother always seemed to be in a good mood and was never angry. She made few, if any, demands on me.

For reasons unknown to me, I always had to return home to Madea's house. While I lived there, I had little contact with the other members of my large family who lived in the area. I cannot remember a time when any of my aunts and uncles visited me at Madea's house. If I saw them or their children, it was when my mother came to town. We would go to their houses, or they would come to my grandparents' house for a visit. I missed the relationships that I never had with them, but mostly I felt alone, abandoned, and unwanted.

Then, the unexpected and unimaginable began to happen—people started to leave my life. At various times during the 1960s, people left. My grandmother—Madea's mother—died; my aunt—Madea's sister— got married and moved to New Jersey; and my sister went away to attend high school. I missed her most of all. She was accepted into a national program, A Better Chance (ABC), that started in 1963, at the height of the civil rights movement. In an attempt to address academic racial disparities, ABC started to "cream" by taking the brightest black students in racially segregated schools and providing them with an opportunity to attend select and largely all-white public and private high schools up north. Because she was a good student, my sister was selected to participate, and she left home for Minnesota in 1967. When she did, only Madea, her youngest sister, and I remained.

Shortly thereafter, Madea was diagnosed with late-stage uterine cancer. For the next year and a half, she suffered tremendous pain and agony from her illness. As she began to die, I became responsible for this proud woman's basic needs. I made sure that she was clean and had taken her medication; I prepared all of the meals, cleaned the house, and washed the clothes; and I did all of the necessary errands. I was responsible for everything else that kept the family functioning. Madea was still receiving her small teacher's salary, and we managed, with the help of her married sister and friends. But the day-to-day responsibilities were largely mine, even though, as a child, I was not adequate for the job. It was extremely stressful and tiring. I would sometimes miss days from school, but I was not resentful. I did not mind caring for Madea's needs.

As I look back now on Madea's life—my other mother—I recall that she was never affectionate toward me. I cannot remember ever receiving a hug or a kiss from her, but what she gave me was what she had: a home. I needed a home, even though it came with physical and emotional pain. She also taught me one of the most important lessons that I would ever learn in life: the meaning of compassion. For this I am grateful, and I will never forget it. I do not know if she loved me, but I do know that she cared for me when there was no one else willing to provide food, clothing, and shelter. Madea tried to do the right thing. I think she did not adopt me because she really could not afford the legal cost of doing so.

I define caring as a concrete action: for me, it is what you do in an attempt to prevent or alleviate the pain of others. Your effort may be completely inadequate or not ideal; you may not completely rise to the occasion at the moment, but at least you try to interrupt what is surely to come. It is the kind of thing that would happen when I would ride with Madea in the front seat of the car and she would need to slam on the brakes—her large protective arm would immediately extend toward me in an attempt to prevent my body from smashing into the dashboard. Madea died from cancer, and I stood before her grave with tears rolling down my cheeks. I had compassion for Madea's indomitable spirit and admired how she fought for her life against incredible odds. But my tears were also for myself and the uncertainty of what would happen to me next.

* * *

I have not experienced that process by which a woman negotiates the day-to-day demands of motherhood along with her desire to utilize her abilities and talents to the fullest extent possible. I am childless by choice. My decision, I know, is deeply rooted in the trajectory of my own childhood experience. I decided that if, through my own efforts, I could not provide adequate food, clothing, and shelter as well as a stable, secure, and loving home, I would not bring a child into the world. This was not a purely economic decision; I considered very seriously the quality of life that I could provide for a child. It was a planned decision that went against cultural and social norms and, for some people, challenged the very essence of what it means to be a woman. Over the years, I have endured the sly suggestions and opinions of others who deemed me incomplete without a child—dare I say a husband—to make me whole. But I still maintain that the quality of a child's life is as significant as life itself, and there are many examples of hurt, harm, and simple cruelty to children on which to draw.

My decision is deeply personal, and I have embraced the implications and consequences it holds for my life: I render no judgment on other women who have also made different and difficult decisions about their lives, although those decisions may have been different from mine. My decision was made possible only because of the sacrifices made and the price paid by other women who had more limited choices. My mother paid an enormous price for the sacrifices she made in giving what she thought was the best she had to the world and in trying to make a better life for her children and herself. Not only did it take tremendous courage to give up her children, but that decision also took a tremendous toll on her life. I have often wondered whether my decision not to have children was substantially different from the one my mother made in giving up her children. She brought us into the world but could not take care of us. My mother negotiated the best she could out of her life as a single mother of five children and as a black woman limited by racial inequality and injustice. What of her dreams and what of her hopes?

When my mother moved to Florida in the early 1960s, she had little difficulty in finding a job as a maid working for resort hotels on Collins Avenue, next to the pristine, sandy beaches of Miami. There was always work to be had cleaning up the waste and filth of wealthy white people. After finding her footing and getting the lay of the land, she mostly worked for white families on the beach. Initially, when she moved, her intention was to save enough money and go back home to Georgia to "build a large house for me and my children." But as my mother said, "Once you get that Miami sand in your shoes, you can't leave." She stayed in Miami for thirty years.

Never unemployed, my mother worked for a number of households and did a variety of jobs. She once told me the only thing that she would not do was get down on her hands and knees and scrub floors, and if such a request was made, she quit. Usually, my mother liked working in homes where there were children. Maybe she could shower on them what she could not give to her own children. Maybe children were more pleasant to be around, and the power relations between them were not as stark as those between my mother and her white bosses. Or maybe it was because of the added benefits of working with families who had children—they had useful items they discarded, such as clothing and toys, which she could take and send to her own children. Often she did just that.

I cannot recall a time when my mother said that the people she worked for were ever intentionally mean or cruel to her. Friendly, with an easy laugh, she was accommodating to their needs but was never a live-in maid. Generally, she would start her day at around 6:00 a.m. each morning, except for Sundays, by preparing breakfast. During the mid-1960s, while working for a wealthy woman, something different happened one morning. My mother said, "Normally, I would serve her, but this particular morning, she wanted to serve me." Taking the last sip of her coffee, "I went haywire and did not know exactly at that time what was going on with me," she said. The woman had spiked my mother's coffee with LSD, a psychedelic drug that produces hallucinations by altering cognition and perception, to see how she would react. My mother reacted badly to the drug.

Consequently, she was committed to a psychiatric hospital for six months; she said, "The doctors said that my nerves were shattered." When this happened, I was a child, and Madea told me that my mother had a nervous breakdown. Still, I heard whispers—I do not recall from where or by whom—that speculated that it was due largely to the stress brought on by her decision to give up her children rather than solely a reaction to the white woman's abusive action. I do not know whether it was the LSD alone or the LSD in tandem with the pressure she felt over her ever-haunting decision to give her children up, but I do know that the next time I saw my mother, following her stay in the psychiatric hospital, she seemed different to me. The light that had shone so brightly in her was dimmer; something inside her had been lost, and she would never fully regain it or recover from the incident. Repeatedly during her life, she returned to psychiatric hospitals for care.

My mother's decision to give up her children caused her to carry a heavy burden of shame and guilt. It was omnipresent. It was in the way she talked, embellishing the truth and never being completely forthright; it was in the way she walked, with a cautious gait, slowed by fear of judgment from others; and it was in her laughter, when it appeared at inappropriate moments. My mother's decision was always there, lurking in the shadows of her life, and as her children, those dark shadows became a part of our lives as well.

Weighed down by shame and guilt, my mother lacked the tools for raising her children successfully. My eldest and youngest brothers especially added to her burden by drawing the dark shadows out into the open for her to see. My eldest brother is about ten years older than I. I do not know of his dreams and hopes, only that they were never realized. When my mother resettled in Miami, my eldest brother went to live with her; on the occasions when I visited my mother during the summer, I rarely saw him; he had moved out of the house and was living his own life.

He was the darkest of my siblings. He was simply beautiful, with shiny eyes and a warm and easy smile. He was a ladies' man, but the last summer I saw my brother, he was completely broken and ravaged by alcoholism. When he drank, his unmasked anger was often aimed at my mother. Out of fear, she would usually lock the doors of her house so that he could not gain entry, but she could not lock out the contours of pain on her face from having to do so. That pain is indescribable. My brother would stand in my mother's yard yelling, cursing, and calling her all kinds of names for the world to hear and see. He never got over the anger and disappointment he felt from my mother's decision. Like his father, he, too, would one day walk away forever, and my other siblings and I do not know in what direction he went. I miss the relationship that I never had with him.

Meanwhile, my youngest brother's paternal grandmother died when he was about thirteen years old. Upon her death, he, too, went to live with my mother in Miami. Working long hours, my mother and her husband would leave the house before daylight broke and return during the setting of the sun. This gave my brother unfettered freedom from rules and restrictions, and he took full advantage by running the streets of Miami. My mother's guilt would not allow her to say no to his demands, no matter how unreasonable they were.

Shortly after his arrival in Miami, he harassed my mother into buying him a BB gun that had the appearance of a .45 Magnum handgun. The outcome was predictable. After playing with the gun, he and a friend decided to go into a convenience store to purchase sodas. On entering, they were met by a hail of gunfire; buckshot peppered his body, and one pellet lodged so close to his heart that it was deemed more risky to remove it than to just leave it in his body. My brother was near death, but after weeks of intensive care, his youthful body slowly recovered.

This incident only heightened my mother's sense of guilt and shame. After almost losing him, she overcompensated in her permissiveness toward him. My brother took full advantage of the situation and did whatever came to mind. He dropped out of school and started taking and selling drugs. As a juvenile offender, he was constantly reprimanded and placed in detention by the judge. My mother, ever the apologist, was complicit by accepting and watching his glaring self-destructive, illegal activities. At times she even participated by depositing large amounts of drug money into her bank account and attempting to justify this action as a way of getting him to save for his future. Over the years, my brother and mother became dependent on each other's weaknesses. As an adult, he would spend most of his life in and out of prison. What of his dreams and hopes?

Once, while in college, I tried to help, sending for him to come and live with me so that he could get a new start in life. One evening, after finishing dinner, we talked about what was important to him. Unflinchingly, he told me that all he wanted out of life "was a bitch with a car." I neither saw myself as a "bitch" nor owned "a car." Deeply offended by his remarks, I borrowed money from a friend (at the time I was a struggling undergraduate student trying to make ends meet with limited resources) and immediately sent him back to my mother.

I distanced myself from my brother and his self-destructive behavior, but I loved him and could never completely abandon him. I detested the pain and misery he brought on others, especially those people who were important to him. I was insistent that he take responsibility for his decisions and actions, but I could not stand to see my brother confined to a cage like an animal, so I never visited him in jail or prison. I would write and send small amounts of money to him. My mother would visit him whenever she could.

Always thrilled when he got out of prison, my mother gradually accepted the trajectory of his life and joked that he was only on vacation and would soon return to his real home. For his part, my brother blamed and placed the responsibility for his perils on my mother. He was also envious of our brother and sister, who had been adopted, and of me, for having been raised in what he thought was a loving and caring home. He felt that we had been provided with opportunities that he had not had. We, he believed, had a real chance in life. He could never reconcile the fact that as an adult, it was he, rather than my mother, who was responsible for his own decisions and actions. He once said to me that although he had done "bad things" in life, he had never killed anyone. I was deeply saddened by his remarks and the extremely low baseline he set in judging his own value. My brother's life became a cruel cycle of using and selling drugs and going in and out of prison up until the point of his death. He died homeless, in Miami, in May 2011, two years after my mother's passing, almost to the day.

Growing up, I occupied a place where dreams and hopes had largely been abandoned. Succinctly, I was a child who grew up in rural poverty with people who did their best to provide a loving and caring home. Amid the unpredictability and nuisances of living on the social and economic margins, demarcated by the rigidity of racial divisions in the United States, sometimes their best was simply not good enough.

Family history and my place within it as a child provides only a partial reference for the question "Who am I?" My other reference is rooted in the rural southern community, where white supremacist cultural norms and racial expectations of Jim Crow segregation of the 1960s dominated social life. This broader community environment played an important role in shaping my view of self; it provides a deeper understanding of not only who I was as a Negro child but who we were as a community and what we came to value as a society during the 1960s.

2

WHO WERE WE?

Race Relations in the Jim Crow South

When I stepped out of Madea's house, I immediately entered another world. I stepped onto the streets of Thomasville, Georgia. My hometown is nestled between the much larger cities of Albany, Georgia, to the north and Tallahassee, Florida, to the south. As a child, even though I occasionally traveled to these cities visiting relatives or family friends, Thomasville was my home and the only world with which I was truly familiar.

My days were often filled with a sense of predictability. Nothing seemed to change in the southern rural community I called home. I knew that the cold, wispy winter mornings of December would gradually give rise to warm, blossoming spring days of May, followed by the blistering noonday summer sun of August. The reliability of the seasons, filled with their rhythm of life, offered a sense of childish assurance. That predictability held my fear and ignorance of the unknown at bay and stood as a firm gatekeeper against fundamental and life-altering changes to the usual ways of daily life. But, like the seasons, life is ever changing; it is the unpredictability and nuances found within and between those seasons of change that produce the uncertainty of life itself.

Inevitably, even amid resistance, change occurs. Sometimes that change creeps in gradually; it requires only minor alterations, here and there, to the known and reliable realities of life. At other times, change occurs in one fell swoop, and the dramatic transformation it creates can have a dizzying and disorienting effect, completely distorting the known realities of life. Regardless of the meaning or nature of change, its unpredictability and nuances can, and often do, bring out people's very best as well as very worst attributes. This is particularly true for those who have a vested interest in the outcome. In the early 1960s, the events of the civil rights movement, especially those in Albany, Georgia, intruded on the comfort of my familiar home life. I had a vested interest in the outcome of the changes demanded by the civil rights movement of the early 1960s, even though at the time I was completely unaware of that fact.

As I reflect on my childhood, I am reminded of what Jan Pieterse said: "The world which adults shape for children reflects the logic of the adults' world. It is no wonder then that it is no easier being black in the children's world than in the adults' world."[1] As a child, when I stepped onto the streets of Thomasville, I stepped into my racial identity: whites considered me a Negro, while blacks usually called me a little colored child. In this sharply defined black or white world, my racial definition was not predicated on how I saw myself but rather on how others saw and positioned me in their social order. In other words, family, friends, neighbors, and people at large determined my racial worth and value, or the complete lack thereof, based on their definitions of my skin color—even though I just called myself "me." I would gradually come to understand the meaning of the Duboisian question: Was I an American, or was I a Negro? To be a Negro in the early 1960s was by no means the same as being an American.

As I went about my days, I experienced social changes that were as real as night turning into day. The stakes were high. At the time, I did not necessarily understand the meaning of or fully appreciate the nature of the changes occurring. This vague understanding, however, was not solely a result of my youthfulness; the changes were cloaked by continuity of southern customs that dictated the usual ways of doing things. This was especially the case in the politically charged climate of the early 1960s, where the struggle to get rid of Jim Crow segregation in the rural South was met head-on by the push back to maintain it.

As the season of change swept through my small rural community during my growing-up years, in the early 1960s, I continued to wonder about "Who am I?" Intricately linked to and defined by the people of my community, I also wondered about my family, friends, and neighbors and who they were as unsettling changes began to disrupt the customary ways of doing things. There is no doubt that this disruption was essential to creating one of the historical paths of change that occurred in race and race relations in our nation.

My childhood journey is deeply personal, yet I believe it is a shared experience of my generation, for after all, the struggle for fundamental human rights (as embodied in the modern civil rights movement of the 1950s and 1960s) defines who we once were as a nation. Its importance underlies the trajectory that we have since followed, where our footprints eventually led down a path to the historical moment in which we now find ourselves, the age of Obama. For me, that trajectory began with the absence of Negro civil rights in the United States and the teetering steps taken on the racial tightrope toward inclusion in our vibrant and ever-changing democracy.

o o o

As a child living under Jim Crow segregation, it never dawned on me that someday there might be such a thing as a Negro politician, to say nothing of a Negro president elected by people who could freely vote their preference for the office. But change was gradually closing in on the usual ways of doing things in Thomasville.

Of course, I was well aware of the fact that politicians existed, and by the early 1960s, I could probably name a few of the past presidents from memory, or at least one—my favorite, Abraham Lincoln, the Great Emancipator who freed the slaves. Nevertheless, the possibility of a Negro holding political office simply did not enter my consciousness. This was not just youthful naïveté. During the early 1960s, I also did not know that there could be Negro judges and lawyers; police, firefighters, and mail carriers; or Negro tellers in a bank; or Negro sales clerks in a department store. I did not think about such things because they simply did not exist in my reality.

There was a reality, however, that was widely known within my community. A mutual understanding existed between blacks and whites, old and young Thomasvillians alike, regarding how things were supposed to be. Custom, created out of history, dictated a certain way; and even as a child I was aware of this particular reality.

Since the days of slavery, blacks constituted the majority of the population in my community, but in Thomasville, the county seat of Thomas County, the majority did not rule. To the contrary, Negroes had no political say in who governed the social and economic life of the community. They were effectively disenfranchised solely because of the color of their skin. If somehow Negroes forgot their place in the social pecking order—forgot the fact that they were not citizens with equal rights or were bold enough to think that they were—then black men, women, and children were dealt with according to the established customs and rules of white supremacy. History—built on the solid foundation of racial fear, hatred, and anger—rather than democracy dictated how things were done. That fear, hatred, and anger determined how Negroes and whites were supposed to interact in the presence of each other. Both blacks and whites drew on the shared lessons learned from that violent history; it was a stark reminder of the realities of life shaped by racial custom.

In Thomasville, that history included lynching, rape, and the cold-blooded murder of blacks. In the 1930s, shortly after my family arrived there, terrorism against blacks by white supremacists was rampant. Over a one-month period, a Negro man was lynched and hanged in the courthouse square; a Negro woman was repeatedly raped in a field; and another Negro man was shot and killed in the doorway of his home. On August 29, 1930, as Scott McAleer describes in his article "Great Indignation: A Study of Racial Violence in Thomas County, Georgia, 1930":

> Henry Price and C. V. Moore arrived at the house of Alec and Minnie Lee Thomas. Alec Thomas was away driving his cotton to market in nearby Pavo, but his wife was home. The two men kicked in the doors and chased Minnie Lee Thomas into a field. They knocked her to the ground and while her children stood on the porch calling for their mother, put a gun to her head and raped her, choking her each time she called for help. Price and Moore were both white. The Thomases were black.[2]

On September 24, Willie Kirkland was accused of attempting to rape a nine-year-old white girl. He was hunted down, and

> By nightfall a twenty-year-old convicted horse thief named Willie Kirkland had been arrested, and approximately one thousand people

> soon converged on the stockade where he was in custody. . . . A
> crowd of angry men hurried Kirkland away to nearby Magnolia Park
> where he was shot. His corpse was dragged through town behind a
> car and put on display in front of the courthouse.[3]

Three days after Kirkland had been lynched, "Minnie Lee Thomas'
cousin Lacy Mitchell, who had been scheduled to testify at the trial of
her rapists, was at home with his family when a small group of men
arrived at his door and shot him in the stomach." He died two days
later.[4]

Even though these three terrorist acts happened during the fall of
1930, white vigilantism was by no means limited to a specific season of
Thomasville's history; this was simply one of its more dramatic moments.[5] Racially motivated violence was an unequivocal and unambiguous part of the dual message sent to Thomasvillians: Negroes must not
challenge or offer resistance to white social and economic rule in any
way; and whites must not tolerate even the perception of rebellion
against the system, let alone the actual transgressions, of Negroes. Surely my family knew of this violence and the message it conveyed while
working at Pebble Hill Plantation. I wonder whether their position at
the plantation provided them with a kind of protective cocoon offered
by the powerful and prominent—if not paternalistic and benevolent—
owner of the estate, Kate Benedict Hanna Ireland.

Nonetheless, these three incidents, along with other examples of
lynchings, rapes, and killings in Thomasville's past, represent yet more
examples of the collective blind eye that people turned toward racial
violence. Even today, residents rarely talk openly about the ugly racial
violence that lurks in the shadows of the town's history. By the early
1960s, there was not only an obvious silence regarding such violence,
but there was also a shared understanding between blacks and whites of
it. That shared meaning pierced the stillness of that silence and per-
meated everyday behavior.

On Election Day, only a few Negroes could enter the back, or segregated, doors of the courthouse and exercise their right of citizenship—
the right to vote. The majority of them were intentionally excluded
from voting due to the highly subjective criteria for passing a literacy
test. There were few Negroes who even attempted to register to vote,
since the humiliation of trying to do so was often enough of a deter-
rence. It did not matter whether you were educated or uneducated or

whether you actually got the answers right or wrong on the test; if you were black, then you were effectively disenfranchised. Not even the slightest pretext of democracy existed for blacks in Thomasville.

In my hometown, all of the notable liberal ideas and fundamental premises of democratic citizenship, including the foundational right to vote, were summarily discarded, like trash, when it came to Negroes. The guardian and concurrently the white community's conscience of this status quo was the local newspaper, the *Thomasville Times-Enterprise*, which actively encouraged Thomasvillians during each election season to "exercise your right to vote." White citizens were wholeheartedly encouraged by the paper to assert their political interests through voting. And, as the paper's editorials constantly reminded the citizens of Thomasville, throughout the early 1960s there was no interest more important to the white people of Thomas County than that of maintaining Jim Crow segregation.

The battle line had already been drawn by the 1954 landmark decision of *Brown v. Board of Education of Topeka*, when the United States Supreme Court unanimously declared separate public schools for Negroes and white students unconstitutional. Specifically, the court held the following:

> To separate them [Negro children] from others of similar age and qualifications solely because of their race generates a feeling of inferiority as to their status in the community that may affect their hearts and minds in a way unlikely ever to be undone. . . . We conclude that, in the field of public education, the doctrine of "separate but equal" has no place. Separate educational facilities are inherently unequal.[6]

Everyone knew, blacks as well as whites, that the US Supreme Court ruling on this case had broader implications than simply dismantling de jure, or legal, segregation in public education; it opened the door for dismantling Jim Crow segregation as a whole in the South. By discarding the "separate but equal doctrine," a critical legal precedent was established. When the 1960 presidential election between John F. Kennedy and Richard M. Nixon rolled around, the *Thomasville Times-Enterprise* viewed the voters' choice as a clear referendum on segregation. Leading up to the presidential election, the editorials printed in the paper repeatedly warned the white community of what was at stake. On September 7, 1960, "Time for the South to Think," an editorial, subtly

suggested that white citizens rethink their historical allegiance to the
Democratic Party:

> For the past 100 years the people of the South generally have voted
> for anything and everything bearing the Democratic label, even
> though the garment of the party often looked and smelled bad. Yet
> because it bore the party label it was accepted.
>
> But we should never forget the eyes of the nation are upon the
> South today, and if the South is willing to continue to accept insults
> and impositions submissively and without effective protest, we
> should not be surprised if more are hurled at us.

By October 29, 1960, days before the election, the *Thomasville Times-
Enterprise* printed a more strident editorial titled "Worth Remembering" and warned white citizens of even direr consequences of supporting the Democratic Party. It said:

> Some may have forgotten the history of the 1954 Supreme Court
> desegregation decision and subsequent developments at Little Rock,
> Arkansas, and some of the nation's leading politicians, seemingly
> would lay all the blame at the door of the Republicans.
>
> For this reason it is well to point out that the Supreme Court that
> made that decision, was made up of eight Democrats and one Re-
> publican. One of the Judges, a staunch Democrat, Hugo Black, was
> from the neighboring state of Alabama. . . .
>
> It should also be pointed out that while both platforms, Demo-
> cratic and Republican, pledge further efforts to strengthen civil
> rights legislation, it is the Democratic platform which promises
> COMPLETE DESEGREGATION BY 1963.

White Thomasvillians did not heed the paper's warning. Similar to
voting patterns of the past, in the 1960 presidential election, white
Georgians threw their support to the Democratic Party. John F. Kennedy, the Democratic presidential candidate, and his vice-presidential
running mate, Lyndon B. Johnson, a son of the South, won the election.
There was a deep-seated political history at work here. White Georgians' close ties to the Democratic Party began during the days of the
Republican emancipator, President Abraham Lincoln, and had been a
reliable and consistent source of Democratic political power. Yet it was
not the popular vote that made support for the Democratic Party pre-

dictable during the 1960 presidential election; rather, it was Georgia's county unit system, which divvied up the popular vote into units based on population rates and was controlled by white supremacist politicians.

Geographically, Georgia is composed of counties that are made up largely of small towns and rural villages. Under the county unit system, each county was allotted a certain number of units—urban counties received six unit votes, town counties received four unit votes, and rural counties received two unit votes, respectively.[7] Statewide, in 1960, there were 410 county unit votes. The county unit system allowed candidates to focus on winning county support rather than popular support or individual votes. This had strong political implications for national and statewide elections.

One of the more notorious examples of how the county unit system worked in influencing the outcome of elections was seen in 1956. White supremacist Herman Eugene Talmadge lost the popular vote for the United States Senate by 16,000 votes but won the election anyway because he received 244 county unit votes. Talmadge would become one of the staunch bulwarks against desegregation in the US Congress.[8]

The county unit system served two important political purposes. First, by condensing individual votes into county unit votes, weighted by population, rural areas such as Thomas County could effectively negate the voting strength of more populous urban areas such as Atlanta, because smaller counties were more numerous than larger counties. During the 1960s, rural counties constituted 32 percent of the state population, but they controlled 59 percent of the total unit votes in Georgia. Therefore, candidates who often received the majority of unit votes defeated those who won the popular vote, no matter what the margin. Second, statewide elections could be controlled: rural areas could exert undue influence over state policies and laws, such as de jure segregation, by electing white supremacists to the state legislature and governor's office, with an eye toward maintaining racial laws and customs. Consequently, the county unit system in Georgia was a cunning political ploy that enabled white supremacists to not only dilute the strength of the black vote, especially in urban areas, but also systematically maintain Jim Crow segregation through state elections.

This same political system enabled Kennedy to win Georgia in the primary and general election by garnering support from political bosses in the majority of the state's counties. Arguably, given what we now

know, neither white Georgians nor Thomasvillians voted for their interests during that fateful 1960 presidential election. Kennedy became
president by a close margin, but his presidential victory would come
back to haunt his white southern supporters. Under the Kennedy administration, in tandem with a Democratic-led Congress and a liberal-
leaning US Supreme Court, a major executive, legislative, and legal
assault was mounted to dismantle Jim Crow segregation in the South.
In opposition, the *Thomasville Times-Enterprise* kept up a steady editorial drumbeat that constantly reminded white Thomasvillians of their
racial agenda.

❊ ❊ ❊

As a child, my usual response to a difficult question was, "I don't know."
An aunt, Madea's unmarried sister, who rarely strayed beyond the city
limits of Thomasville, would always reply, "A whole new world could be
made from all of the things you don't know." Over the years, I have
come to understand and appreciate the fact that she was absolutely
right. But growing up, there were certain things that I did know, for
sure. I knew there were Negro teachers like Madea, Negro preachers
like Reverend Mullins, and Negro businessmen like my father. I also
knew, or at least knew something about, most of the people in my
hometown, especially the blacks.

During the early 1960s, there were about twenty thousand people in
and around my hometown. The majority were Negroes. Many had the
same last names as the names of the plantations that surrounded our
community and gave it its scenic character. Or their names were taken
from the individual slave owners—but without the wealth, power, and
prestige accumulated with the help of black slave labor on their plantations. Hence, it was not uncommon to have many different black famil-
ial groups with the same surname of Hill, for instance, who were not
related by blood but whose people had worked at Pebble Hill Plantation throughout the generations.

Regardless of race, everybody in town seemed to know everybody
else or at least someone in, or something about, their family. In the
black community, Mr. Elijah Hill Jr. was a highly respected and successful Negro businessman; everybody knew or knew something about
Mr. Hill. He was a housing contractor for the black community who

built homes from the ground up or renovated them. He was part of the small Negro middle class in Thomasville and considered by many to be a community leader because of his active involvement with the Progressive Club, the only black political organization in town. Mr. Hill had social standing in the Negro community.

When I visited Madea's married sister, my aunt, on weekends, sometimes she would let me play with Mr. Hill's daughters, who did not live far away. Occasionally, I spent the night at their home—a large red brick structure with plenty of unused rooms and lots of toys, especially white dolls. It was bigger, and seemingly better, than any of the other Negroes' home I had entered.

Among white Thomasvillians, however, Elijah Hill was of little importance. He was just another no-account Negro. I remember hearing the rumor that he was running for a seat on the county commission, the local seat of political power and the governing body of the town. The county commission appointed the mayor. The rumor was true. Word got out that he was running for office, but before he officially filed for candidacy, he decided not to enter the race. Eavesdropping on adult conversation one day, I overheard my aunt say that Mr. Hill withdrew because local whites had filed papers for a *dog* to run against him in the upcoming election. Even as a child, I knew that there was something seriously wrong with that picture. Although young, I was aware enough to know that if Mr. Elijah Hill stayed in the race, the *dog* would surely win the election. Humiliated, he was forced to withhold his candidacy or suffer the indignity of having a dog win over him.

Who votes for a dog over a human being in a political election? What does that say about the value that society put on the Negro's life?

As my aunt said, a whole new world could be made out of what I did not know. However, I now know that there are many new worlds—not just the ones that lie across distant shores or are gated by national boundaries—whose people and daily lives are completely foreign and unfamiliar. There are also worlds of fear that lie deep within us. They are constructed out of the illogical and irrational anticipation of danger that is embodied in the mere presence of those who appear to be different. Concomitantly, there are worlds of hate, which are rooted in ignorance that gnaws at our very being until we lash out in violence and attempt to destroy those whose presence merely gets on our nerves or irritates us in some way. There are worlds of anger over perceived threats to what are seen as unique endowments—whether given by God or sheer entitlement—in which privilege is somehow undermined. When I stepped onto the familiar streets of Thomasville, I stepped into a world of intolerance, bigotry, and racism, a world of fear, hatred, and anger about the mere existence of the Negro race.

This world, however, was seemingly separate and set apart from the other world in which I grew up—the Negro world. Since I attended an all-black elementary school, junior high, and later a high school named after Frederick Douglass, each year we proudly celebrated Negro History Week. We focused on the achievements that individual Negroes made to the greatness of the United States—scholars, inventors, artists, athletics, and the like. This was a different history—one that seldom appeared on the pages of our hand-me-down schoolbooks that were no longer needed by white students. It was a history that mapped African American progress in the United States; a history that said to us—little black children—that Negroes were a valued and worthy people—just look at the important contributions they made to the well-being of humanity! I particularly loved the focus on great black leaders and their feats of real heroism that always seemed to occur in the context of the struggle against racial inequality and injustice.

Harriet Tubman, more than most, captured my childhood imagination. What I liked about her was her insistence that human bondage was simply wrong. Against the odds, she took it upon herself to do something about her convictions, escaping from slavery herself and then going back to guide family members and others to freedom. She helped John Brown recruit men for his Harper's Ferry raid, worked as a Union army guide, and participated in the struggle for women's suffrage. These were truly amazing feats of courage and daring, particularly for a woman who was small in stature and had a debilitating health problem that made her appear peculiar. I liked the fact that she was odd. As a result of having been hit in the head by a white man as a child, she developed seizures and would fall into an unconscious, dreamlike state, regardless of where she was or what she was doing at the time. From the physical and mental abuse heaped on her during her enslavement, she started to have visions and revelations from God, and along with the North Star, they guided her actions.

As a child, I, too, searched for the North Star and came to love a clear, cloudless night. The Negro world that I grew up in appeared to be as unambiguous as the night sky, but in the distance, there were always the little twinkling white stars, keeping a watchful eye over the darkness.

My family, friends, and most of the people with whom I interacted were black. There were four exceptions, however. Mr. Mallette, who dripped of sweat from riding his bicycle in the summer heat to deliver Avon products; insurance men, who came to collect the ten-cent life insurance policies each week; peddlers, who sold seemingly anything and everything from pots and pans to ankle socks out of the trunks of their beat-up, dusty cars; and Mr. Goldstein, who allowed black folks to buy food on credit from his grocery store, with the accounts due at the end of each month. To me, these were, and were not, white people; they, like Harriet Tubman, were peculiar and odd in some unidentifiable way. They were hard-working and decent people trying to make a living the best they could; they were just people, and in our interactions with them, we seemed to be just people to them, also.

The real white people were mostly downtown, or across town, or in passing cars. Rarely did I interact with them, but they were very much a part of my reality. They were everywhere—little twinkling white stars scattered across a black sky. They appeared in miniature form on television in *The Edge of Night*, *The Lawrence Welk Show*, or the Colgate toothpaste commercials. They were scattered throughout the pages of my schoolbooks and smiling on the pages of the *Thomasville Times-Enterprise*. What I noticed is that they always seemed to be enjoying themselves, smiling and having a good time. Nowhere did they have a better time than at a parade, especially the annual Rose Parade.

Thomasville is advertised as the "City of Roses," and true to its billing, the community is teeming with rose gardens. Everyone seems to have at least one rosebush, and roses even grow wild in the surrounding woods. Since 1920, my hometown has held a Rose Festival that celebrates not only the arrival of spring but also the history of the town. The festival includes a flower show, tours of plantations, and a pageant featuring the crowning of Miss Thomasville. All of this culminates with a parade. During the early 1960s, it was not uncommon for the parade to have floats plastered with colorful roses and featuring white girls as southern belles in antebellum dresses and white boys in the gray uniforms of Confederate soldiers. Clearly, this was reminiscent of the "good ol' days."

The parade was always held on Broad Street, in the heart of the shopping district, lined with its antique shops, small businesses, and restaurants. We would attend, not because of the cars and floats peppered with colorful arrangements or the white, smiling faces of people who were waving and tossing candy to the onlooking crowd, but because Negroes were also a part of the parade. The Miss Douglass royal court and the Frederick Douglass High School marching band always brought up the rear. When the parade got to the corner of Broad and Jackson Streets, the queen's court veered off and entered "the Bottom," the black part of town, where the band would play the latest popular tune and put on a high-stepping show just for us. We waited in eager anticipation for this special performance.

One year, while waiting for Miss Douglass and the band to appear, something unusual happened. The float that preceded them was in the shape of a large green watermelon sliced in half, with the fleshy red center divided by two rows of black seeds. The watermelon seeds, however, were not paper painted black; they were children's faces. Initially, I thought that they were little black children. But no! The watermelon seeds were little white children with their faces painted black. I really did not understand what this particular image was supposed to symbolize—at the time I loved watermelon—so I just thought it was funny, until my sister told me to stop laughing and tried to explain the insult that was being hurled at us.

My reaction at the time was similar to the one recalled by Andrew Young, who had also observed the Rose Parade—the year following the landmark *Brown v. Board of Education of Topeka* decision of the US Supreme Court—during his stay in Thomasville. Of the parade, he said:

> The town's approach to race relations was clearly illustrated in a parade float by one of the county's largest employers. The Sunnyland Packing Company float featured two huge egg cartons. One carton had twelve white children and a sign that said GRADE A WHITE. The other carton had twelve black children and a sign that said GRADE A BROWN. That was Sunnyland's version of separate but equal. The sad thing was, we thought it was good. [9]

What he saw was a visual representation and reaffirmation of the "separate but equal doctrine" established in the landmark 1896 US

Supreme Court case of *Plessy v. Ferguson*, which *Brown v. Board of Education* overturned.

I have since learned both the explicit and implicit meaning of the messages contained within such racial images. Racist imagery is used as an attempt to strip away another's humanity, to demonize and deprive individuals of human worth and value. If a person no longer seems human and thus deserving of basic human dignity, then it becomes much easier to treat him or her as a lesser being.

The watermelon float was not the only sign conveying the message of black racial inferiority in Thomasville. Accompanying the prized roses that dotted my idyllic community were many racist signs and symbols, which you could not avoid noticing: the Georgia state flag, mimicking the Confederate flag with its Confederate bars, flying aloft the courthouse and other government buildings; the Confederate flag appearing in miniature form on cars' and trucks' license plates as they sped along local streets; and, of course, the signs that boldly proclaimed where colored people were allowed to go. Up and down Broad Street and the side streets as well, businesses labeled their back entrances or side windows for serving Negroes while their front doors simply read, "No Negroes Allowed." Bus and train stations had signs and arrows that read "For Coloreds Only," accompanied by seats labeled "White Only."

Justifying Jim Crow segregation, the voice of the community, the *Thomasville Times-Enterprise*, on June 29, 1963, published a lengthy editorial called "A Discriminating World," which said in part:

> One look at the map of the world and a brief review of history shows that human nature is such that discrimination is almost everywhere to be found and while in the United States efforts are being made to eliminate discrimination by legislative processes, it is recognized this can not change man's basic nature. . . .
>
> The old adages that "birds of a feather flock together" and "like begets like" still hold good. It's true in the animal kingdom and with the fishes of the sea, just as with birds. God made the earth and all therein, creating mankind in his image and giving to each racial group certain characteristics which differentiate them from others. . . . Why, we do not know, other than God wanted them different. . . .

Each human being by nature is distinctively different from all others and no amount of brain-washing is likely to change the ideologies of entire nations and groups of people against their will. . . .

Those who advocate a multiracial nation and world certainly cannot be said to have the best interest of any race at heart. . . .

Legislative enactments, no matter how well intended, cannot serve to change human nature. Forced legislation will only substitute racial bitterness for the milk of human kindness.

What, if anything, is the worth and value of a little Negro girl in the sociopolitical climate of Jim Crow segregation?

Ironically, the very same institutions designed to reaffirm the notion that Negro children were less than white children—our segregated schools—tempered the racism we experienced. Teachers tried, as best they could, to protect us, largely by keeping us busy with learning. They were the unsung heroines and heroes in this racial drama that was being played out under Jim Crow segregation. Frederick Douglass schools—with their celebration of Negro History Week, queens, and marching band—taught us in one way or another, "Little Negro children, you are of human worth and value." But who protected the Negro teachers as they engaged the harsh realities of trying to educate us under segregation?

Frederick Douglass Elementary, Junior High, and High School were not the only institutions in the black community that attempted to thaw the icy mental and emotional effects of Jim Crow segregation on the minds and bodies of Negro children. The Negro church was instrumental in our development as well.

* * *

Growing up, my Saturday afternoons were usually spent preparing for Sunday mornings, specifically, getting ready for Sunday school and church services. Preparations consisted of the weekly rituals of getting my hair straightened and making sure that my only church dress was washed, starched, and ironed.

I hated going to church, and I hated the rituals of preparing to go to church even more, especially getting my hair done. Madea would send my sister and me next door to Mrs. Mary, who did hair, while she went off to the Saturday matinee at the dog track. Even now, I can hear the

Georgia Peach or Royal Crown hair grease sizzle each time Mrs. Mary stuck the hot straightening comb into my hair as hot oil scalded my scalp and burned my ears. If I was lucky, I would leave Mrs. Mary's house with the prize of having black, shiny, straightened hair, coifed with bangs and pigtails, without burns on my scalp and ears. Usually I was unlucky, and the bangs and pigtails had to suffice.

Sunday mornings were always filled with high drama. I had gradually adopted a Sunday morning ritual that was all my own: after donning my crinoline slip and starched Sunday dress, white ankle socks, and Vaseline-shined patent leather church shoes, I would promptly throw a tantrum—a major fit. My sister thought that I was losing my mind. Undaunted by my Sunday morning hysterics, she would pronounce me strange and then go off to church, leaving me behind.

Sometimes I could tolerate Sunday School because it was only the children and their teacher in the basement of the First African Baptist Church, having a lesson about Christian morals and parables. After the lesson or the recitation of Bible verses we had learned the night before, we would get a treat, usually cookies and punch; because of this, Sunday school was tolerable. However, I had no tolerance for the long church service itself. There were always adult eyes peering and monitoring every laugh and whisper. Then there was Reverend I. L. Mullins talking incessantly about God. All you could do was sit and listen to Reverend Mullins preach while swinging your legs back and forth, or playing with the hymnbook, or looking at the church fan that had a picture of a white Jesus on one side and a Grooms Funeral Home advertisement on the other. When the pitch of Reverend Mullins's voice rose to a boisterous crescendo, signaling an end to his sermon, the boredom was finally over. The chorus would rise, and shortly thereafter, Reverend Mullins would offer the benediction. Even though I could not carry a tune, I must admit I loved the singing and hand clapping.

Simply put, what I hated most about church was sitting passively and being preached to—and to this day, I feel the same way. So on Sunday mornings, I would throw a major fit and announce, in no uncertain terms, that I was not going to church. As you may suspect, Madea was not having any of that attitude, and I would often get a beating and be forced to go to church. The beating was well worth the punishment, though, if my fit accomplished the aim and I did not have to go to church. On rare occasions Madea relented without the beating, and I did not have to go.

I can count on one hand the number of times Madea actually attended church. Even though she would dutifully try to send my sister and me to church for our religious education, rarely did she, my aunts, or my grandmother attend, and they seemed to have turned out fine to me. Given their delinquency, I did not feel that I should attend either.

My attitude toward church attendance started to shift because the rituals changed. This was largely due to the guidance of Reverend Mullins. He was dark-complexioned, short, handsome, and always immaculately dressed in a dark-colored suit with a crisp, white shirt and tie—no matter what the occasion or how hot it was. The women, who really ran the church, absolutely loved him. It did not hurt in the least that he was a Morehouse man—a graduate of Morehouse College—and a trained minister from the Interdenominational Theological Center in Atlanta, Georgia. He had also served in the navy and had been a boxer there. All of this garnered respect from the men of the church, but to me, what was endearing about Reverend Mullins was his warm smile, an appropriate joke for every occasion, and the fact that he would visit the sick and shut-ins every first Sunday to offer communion.

Reverend Mullins knew by name those who attended church regularly and those who did not. Dutifully, he would stop by our house on the evening of the first Sunday of the month to give my grandmother, wheelchair-bound by a stroke, communion. He would take the opportunity to chide Madea, my aunts, and me for not attending church services—only my sister escaped this slight embarrassment because she enjoyed the whole church ritual and was an eager participant each Sunday. Then he would offer communion to us as well. From these visits, Madea and Reverend Mullins became unlikely friends. I always knew that he kept a watchful eye over his ministerial flock, including me.

Traditionally, the First African Baptist Church had been a reliable stalwart in the effort to bring racial and social justice to Thomasville and was seen, even among other Negro churches, as a leader in the community. It was organized by the diligence of former slaves. Initially, during slavery, blacks and whites worshipped at the white Thomasville Baptist Church, but not together—Negro services were separate; they were conducted by a white minister and held only on Sabbath afternoons in the basement. In 1860, a white citizen, Alex Smith, donated land to be used exclusively for building a Negro church. Withdrawing their membership from the Thomasville Baptist Church, 129 Negroes, guided by Reverend Jacob Wade, began to worship outdoors in 1866. They first built a "bush arbor"—a rough, open-sided shelter constructed to protect them from exposure to the elements—until they could afford to erect a church building. The construction of the First African Baptist Church was completed on July 29, 1900.

Reverend Mullins brought change to the First African Baptist Church. That change was not, however, seen in Sunday services, for after all, it was a house of worship. As a young preacher in 1961, Reverend Mullins became the nineteenth minister to head the church, and he readily took up the traditional mantle of leadership for racial and social justice.

He was well suited for the task at hand. Reverend Mullins was smart and socially conscious. Through his theological and collegiate connections in Atlanta, he marched with Dr. Martin Luther King in Montgomery, Alabama, and was a friend of other ministers who formed the leadership of the civil rights movement. Shortly after his arrival in Thomasville, he organized a local branch of the National Association for the Advancement of Colored People (NAACP). Madea readily supported this effort and gave my sister and me a dime to join the Youth Council. I was proud of my NAACP membership card with my name boldly typed on it, and I kept it securely in my Sunday pocketbook.

With the support of the Progressive Club, headed by Mr. Elijah Hill and Mr. William "Bill" Morris, and the local chapter of the NAACP (which Mr. Curtis Thomas had assumed leadership of), Reverend Mullins started to hold weekly Monday night public meetings at the First African Baptist Church to discuss the state of race relations in Thomasville. At the top of the list of priorities was voter registration, but the collective black memory of what happened to the first Negro who tried to register to vote in Thomasville was omnipresent and oppressive. In 1948, when an unidentified black man tried to register, he was summarily lassoed on the courthouse steps; the rope was tied to the back bumper of a pickup truck; and he was dragged around the black community. He was then cut loose in front of the jail, where he was left to die.[10] Black voter registration under Jim Crow segregation carried the dire possibility of death.

It was not the first time that a call for a voter registration drive in Thomasville was issued. In 1956, Andrew Young, along with Hubert Thomas, Elijah Hill, and Bill Morris, tried to organize a voter registration drive, but their efforts were unsuccessful. It was organized to coincide with the 1956 presidential election between Adlai Stevenson and Dwight Eisenhower. Andrew Young and others solicited the help of the legendary activist John Wesley Dobbs of Macon, Georgia—the grandfather of Maynard Jackson, who would become the first black mayor of Atlanta in 1973—to speak at a mass registration rally in Thomasville. In that effort, as Young said, they soon learned that "the Klan had been gathering from all over southwest Georgia, and their destination was Thomasville, where they were going to try to intimidate us. We had publicized our planned registration rally quite openly and expected a large attendance, so it was no surprise that the Klan knew about us."[11]

On Saturday, the day a rally was to be held at Frederick Douglass High School, the Klan had gathered at the courthouse square. But nothing happened. Young said: "When it was discovered there might be violence or threats by the Klan, the black elders of Thomasville went to the white business community leaders and, in effect, told them, 'If you let these Klansmen come into our community and harass us you can forget about us shopping at your businesses from now on. So you all stop them before they get started.'"[12] Even though no violence was reported, the Klan had accomplished its intended aim: few black Thomasvillians attended the rally, even fewer attempted to register, and only a handful actually voted in the 1956 presidential election.

Reverend Mullins and the others were determined to mount another registration drive. It seemed as if all of the Negroes in Thomasville, even those from other churches, came to the weekly NAACP meetings. The only ones not in attendance were the schoolteachers—they would have been fired immediately if word of their participation got back to the all-white board of education. Some of the teachers, like Madea, sent their children in their stead, and I eagerly stepped into the role of a little surrogate activist.

The meetings were exciting, and I could not wait to go to church on Monday nights, even though I really did not understand what was going on. Sometimes there would be special meetings following church services or on Sunday evenings. If there were guest speakers such as Andrew Young or Julian Bond, the small children such as myself usually sat on the floor because of the crowd. Unlike my boredom with listening to Reverend Mullins's dry Sunday morning sermons about God, I was riveted and entertained by the cadence of the speeches about overcoming racial barriers. I loved holding hands and singing "We Shall Overcome" at those Monday night gatherings. Quite simply, I enjoyed the festive atmosphere—for me, it was like a Monday night party where everybody was singing and happy. I knew something wonderful was happening in the lives of Negroes and that I was a part of whatever it was; but at the time, I had absolutely no idea of its significance. All I understood was that something big was going on, especially in Albany, Georgia.

* * *

The *Thomasville Times-Enterprise* was also aware that something big was happening, that a season of change was enveloping the South and threatening its traditional ways of doing things. On January 18, 1961, the paper published an editorial titled "History Repeating Itself" that said:

> THERE IS MUCH in common between the events of the 1850s and 1860s and those of the 1950s and 1960s.
>
> The issue a hundred years ago was that of slavery, and to settle it a bloody war was fought in which some 600,000 men died, hundreds of thousand of others were wounded and maimed for life and the South left in ashes, victim of the venomous hatred of those who wanted the white people of the South crushed into the dust. It was called Civil War.
>
> The issue of today is what is described as Civil Rights. It is a controversy in which we find a concerted effort being made with the blessing and at the dictation of the federal courts to force racial mixing in the schools of the nation, all of which is designed to bring about full-scale integration at all levels. . . .
>
> This the white people of the South object to and resent because it is contrary to the traditions and heritages of this part of the country.

I now know that in the winter of 1961, Negroes had started conducting mass demonstrations, boycotts, jail-ins, and sit-ins and were filing lawsuits in the district court of Albany to challenge the inhumanity of

Jim Crow segregation. The protesters were emboldened by a ruling of the US Supreme Court a year earlier. The US Supreme Court's decision in *Boynton v. Virginia* upheld the right of interstate travelers to disregard local segregation laws in the South.[13]

By the spring of 1961, the Congress of Racial Equality (CORE) had created a strategy testing the viability of that decision. CORE decided to target interstate travel and recruited biracial Freedom Riders to challenge segregation on bus travel through the South. Unlike my mother and I, who sat in the back of the bus reserved only for Negroes when we traveled to Albany to visit my sister, the Freedom Riders refused to accept this seating arrangement. The activists challenged Jim Crow laws regarding segregated seating on buses, in waiting areas, and in restaurants and in regard to the use of separate water fountains and restrooms in bus terminals.

In May of 1961, starting out from Washington, D.C., the Freedom Riders took buses traveling throughout the South and encountered various degrees of white resistance along the way—everything from bloody mob violence to the refusal of services or the closing of restaurants at bus terminals altogether. A group of Freedom Riders briefly ventured into Thomasville without incident. On June 16, 1961, the *New York Times* reported, in a story titled "Bus Riders Press to North Florida; Meet Little Trouble as They Also Test South Georgia," that a group of Freedom Riders was coming across Florida, and at Tallahassee, they took a bus "northward, making a brief round trip to Thomasville, Ga. thirty miles away. The purpose of the trip, the leader of the group said, was to certify themselves as interstate passengers in preparation for a swing through Florida."

On November 1, 1961, the federal Interstate Commerce Commission banned racial segregation on interstate buses and in bus terminals. To test whether Albany's bus terminal was in compliance, high-school students from the NAACP Youth Council went to the Trailways bus station to stage a sit-in, but before they could accomplish their task, they were ordered to leave by the police. They complied. Nine students from the all-black Albany State College conducted another test on December 10, 1961, but this time they were arrested. In the weeks to follow, more than seven hundred blacks were arrested for civil disobedience. As a result, the Albany movement was born.[14] The leadership of this movement was composed of a coalition that included the Student

Nonviolent Coordinating Committee (SNCC), the NAACP, the Ministerial Alliance, the Federation of Women's Clubs, and the Negro Voters League. Dr. William Anderson, a local osteopath, was elected president of the coalition. An invitation was also extended to Dr. Martin Luther King Jr., chairman of the Southern Christian Leadership Conference (SCLC), to join the coalition.

Nonviolent protests were occurring in other cities and towns across Georgia, where strategies concentrated on voter registration, equal access to public accommodations, or school desegregation. But in Albany, the approach was a bit different. A multifaceted strategy was being employed—an all-out attack—which included economic boycotts, protest marches, voter registration drives, and lawsuits. Negroes were demanding an immediate end to Jim Crow segregation in that city.

The tactics used by law enforcement to deter the protestors were also a bit different. Having carefully observed civil rights protests in other places, police chief Laurie Pritchett implemented strategies to subvert the protest in Albany. Unlike in other places, such as Montgomery and Atlanta, Pritchett strategically refrained from using public police brutality during mass arrest—in an attempt to minimize media coverage and/or the possibility of federal involvement, which would draw national attention. Furthermore, he arranged to disperse protesters to nearby county jails to avoid filling up the local jail, in order to continue to make mass arrests and to hold demonstrators for longer periods of time. Detainees may even have been moved to the Thomas County jail.

Nevertheless, the arrival of Dr. Martin Luther King catapulted the Albany movement into the forefront of the civil rights struggle. By August 1962, during the sweltering heat of the late summer days in Georgia, tensions had reached a boiling point in the city. The Ku Klux Klan (KKK) was rallying; two Negro churches were burned to the ground; about eighty ministers from the North were jailed for holding public prayer vigils; a door-to-door voter registration drive was under way; the city bus company suspended services; local businesses were losing money because of the economic boycott; fourteen Negro children had been turned away from white schools; and the district court was being bombarded with bail hearings, petitions, and lawsuits in regard to the desegregation of public accommodations, including the library, swimming pool, and parks. The mass arrests from marches and demonstrations continued.

Mayor Kelley and other city officials refused to meet with movement leaders. During this period, President Kennedy drew the ire of Georgia politicians, many of whom had supported his presidential candidacy, when at a news conference on August 1, 1962, he responded to a question about Albany by stating:

> Let me say that I find it wholly inexplicable why the city council of Albany will not sit down with the citizens of Albany, who may be Negroes, and attempt to secure them, in a peaceful way, their rights. The United States government is involved in sitting down at Geneva with the Soviet Union. I can't understand why the government of Albany, city council of Albany, cannot do the same for American citizens.

Responding to the president, Governor Ernest Vandiver said in no uncertain terms: "I stand four-square with the city officials of Albany on their refusal to sit down and negotiate with individuals who are violating the law." Albany's mayor said, "We will never talk to outside agitators relative to local problems. These agitators came in to create turmoil and strife and in their own words to turn Albany upside down." Keeping watch and informing Thomasvillians of what was happening to their neighbor, the *Thomasville Times-Enterprise* denounced President Kennedy's statement and again put the white citizens of Thomasville on alert by proclaiming in a lengthy editorial on August 3, 1962, "The South Is under Attack," that

> Efforts to humiliate the South and make it appear it is a land of brutes and vandals have been made by some of the news agencies and television shows in which one of King's assistants appeared with bandaged head to testify to treatment accorded him. It was a play apparently designed to make the South look bad. Only one side of the affair was given, and the main purpose seems to be designed to create sympathy for the leaders of the Albany movement while at the same time apparently trying to make it appear that the citizenry of Albany through its officials is a band of outlaws.
>
> Reports indicate that at least four big foundations along with various individuals are furnishing money to finance the activities of

King and his associates, whether it is to bail them out of jail or pay legal fees for counsel in their behalf.

For whatever faults that may be attributed to Albany city officials and the South in general, it is an obvious fact the South today is under a vicious attack by outside influences and agencies, all well financed and with one aim only, to break down the traditional way of life below the Mason-Dixon line.

The government (U.S.) itself—a Democratic administration—has been one of the prime movers in this effort. This within itself should serve to remind us that this is the pay-off from the Kennedy administration for the support given him in the Presidential campaign. Because he wore the Democratic label he was supported by party leaders in all parts of the South. They fell under pressure, and like Samson of old, are now shorn of their power.

Almost 1,500 "Jews, Catholics and Protestants, men and women, Negro and White persons, young and old" were arrested for some form of civil disobedience in Albany. Even though city officials attempted to halt the civil rights protest by getting an injunction from district court judge Robert Elliott, a circuit court of appeals judge, Elbert Tuttle, stayed that injunction. But above all else, what city officials really wanted was for Dr. King to leave. They considered Dr. King to be an interloper and a troublemaker; therefore, they refused to negotiate with local leaders until he departed. I speculate that city officials may have believed that if Dr. King left town, the Albany movement would cease to garner national attention, and local resistance would wane. The media spotlight was clearly focused on Dr. King: he was arrested three times for disorderly conduct, charged with parading without a permit, obstructing the sidewalk, and disobeying the orders of law enforcement officials, respectively. As long as Dr. King stayed in Albany, city officials were determined not to show a sign of weakness by negotiating.

Many whites wanted Dr. King to leave Albany; some wanted him to leave the entire state of Georgia; and a few hoped he would quit the country altogether. The "liberal" Democrat Carl Sanders, for instance, then a state senator and a candidate for governor—gave voice to the sentiments of many when he vowed that, if elected, he would "guarantee that neither King nor anyone like him will be permitted to stay in the state and lead violent demonstrations."[15]

By the fall of 1962, civil rights leaders and city officials were at an impasse. Dr. King was arrested for the third time in July, and Judge Durden found him guilty as charged, imposing a sentence of sixty days in jail and a two-hundred-dollar fine. Then the judge suspended Dr. King's sentence and placed him on probation with the condition that he violate no laws. When asked whether he had to obey segregation laws, Judge Durden replied, "No."[16] The judge's response did not denounce segregation, yet it was extremely significant. It was a concession, but one largely designed to hasten Dr. King's departure from Albany.

Finally able to meet with city officials, civil rights leaders and local government officials struck a bargain. Dr. William Anderson, the president of the Albany movement at the time, said years later in a 1985 interview for the documentary series *Eyes on the Prize: America's Civil Rights Years (1954–1965)*, "A tacit agreement had been reached with the city whereby they would set into place mechanisms whereby our concerns would be answered. They included things like desegregation of the bus station. Desegregation of some of the public facilities like lunch counters, the train station and some other facilities." Insistent, Dr. King told the negotiators on behalf of the coalition that he wanted the agreement in writing and the terms publicized in the press. This was done, and as Dr. Anderson said, "We accepted the agreement."[17] Dr. King, however, remained "uncomfortable" with the agreement, but they "all agreed that it was in the best interests of the people of Albany to have the matter resolved and to accept" it.

The matter of Jim Crow segregation was far from being permanently resolved, but Dr. King agreed to leave Albany on August 10, 1962. The Albany movement and Negro protest, albeit with less national attention, persisted. As demonstrations against Jim Crow segregation continued, so, too, did the intransigence of city officials and the retaliation in the form of police brutality.

❊ ❊ ❊

Meanwhile, back in Thomasville, daily life went on as usual, but small shifts began to appear in the usual ways of doing things. In the "Negro News Notes" section published every so often in the *Thomasville Times-Enterprise*, it was reported that on March 9, 1962, "26 Douglass Students Take First Train Ride." Mrs. Pauline Easton asked her fourth-grade class, "How many of you have been on a train?" Only one child responded to this query, so she decided to arrange a train ride for them. The paper listed all of the children in her class who took the twenty-minute train ride from Thomasville to Cairo, Georgia. It also named four first-graders who went along for the ride, and there, in black-and-white print, was my name in the *Thomasville Times-Enterprise*.

Kneeling on the seat so that I could peek out of the huge window to watch the pine trees pass, I was thrilled by my first train ride on the Atlantic Coast Line Railroad. I recall that it was springtime, and I was wearing my starched Sunday dress and shiny shoes. Madea placed a nickel in my hand and told me to be good. I also remember that we could not go into the train station but waited outside on the platform until the train pulled in and then boarded the last car, which was re-served for us. As I think back, I do not know whether this special train ride for little Negro children—which presumably had the approval of the all-white board of education—was simply an innocent school outing or whether it was a way of softening the harsh reality of Jim Crow segregation playing out all around us. Perhaps it was some type of benevolent paternalistic attempt to offer a contrasting picture, drawing on the novelty and sheer pleasure of a child's first train trip, to that of the indignities the Freedom Riders were enduring for violating south-ern customs and laws at the time.

Several older black Thomasvillians have since told me that the ra-cism in my hometown during the early 1960s was not as harsh as it was in other places in the South. In his memoir, Andrew Young seems to confirm this idea by saying: "Thomasville engaged in a gentler form of segregation than the surrounding counties in southwest Georgia."[18] But he readily acknowledged that "it was no less real" in its impact and implications. If Negroes in Thomasville experienced a "gentler" form of segregation—whatever that meant—one thing is certain: just like the harsher form, it denied Negroes the full rights of citizenship.

Reverend Mullins, Curtis Thomas of the NAACP, and Elijah Hill and Bill Morris of the Progressive Club clearly understood this fact. They continued to hold Monday night meetings at the First African Baptist Church, with a firm determination to secure a fundamental right of democracy—the right for Negroes to vote. Sadly, systemic and institutional barriers continued to block the way.

Violations of the Fifteenth Amendment of the US Constitution, which prohibited disenfranchisement based on race, stubbornly persisted in spite of opposition. Many forms of Negro voter discrimination and voter suppression were under judicial and legislative attack. In Georgia, the civil rights movement vigorously mounted challenges to the county unit system and voter literacy tests, challenges which were simultaneously resisted by whites.

In anticipation of a federal court ruling about a lawsuit brought against the state of Tennessee, which had a similar unit voting system, Governor Ernest Vandriver of Georgia called a special session of the state legislature to revise its system in an attempt to thwart federal action and maintain control over the state voting apparatus. Under the governor's reapportionment proposal, Thomas County stood to lose two of four unit votes, thereby diluting its overall political power and influence in the state. Outraged by that proposal, the *Thomasville Times-Enterprise* called for rural counties to secede from the state by posing the question, "Why Not 2 States in Ga.?" in an editorial on April 9, 1962. In part, the editorial said:

> Georgia should correct and revise its voting system before the federal court steps in and makes it mandatory,
>
> While the threat of federal action over the state hangs heavily, as a result of the decision, we do not think the Governor ought to jump at the crack of the whip and command the members of the General Assembly to rush to the Capitol and join in the jumping.
>
> If each county other than the several metropolitan areas, is to be reduced to a one representative and two unit basis, then Thomas County will have no more voice in state affairs than will Echols County with a few hundred citizens. . . .
>
> Possibly the solution of the problem would be to let Atlanta and some of the more populous areas in North Georgia secede from the state and create a state to be known as North Georgia. They have a North and South Carolina and a North and South Dakota, why not a North and South Georgia?

This call for secession fell on deaf ears. But, as Laughlin McDonald describes in his book *A Voting Rights Odyssey: Black Enfranchisement in Georgia*, change in the usual ways of doing things was gradually closing in, but not without strong resistance. Adjusting their strategies to meet the political realities of the time, state power brokers employed legal, quasi-legal, or illegal means in an attempt to maintain their vested interests in white supremacy.[19]

In the spring of 1963, before the governor's reapportionment plan could be implemented in the state, the US Supreme Court heard the case of *Gray v. Sanders*.[20] This case directly challenged the legality of the county unit system in Georgia. The justices found the system unconstitutional in a majority decision of eight to one because it violated the "one person, one vote" principle of political equality. In the fall elections, with the governor's office up for grabs, Georgians voted under a new system—popular vote balloting.

Still undeterred by the US Supreme Court's decision, during the 1963–1964 legislative session in Georgia, another voting proposal was adopted. This time it was sponsored by the newly elected governor of Georgia, Carl Sanders Sr.—the same "liberal" politician who had vowed to run Dr. King out of the state. His plan called for an at-large election, particularly for state senate seats in counties with more than one state senator. With an at-large system, the candidate who gets the most votes wins the election. Unfortunately, this system opens up the possibility of gerrymandering—allowing state legislators to draw voting district boundaries in such a way as to give themselves electoral advantage over their political rivals.

Sanders's proposal was a political ploy specifically designed to undermine the voting bloc power of Negroes in urban areas. In particular, it was aimed at thwarting the efforts of attorney Leroy Johnson, a Negro from Atlanta, who was running for the office of state senator in 1964. Governor Sanders's strategy failed, however, because the at-large proposal violated Georgia's state constitution. There was not enough time to amend the state constitution and then redraw the voting districts to favor the white candidates before the upcoming election. As a result, Johnson became the first black state legislator elected in Georgia since the Reconstruction era.

Even though in the early 1960s minor changes were occurring on the political landscape in Georgia, those shifts did not fundamentally alter white supremacists' intent to maintain the status quo. Ongoing and systematic barriers continued to block black voting rights. In addition to state politicians, local officials also used their discretionary political authority to impose discriminatory rules and structures that inhibited voter rights. Nowhere was this more evident than in the use of literacy tests. The *Thomasville Times-Enterprise* justified their continuing use in a February 8, 1962, editorial titled "Ignorant and Uninformed," by arguing that

> Eligibility to vote should include the ability to read, to write and to know something about the people running for office, what they stand for and what they propose to do if elected.
>
> It is part of the democratic processes of government for the people to vote and elect their officials. This naturally presumes they shall know how to read and write. Without that qualification they, like sheep, can easily be herded into groups, marched to the polls and vote as they are told or as their ballots may be marked for them.
>
> As this situation develops it will more than ever become necessary that the educated, the best informed, intelligent people must for their own protection take time to go to the polls and vote. Otherwise the ignorant and uninformed may easily take over.

The use of literacy tests had legal protection. In 1959, the US Supreme Court upheld the constitutionality of literacy tests in *Lassiter v. Northampton Board of Elections*.[21] States such as Georgia could legally require literacy tests as long as they were shown not to be racially discriminatory. Therefore, whites—especially the poor and uneducated—were not legally exempt from taking a literacy test before they could vote. In practice, however, local registrars and clerks used their discretion in administering the test; they arbitrarily determined who would and would not be required to take the test. The examiners had various versions of the literary test on which to draw and many questions to choose from, and, most important, whites were sometimes exempted from the test altogether.

In Georgia, generally the test was composed of thirty questions, and in order to pass it, respondents were required to get at least twenty answers correct. The test could include such questions as: "What is a republican form of government?" "What is the name of the state judicial circuit in which you live, and what are the names of the counties or county in such circuit?" "What is the definition of a felony in Georgia?" "Who is the solicitor general of the state judicial circuit in which you live and who is the judge of such circuit? (If such circuit has more than one judge, name them all.)" "How does the Constitution of Georgia provide that a county site may be changed?" "How many electoral votes does Georgia have in the Electoral College?" "Who are citizens of Georgia?"[22]

Clearly, such questions were designed to encourage failure and to deny the franchise. Indirectly, they were a way of keeping blacks from voting, for if challenged, blame could easily be attributed to the inadequate educational level of Negroes themselves rather than the seemingly benign and rational questions on the test. Given the US Constitution's protection of literacy tests, it was difficult for advocates to mount effective challenges against their widespread use. However, for whatever reasons, the newly elected governor of Georgia, the "liberal" Carl Sanders, wanted to suspend the use of such tests. He was reported as saying, "One's inability to read should not be a bar to voting." In response, expressing umbrage at this notion, the *Thomasville Times-Enterprise* repeated its support of literacy tests in a November 2, 1963, editorial titled "An Inconsistency," where it said:

> This means of course that if one cannot read for himself, he would likely be used by those who can do so, to vote, as they wish.
>
> If reading is not to be required as a condition of qualified citizenship to be exhibited at the polls in the selection of those who are to run the government, levy taxes, collect taxes, declare wars and fight wars and all the other acts incident to government, then we might as well forego the need for educating the people—just let them be dumbbells or pawns in the hands of those who would use them for their own selfish ends.
>
> The advantages of a good education, or even a high school education are too well known to require repeating but it does seem some of our leaders are somewhat inconsistent in advocating dropping the literacy requirement for voting while insisting on more money for education.

Immediately on assuming office, state senator Leroy Johnson of Atlanta offered an amendment to an election law proposal that would alter the literacy test in Georgia.[23] Rather than thirty questions, under his amendment potential voters would be required to answer four of only six questions. They were:

1. Name the president of the United States of America.
2. Name the vice president of the United States of America.

3. Name the two US senators from Georgia.
4. Name the governor of Georgia.
5. Who are the members of the general assembly who represent you?
6. Name the sheriff of your county.

The state senate adopted the amendment by a vote of thirty-five to two, but passage by the Georgia General Assembly was an uphill battle because of strong opposition.

Then something quite unexpected appeared in the *Thomasville Times-Enterprise* on April 20, 1964. Under the title "125 Thomasville Students Become Registered Voters," the paper reported that both white and Negro students had exercised their rights of citizenship by registering to vote. Describing what happened, it said: "The students, all 19 years of age, added their names to the voter list by appearing before Thomas K. Vann Jr., Chairman of the County Board of Registrars." And, discussing the registration process, it said: "Registration takes only a few minutes of anyone's time. To register a person need only apply at the office of Tax Collector W. S. Stewart." In this article, the *Thomasville Times-Enterprise* went on to list the newly registered voters by name: of the 125, 66 were white, but importantly, 59 were listed as Negroes.

If the *Thomasville Times-Enterprise* reporting was correct and all you needed to do was go to the tax collector's office, take five minutes out of the day, and register to vote, then something clearly had shifted in Thomas County's voting process. Could this mean that officials—without informing the residents—quietly abolished the literacy test requirement for voter registration? No, the literacy test continued to be used as a useful tool in black voter suppression. But why was it important to announce the voting registrations of Negro students? What was the Thomas County Board of Registrars signaling to the community? And what was the impetus for this slight alteration in the voting process for Negroes? The precise answers to these questions are unknown to me.

At the same time, the rationale for separate racial polling precincts was becoming a bit more difficult to justify. As reported by the *Thomasville Times-Enterprise*, even a member of the Thomasville Chamber of Commerce thought such segregation unwarranted. When a federal judge ruled that separate voting sites were unconstitutional in Georgia, Bob Ausley, a local businessman, recommended that the Chamber of Commerce contact "the Board of Registrars and ask that such practices here be discontinued." He argued that Negroes stood in lines with whites to purchase automobile tags, "so I say, let's take the lead in abolishing the procedure here."[24] The recommendation was made, but the board said that it would "consider the matter at a future meeting."

Evidently the board did take up the matter of segregated polling, and by the fall another change had occurred. On September 12, 1964, the *Thomasville Times-Enterprise* announced in an editorial titled "Integrated Voting Here," that

> INTEGRATED VOTING in a Thomas County primary election Wednesday, was the first of its kind here on a county-wide basis. . . .
>
> That there were no incidents of any kind to mar good racial relations is a matter of community pride, reflecting the good citizenship of both white and colored citizens.

Were these shifts in the voter registration process a paternalistic attempt to do the right thing and ensure black voter participation? Given the long history of voter discrimination and suppression in Thomasville and the county as a whole, why did these shifts occur at that particular moment in history? The answers, I believe, rest in the fact that these procedural shifts were largely a temperate attempt to abide by the law in order to avoid the risk of federal involvement in local practices. They were a local response to the enactment of federal legislation—the Civil Rights Act of 1964—especially Title I, which outlawed voter discrimination.

o o o

While campaigning for president in 1959, John F. Kennedy did not want to antagonize, alienate, or risk political backlash from southern white voters. He needed their support, so he avoided speaking on issues of race and race relations, especially in the context of civil rights. After he was elected president, as legal challenges and public protest against Jim Crow segregation increased, he could no longer avoid the issue. The blatant political contradictions that undermined both his domestic and foreign policy agenda galvanized the attention of the nation, if not the world. On June 11, 1963, in a nationally televised address, he called on Congress to pass a major piece of legislation, a civil rights bill, to respond to discriminatory treatment against Negroes. In his remarks, Kennedy affirmed an essential premise of a democratic society, by saying: "The right to vote in a free American election is the most powerful and precious right in the world—and it must not be denied on the ground of race or color."[25]

On the centennial of Abraham Lincoln's issuance of the Emancipation Proclamation, the meaning of black freedom under a democratic government came full circle. Kennedy called on the nation to "rededicate itself to the goals of freedom" by proposing that Congress pass sweeping civil rights legislation against racial disfranchisement and discrimination. This landmark proposal offered provisions dealing with voting rights, public accommodations, desegregation of public schools, establishment of the Community Relations Service, continuation of the US Commission on Civil Rights, nondiscrimination in federally assisted programs, and the formation of the Equal Employment Opportunity Commission. As Kennedy told the nation on that summer evening in June, "Surely there could be no more meaningful observance of the centennial than the enactment of effective civil rights legislation and the continuation of effective executive action." Sadly, five months later, in the winter of 1963, President John F. Kennedy died from an assassin's bullet to the head.

Like the rest of the nation, both black and white Thomasvillians were deeply stunned and mourned this senseless tragedy. On the day following Kennedy's assassination, the *Thomasville Times-Enterprise* gave voice to the general sentiment of the community in a November 23, 1963, editorial titled "JFK, Warm Human Man." It said: "For, no matter what our politics, we know that this was a warmly human man who so obviously loved his family, his country and all human-kind that he was, in a sense, irresistible. . . . We must with one voice call upon the Divine Providence to guide the hand of now president Lyndon Johnson as he takes over the helm of government." But soon thereafter, on November 30, 1963, the paper asked, "Can There Be Unity?" Generally, this question of unity was raised in regard to the contentious state of race and race relations, but specifically to the proposed Civil Rights Act and the threats it posed to white supremacy. In its argument, the paper said

In his appeal for unity the President again pointed out the need for tolerance and understanding on the part of the people having . . . called for passage of the civil rights bill as a tribute to the memory of the late President.

It will be a little difficult to reconcile the idea of unity with the controversial issue of civil rights which legislation has been denounced by Southern Congressmen as a vicious bill. . . . There can be no denying the need for unity on a national basis, but its realization will be made more difficult when the administration seeks to enact legislation which ignores the traditional heritage of a large segment of the people. . . .

The civil rights bill has been castigated by Southerners as one which would give special rights to Negroes, while ignoring the basic constitutional rights of white people. As long as such legislation is sponsored by the government it is difficult to see how the spirit of unity can prevail. Can there be unity under these conditions?

The task of shepherding the Civil Rights Act through Congress was now in the hands of President Lyndon Johnson, a son of the South. After Congress passed the act, President Johnson signed it into law on July 2, 1964. The *Thomasville Times-Enterprise* viewed his action as a tremendous betrayal to the South, saying in a February 6, 1964, editorial titled "Steam-Roller Rolling":

President Johnson, a Texan and Southerner, who once professed to be in opposition to radical civil rights legislation, changed horses back in 1957 when he, as Senate Majority leader, pushed through the first major bill. First, he appeared to want to apologize to the South for his action, saying it was either that bill or something worse. Later he became proud of the fact he was the first to pass a civil rights bill and boasted of it, in his efforts to woo support as a candidate for the Presidential nomination in 1960. He has since become an open champion of civil rights, causing Southerners to wonder whether he is a friend of the South or willing servant of the NAACP.

Also responding to President Johnson's action was Reverend Rutledge Courtney of the Dawson Street Baptist Church, who told the Rotary Club of Thomasville on June 17, 1964, that "the nation is governed by a dictatorship of the President, the Justice Department and nine members of the Supreme Court." The *Thomasville Times-Enter-*

prise reported his affirmation and commitment to Jim Crow segregation and white supremacy in "Pastor Here Sails into Rights Bill." In his
remarks, the reverend said:

> There is hatred that will be in our bosoms for another hundred
> years. . . . I believe we do better if we're left to ourselves, I believe
> the colored man does better among his people and the white man
> among his people. I believe God made us as we are, and we should
> stay as we are.

Given such racial sentiments, especially among white community
leaders, city officials were confronted with a major dilemma: how to
uphold traditional racial values and customs while complying with the
newly enacted Civil Rights Act of 1964. This dilemma was quite evident
in the mixed message conveyed in the official public announcement
that appeared in the *Thomasville Times-Enterprise* under the title
"New Law and Your City." In its entirety, it read:

> The Thomasville City Commission recognizes that the new Civil
> Rights Bill has been signed, thereby becoming law. We urge re-
> straint, understanding, and good faith between all citizens of this
> community in observing the provisions of the act.
> The new Civil Rights Law does not invalidate local and state laws
> dealing with creating a disturbance, disorderly conduct, or any other
> laws dealing with orderly government. The present police proce-
> dures in regard to such laws shall continue to be enforced fairly and
> equally upon all offenders.
> —Mayor Roy M. Lilly and City Commissioners, City of Thomasville.

Did this announcement signal an end to Jim Crow segregation and
the usual ways of doing things in Thomasville? In theory, racial discrimination was now prohibited under the Civil Rights Act, but in practice,
adjustments were made to conceal blatant violations of the law. In their
announcement, city officials did not call on Thomasvillians to comply
with the new act; rather, they urged "restraint, understanding, and good
faith." Nor did they announce that they would enforce the new civil
rights laws, only that they would not tolerate disturbance, disorderly
conduct, or breaking any other laws dealing with orderly government.
Therefore, in the absence of compliance and enforcement, what did

their announcement mean, especially in regard to eliminating Jim Crow segregation and discriminatory practices?

Desegregation in Thomasville was a gradual process that was many years in the making. By 1964, it had been almost ten years since the US Supreme Court ruling on *Brown v. Board of Education*, and the public schools in Thomasville remained segregated, with no indication of change. More than anything else, the procedural shifts concerning voting in the community were attempts to ward off fundamental changes that were lurking in the shadows. It appeared that both black and white Thomasvillians wanted to avoid the racial drama and tensions that came with it, as played out by their northern neighbors in Albany. Reverend Mullins and the other local civil rights advocates knew that they could not simply wait for white citizens in Thomasville to do the right thing, even with the enactment of the Civil Rights Act of 1964.

A Negro Inter-denominational Ministerial Alliance headed by Reverend Mullins and representing the local branch of the NAACP, the Progressive Club, the Beauty Culture League, the Committee on Public Assistance, and the Negro Business and Civic League presented a resolution to the Thomasville City Commission. Reverend Mullins told the commissioners, "We are working for peace and harmony, but many of our people do not even realize they are free." The alliance asked commissioners to use their influence in getting white businesses to stop discriminatory practices. Reverend Mullins stressed the desire for "keeping good race relations a local matter, without calling on any outside agitators." But he also emphasized "the need for Negro participation in local political and economic life." The commission said it would take this matter under full consideration.

The Ministerial Alliance called on black Thomasvillians for an economic boycott against the intransigence of white-owned business "until blacks were hired as clerks in department stores and grocery stores and treated fairly." Furthermore, in its plan of action, the alliance also set aside a "Freedom Sunday" to commemorate "100 years of freedom for the Negro." The alliance asked people to march and assured the audience that it would be a local affair and "different from Selma." The alliance's goal was twofold: to get Negroes in Thomasville to understand that they were free, and to get white Thomasvillians to understand that also. This would be the first march organized by Negroes to ever be held in the community.[26]

For many blacks as well as whites, this was an unthinkable endeavor—a march down Broad Street by Negroes in an effort to force change. Still, there I was, along with about four hundred other Negroes, out of the shadows, wearing my church dress and shiny shoes—after all, it was a Sunday afternoon in late August of 1964—participating in my first march. Following the corps of drummers and the lead of Reverend Mullins and the other ministers, we were in no hurry, so I could easily keep up with the adults that surrounded me. Even though it was a demonstration and there were no floats or cars, to my childish eyes I thought it was a Negro parade. Never having actually participated in a "parade" before, I was elated by the spectacle of it all. We marched in silence while Thomasville police in their new powder-blue riot helmets kept a watchful eye on our movements. The *Thomasville Times-Enterprise*, reporting on the march in an editorial titled "With Dignity," said:

> Freedom Sunday, as promised by Thomasville Negro Leaders, was a quiet and solemn affair . . . marching about six abreast, progressed slowly—and without any particular fanfare—through the main business district. . . . The proceedings were conducted in a worshipful manner in keeping with the solemnity of the occasion and the quietness of the Sabbath.
>
> Thomasvillians have long enjoyed fine race relations. The progress made by Negroes here could be used as a model for other areas. Everyone, white and colored, is to be commended on the dignity of "Freedom Sunday."

3

WHO ARE WE BECOMING?

The Civil Rights Era

After years of pursuing other paths in life, I decided to become an educator—teacher and scholar—in order to share the lessons that I have learned during my life with my students as they begin to travel down their own particular paths. Admittedly, my choice seems a bit strange to me. If, when I was a child, an insistent adult had pressed on me the question, "What do you want to be when you grow up?" I probably would have said, "I don't know." Maybe I did not know because, as a Negro girl, teaching and nursing were my only clear professional choices. However, neither inspired my curiosity. Choice implies having the opportunity to select freely; it suggests knowledge of the range and variety of options available. But what if there are no good options, opportunities are limited, and the choices of others are forced on you? What, then, are the consequences of one's personal choice? Entering the world of desegregated schools, I would come to learn the meaning of freedom of choice.

Growing up, there was no room for doubt; I was going to get a formal education, regardless of what options were available to me later in life. After all, this was one of the main reasons why my mother was so intent on placing my siblings and me with teachers. It was her way of trying to ensure that we would at least become educated people, and it worked. As a teacher, Madea instilled into my sister and me that we would be educated or else we would become nothing in life. Seemingly contrary to both my mother's and Madea's life experiences, they firmly believed that formal education was some kind of magical key to unlocking the doors to a better, prosperous, and successful future.

Historically, and even now, many in my community believe that obtaining a formal education transforms one's fate. The power of knowledge, the nimbleness of ideas, and the creativity of thought gained in the process of formal learning is thought to be the key to opening doors long sealed shut to blacks. It allows them to envision alternatives to the human condition. This partial truth rests on the systematic exclusion of blacks from equal access to formal education for generations. It also rests on the response to that exclusion, as evidenced by the struggle of black parents to obtain quality education for their children if not for themselves. In the 1960s, even though school desegregation was but one battleground in a much larger struggle for black equality and justice, it was a critical pathway toward legally eliminating Jim Crow restrictions that had long dammed the way to choice and opportunity for blacks; it was the crucible for challenging the deep-seated attitudes and behaviors that lay at the root of inequality and injustice on the racial tightrope during the 1960s.

Without questioning the merits of my community's firm belief in the power of education, I went about the formal process of learning, even when, through my childish eyes, the knowledge acquired did not seem particularly useful. Early on, Mrs. Stoops, my kindergarten teacher, taught me how to read and write simple words from the adventures of Dick and Jane going up the hill to get a pail of water. It was at Mrs. Stoops's kindergarten, an old, unpainted, drab schoolhouse with a huge potbellied, wood-burning stove, that I first met many of the other Negro students with whom I would travel through the educational process.

Following our adventure into kindergarten in the small town of Thomasville, we all went to Frederick Douglass Elementary School, Douglass Junior High, and Douglass High School to become educated. We journeyed down the same segregated educational path that our family members, friends, neighbors, and the other masses of black Thomasvillians had followed for generations. Like them, we embraced our beloved Douglass school campus and understood the important place it held in our intellectual growth and development as Negroes living under Jim Crow segregation. But unlike previous generations, the introduction of school desegregation would dramatically alter our steps on the racial tightrope.

* * *

During slavery, it was illegal in the South to formally educate Negroes; indeed, some of the strongest penalties imposed by Southern law centered on keeping blacks illiterate. A. Leon Higginbotham documents in *In the Matter of Color: Race and the American Legal Process* that the legal restrictions on slave life were extensive. During the colonial era, as Higginbotham says, "Particularly revealing was the prohibition against teaching a slave to read or write . . . the financial penalty for teaching a slave was 50 percent greater than that for willfully castrating or cutting off the limb of a slave."[1] It was thought that ignorance was necessary in order to control the enslaved population, to aid in maintaining the institution of slavery. Slave owners seemed to believe that knowledge was attainable only in the written word and that the lack thereof would inhibit free will and limit the number of alternatives to their enslavement for slaves to pursue.

Immediately following emancipation, newly freed slaves were intent on learning to read and write in order to pursue the possibilities that freedom held. In their determination, W. E. B. Du Bois points out that "the uprising of the black man, and the pouring of himself into organized effort for education, in those years between 1861 and 1871, was one of the marvelous occurrences of the modern world; almost without parallel in the history of civilization."[2] Supporting Du Bois's contention, Gunnar Myrdal said: "The history of Negro education in the South is one of heroic deeds as well as of patient, high-minded and self-sacrificing toil."[3] With the encouragement of the Bureau of Refugees, Freedmen, and Abandoned Lands—known as the Freedmen's Bureau—northern benevolent societies and churches helped to establish Negro schools throughout the South. Blacks played a critical role in supporting and managing these Negro institutions from their inception by forming self-help educational societies.

In Georgia, during the Reconstruction era, these early Freedmen's schools were divided into six subdistricts, located in the towns of Bainbridge, Albany, Georgetown, Cuthbert, Americus, and Thomasville, respectively. These Negro schools constituted the first formal educational system in Georgia.[4] Prior to this, the state had attempted to establish a general education system for white children, but that effort soon petered out because of a lack of adequate funding. With the passage of a new state constitution in 1868, "a thorough system of general education, to be forever free to all children of the State" was proposed; and it was to be funded by poll and liquor taxes.[5] A few public schools were established throughout the state; however, again due to a lack of sufficient funding, these schools could afford to remain open for only three or four months during the year.

In 1877, following the Reconstruction era, the Democratic Party regained control of Georgia and began a political movement known as "home rule." At this time, the Georgia General Assembly officially segregated schools by race—nineteen years before the 1896 landmark US Supreme Court decision concerning *Plessy v. Ferguson*, which legalized the "separate but equal" doctrine.[6] This would stand as law until *Brown v. Board of Education* overturned it in 1954.

It was not until 1949, under the Minimum Foundation Program of Education, that a comprehensive nine-month segregated educational system was established in Georgia.[7] This time it was funded largely through sales taxes.

Many early schools in Georgia were privately run. Similar to other local educational systems in the United States, the availability of formal education in Thomasville did not evolve from egalitarian principles; rather, it was based on class, gender, and most particularly, race—especially in the South. Thomasville followed the same rigid, race-based educational system, with one path primarily for Negroes and the other for white students, especially for those whose parents could afford to pay.

The early days of Negro education in Thomasville can be traced back to church-run private schools, where missionary teachers, both black and white, played prominent roles in the educational process. Foremost among these schools were those affiliated with the American Missionary Association (AMA). In 1885, Mrs. F. L. Allen donated her hotel property in Quitman, Georgia, to the AMA to be used as a Negro school. Within months, this school was burned down to the ground by arsonists. The archival records of the AMA document the circumstances that led up to that the harrowing event.[8]

Quitman, Georgia, had never had a school for Negroes and utilized only one dilapidated school building for white children. Mrs. Allen, of Waterbury, Connecticut, donated a hotel worth about ten thousand dollars for a Negro school, and members of the Congregational church in Waterbury raised an initial thousand dollars and also pledged continuing support for the school. Notably, Mrs. Allen's hotel was located in the heart of downtown Quitman, and on hearing of the Negro school, town officials asked the AMA to exchange the hotel for an old factory building located outside of town. In an attempt to avoid potential racial tensions, the AMA agreed, but with the stipulation that "the exchange be of equal value and made so as not to hinder the opening of school in the fall."[9] Town officials were unable to raise the agreed-on amount to make the exchange financially equal, so the school opened as planned. It was a boarding school for Negro girls, named "The Connecticut Industrial School for Colored Girls." Local whites resented the fact that a Negro boarding school was located in the heart of downtown Quitman.

Reverend Parr, a white minister from Chicago, Illinois, was the school's principal, and three northern Negro women were the teachers. The boarding school opened with 141 students, but fearing for their safety, "only twelve girls were willing to come to board." Even though the school opened without interference from the townspeople, Reverend Parr was leery of potential racial trouble and hired a Negro watchman to keep an eye on things. As the weeks passed with no problems, the watchman was dismissed. But on November 17, 1885, at around one o'clock in the morning, the "teachers heard a great noise in the house. Upon investigating they found the building on fire and the boarding pupils pulling their trunks downstairs." Students, teachers, and Reverend Parr fled the burning building. As Reverend Parr said in a letter to AMA officials:

> The white citizens stood on one street watching and the faculty and pupils on another. The fire engine came to prevent the burning of adjacent buildings. By three o'clock all was in ashes and three cheers were sent up by the white crowd. The children were sent to their homes. The mayor of the town came and said, "they did not wish to be inhuman, and the teachers could go to the hotel at the city's expense." The accommodations given "at the City's expense" was one small room, with a fireplace, a pistol on the mantle, one bed, one

chair, a washstand, so as not "to be inhuman" to one man and four women!!

It was found that the floors of all the buildings and some of the furniture had been soaked with oil. Three large empty oil cans carried from the yard gave abundant proof of the fire being incendiary. It was afterwards learned that the town furnished the oil, and the merchants helped with starting the fire. [10]

Despite the chaos of the fire, Reverend Parr managed to take forty dollars from the building, and this enabled him to purchase train tickets for the staff. On the way to the railroad station, as he said, "With pistols in hand we walked on each side of the carriage guarding the teachers. The train unfortunately was an hour late. Some twenty-five men and boys were at the station to see the party leave. As we boarded the train they sang 'Goodbye my lovers goodbye.'" [11]

The next year, with support from northern Congregationalist churches, the school reopened in a small one-story frame building twenty-four miles away, in Thomasville. [12] Later, two Negro Congregational churches were established to help support the school—Bethany, in Thomasville, and Evergreen (family's congregation), in Beachton. Named the Allen Normal and Industrial School, after Mrs. Allen, the school provided both elementary and secondary education to Negro students, with Bible studies being offered in all grades. In 1933, due to a lack of funding brought on by the Great Depression, the school was forced to close its doors.

Meanwhile, in 1901, Thomasville and Thomas County established separate public school systems—one for students living in town, and the other for those living in outlying areas of the county. [13] Both systems were for white students only. Formal education of Negro children was left to their parents and the Negro community. Undaunted by this race-based exclusion from public education, the black community pooled its meager resources together in 1902 and established the Dewey City Public School inside the city limits of the town of Thomasville. It was the first public school for Negro children. But in 1919, Dewey City Public School was destroyed by fire. Determined to provide formal education, the black community leased space at the Allen Normal and Industrial School so that students could continue their education uninterrupted. In 1925, with a grant from the city, the black community built a new high school on the old Dewey City Public School site. This became Frederick Douglass High School. [14]

As the economic depression swept across the nation, in 1932, the black community somehow managed to raise ten thousand dollars, and the city contributed fifteen thousand dollars to build Douglass Elementary School and Douglass Junior High School. These schools were also located on the site of the old Dewey City Public School. In 1940, with additional financial assistance from the city, blacks constructed a new elementary school located in another Negro residential area of Thomasville. It was initially named the Normal Park Elementary School but was later renamed the Susie H. Dunlap Elementary School, in honor of the first principal of Dewey City Public School.

Consequently, the Negro public school system in Thomasville was composed of two elementary schools, a junior high, and a high school. Throughout each phase of the Negro public school system's development in Thomasville, blacks played critical roles in financing the construction and providing the necessary administrative oversight. The Parent-Teacher Associations (PTAs) raised money through raffles, chicken dinners and fish fries, community fairs, talent shows, and other special events to purchase needed schoolbooks and lab equipment.

Eventually, the all-white Thomasville Board of Education took control of the administration, budget, personnel, and curriculum of the Frederick Douglass schools and also of the Susie H. Dunlap Elementary School. [15]

Nonetheless, we claimed these segregated schools as ours. They were built out of the blood, sweat, tears, and meager funds of the Negro community. Above all else, our schools were built out of the firm commitment to educate Negro children. They offered "principles of scholarship, moral character, integrity, leadership and good fellowship instilled in all who enter these walls," as the motto of Frederick Douglass High School proclaimed.

Along with Negro churches, Negro schools became an abiding institution within the black community. While it was a rare occasion to attend another church's service or religious activity because of the differences between beliefs and rituals, our schools readily served as communal places for meetings, arts and entertainment, and intellectual pursuits. They were central to the vibrancy of our community and, under Jim Crow segregation, to how we viewed ourselves. We were not made to feel small, unworthy, and of less value inside the hallways and class-rooms of the Negro school. To the contrary: they welcomed and af-firmed our human potential, possibilities, and hopes. Within the vener-able walls of our segregated schools, we could validate and give mean-ing to our positive identities.

History, traditions, and identity that we forged within the walls of Frederick Douglass Elementary, Junior, and High Schools were brought to a jarring and disconcerting halt in the fall of 1970. My fellow students and I, having grown up together, were forced to travel down a different path altogether. We followed an unknown course—desegrega-tion of the all-white Thomasville High School. There was no road map to guide us on our rocky journey, which was filled with fear, anger, and hatred because of our race. It would have an indelible impact on what we learned during the process of our formal education, particularly regarding the importance of race and race relations in our lives.

❊ ❊ ❊

After sixteen years, following the landmark US Supreme Court decision in *Brown v. Board of Education*, which overturned *Plessy v. Ferguson*, the dual racially segregated school systems of Thomasville city and of Thomas County were desegregated. Obviously, this desegregation did not involve "deliberate speed," as called for in the 1954 Supreme Court ruling; instead, it was a gradual and arduous process.

It was not until the passage of Title VI of the Civil Rights Act of 1964, banning racial discrimination in educational programs and activ-ities receiving federal funding, that a token school desegregation plan was implemented in Thomasville. Given the law, school officials seemed to understand they could not stand back and do absolutely nothing. In the absence of federal funding, public schools, both black and white, would be in jeopardy of closing. The first strategy to be implemented by the school superintendent, William Ryan, was the grade-a-year integration plan. It was largely a stalling tactic. Starting in 1964, full desegregation would be accomplished over a twelve-year pe-riod by desegregating each first-grade class in the subsequent years.

During the winter of 1964, the all-white Thomasville Board of Edu-cation announced details of how this plan would be implemented. The plan of action was posted on the front page of the *Thomasville Times-Enterprise*. As the paper said in a December 3, 1964, editorial:

> Unemotionally and without fanfare, the Thomasville Board of Education has announced plans for a program that could lead to integration next year in the first grade.
>
> Under the plan, any Negro student applying for admission in white schools would be eligible for the first grade if the white school were nearest his home. A grade would be added each year thereafter until all 12 grades had been desegregated.
>
> Thus the school board has lived up to its obligations. This board is composed of men elected by Thomasville voters. Now the citizens should support their action for the sake of the schools.

Under the grade-a-year plan the superintendent assigned each incoming first-grader to his or her designated elementary school, based on where the child lived; generally, the child went to the elementary school that was nearest home. Of course, the two Negro elementary schools—Frederick Douglass and Susie H. Dunlap—were located in the black community. As a result, few, if any, Negro children attended white elementary schools, and no white students attended Negro schools during the 1964–1965 academic year. Under the grade-a-year integration plan, Thomasville public schools remained fully segregated.

Thomasville was by no means the only area that attempted to employ token integration measures. In fact, the grade-a-year plan was implemented throughout the South. However, civil rights attorneys mounted legal challenges in federal courts against such strategies. In 1964, the Sixth Circuit Court of Appeals in *Northcross v. Board of Education of the City of Memphis* ruled that the grade-a-year plan "was too slow" and that the city must complete the desegregation process within two years. Federal courts also upheld additional challenges to variations on "token" integration strategies. [16]

At the same time as the federal courts were striking down the grade-a-year plan, the US Department of Health, Education, and Welfare (HEW) created even more stringent criteria for public school districts that wished to receive federal funding. Called the "Statement of Policies," these guidelines were composed of three criteria that local school districts had to comply with in order to qualify for educational funding. School districts were required to submit desegregation strategies that included the following elements: first, assurance of nondiscrimination based on race in the assignment of students, faculty, and school staff, as well as in available facilities, activities, and educational services (HEW Form 441); second, a court order, if applicable, which called for the desegregation of a particular local school system; and third, a desegregation plan that laid out the attendance options available to parents. This third factor, called the Freedom of Choice plan, had to either allow parents to decide where to send their child to school; assign students to schools based on nondiscriminatory geographic attendance areas, which were largely targeted at isolated or rural districts where students were assigned to a zone regardless of race; or combine both of these options. School desegregation plans had to receive approval from the Office of Education, and tangible progress combined with good faith efforts had to be shown in the implementation of strategies in order to receive funding. The Office of Education set the fall of 1967 as the goal for achieving full desegregation in all school grades, especially in the South.[17]

The Thomasville Board of Education was therefore forced to abandon its grade-a-year desegregation plan, but not without strong resentment. That resentment was expressed in a lengthy and blatantly racist editorial that ran in the January 11, 1965, edition of the *Thomasville Times-Enterprise*. In part, it read:

> Since the courts are now running the country, there is nothing left for school authorities but to obey the order, it seems.
>
> Historians at some later date will have an opportunity to look backward to the time in which we now live, to point out that the action now being taken to force racial mixing at the school level, was responsible for an attempt to integrate the race and in the end produce a mongrel race.
>
> Maybe that is what the President has in mind when he speaks of the "Great Society;" perhaps he should have referred to it as a new type of society, designed to produce racial conditions similar to those found in some of the South American countries, where they have varying skin shades, and a people who seem to have made little progress over the years.
>
> Forcible race mixing never has been a success, except perhaps in isolated instances. The attempt to build one racial group up by pulling another racial group down can only be viewed with concern by

those who are interested in the future of both the colored and white races.

This editorial did not speak for or express the sentiments of civil rights advocates in Thomasville. On the contrary, with the passage of the Civil Rights Act of 1964, Reverend Mullins, members of the local branch of the NAACP, and the Progressive Club were preparing to test the strength of the law. On March 23, 1965, an obscure little section of the *Thomasville Times-Enterprise* called "Keeping up with Thomasville" noted that "Thomasville Negroes Protest to the Mayor." The paper did not provide any details of this meeting, but noteworthy shifts in the customary ways of doing things in Thomasville following that meeting may provide some indication of what was discussed.

During the year 1965, several notable first-time events occurred in Thomasville. For the first time, black police officers were hired. The *Thomasville Times-Enterprise* featured an article on May 21, 1965, that "Negroes Doing Good Job Here as Policemen," which mentioned that three black police officers "patrol both white and Negro neighborhoods." Also, for the first time, a Negro, William Morris, a member of the Progressive Club and, most important, the principal of Susie H. Dunlap Elementary School, was selected to serve as a juror during the 1965 fall term of the Thomas County Superior Court proceeding held in Thomasville. Another first was the large commercial ad for the Belk-Hudson Department Store, which appeared in the paper with two full-size pictures of smiling Negro men sporting stylish suits.

Furthermore, significant shifts were occurring on the political landscape. The *Thomasville Times-Enterprise* reported on August 12, 1965, that a "large Negro delegation from Thomas County" attended a "massive voting rally in Albany." In reality, this was not a rally at all; rather it was a planned strategy meeting focusing on voter registration tactics. Participants attended workshops and speeches aimed at taking advantage of the newly passed Voting Rights Act of 1965, which outlawed discriminatory voting practices responsible for black disenfranchisement. In this context, another black voter registration drive was aggressively undertaken in Thomasville.

Also, Elijah Hill and Washington Virgil threw their hats into local political races for seats on the Thomas County Board of Commissioners and Board of Education, respectively. Both men mounted vigorous campaigns during the 1965 elections. Even though both positions were seen as vital to the political interests of the black community, it was Mr. Virgil's campaign for a seat on the school board that garnered the most attention in both the Negro and white communities, given the heightened political sensitivities surrounding the inevitability of full school desegregation.

Those sensitivities were spurred on by what had happened during the winter of 1965. In a small town twenty-eight miles away, Moultrie, Georgia, located in Colquitt County, Negro students demanded an end to segregated education. The turmoil over school desegregation there literally landed on the doorstep of the Thomas County Courthouse when legal proceedings were held at the district court. The courtroom gallery was overflowing with onlookers, most of whom were black parents from Moultrie.

In a series of front-page articles during February 1965, the *Thomasville Times-Enterprise* reported on events in Moultrie. To begin with, almost seven hundred students had begun a weeklong boycott of Moultrie's all-black William Bryant High School. The all-white Moultrie Board of Education threatened to arrest the students' parents for violating compulsory education laws if they did not send their children back to classes. On their behalf, civil rights advocates presented a list of demands to the board, which included restoring academic accreditation, improving building maintenance, paving roads around the school, and hiring more teachers, as well as purchasing more textbooks and better science and library equipment. The board responded by saying the city could start paving portions of the school's roads, repair the drainage system, purchase 157 new desks, and buy $167 worth of books for the school library. But beyond this, board members indicated that the school district was not financially able to purchase new laboratory equipment, hire new teachers, or bear the cost of school accreditation. This was unacceptable to the Negro students.

Hence, about three hundred Negro high-school students staged a march on the school superintendent's office, demanding that they be admitted to Moultrie's white high school because of the intolerable and deplorable physical conditions of their school. Local policemen, state patrol officers, and sixteen employees from the Colquitt County Work Farm were there to meet them. The students, ranging from thirteen to eighteen years of age, were arrested for disorderly conduct. The girls were taken to the city jail, while the boys were sent to the county workhouse.

The arraignments for their release were held in the district court in Thomasville, where bail was set at twenty-six dollars per student. Additionally, a hearing about a petition, submitted by the students' parents, which sought an injunction to halt the use of the all-black school facility due to its unsafe and unhealthy conditions, was also held there. Moultrie's city attorneys argued that the conditions at the Negro school were similar to those at the white high school and furthermore that the board of education was in the process of developing a school desegregation plan in compliance with the Office of Education guidelines. The injunction was denied, and the Negro students were forced to return to their dilapidated school, William Bryant High.

The turmoil over school desegregation in Moultrie intruded on the sensitivities of white Thomasvillians as Elijah Hill and Washington Virgil were readying themselves for the December 7, 1965, local election. As president of the Progressive Club and a successful Negro business-man, Elijah Hill was well known in Thomasville. But Washington Virgil was largely unknown, especially to the white community. His support-ers took out several political ads in the paper in order to introduce him to the Thomasville community. The ads pointed out that in 1943, as a junior at Douglass High School, he was drafted into the army and that he participated in the liberation of France during World War II. Returning to Thomasville after the war, he completed the requirements for a high-school diploma. He became a butcher at Sunnyland, a meat-processing and packing company, and married LulaBelle, with whom he had eight children. His civic involvement included twelve years of membership in several church and community organizations, most not-ably the Negro Business and Civic League of Thomasville, and he was president of Susie H. Dunlap PTA and a member of Douglass High School PTA.

In a field of five candidates running for three open seats on the board of education, Washington Virgil's political platform called for change and inclusive representation, as he said:

> I point out the need for a change in our school board's approach in dealing with issues, policies and problems in our school system. This change simply asks the citizens of Thomasville to give to our schools

in this present election a Board consisting of representation of the
total community it serves. . . .

I do not consider my entrance in this race to be a contest. This I
would like to make clear. Rather I consider my candidacy a petition
to the voters of Thomasville. Most of all, I consider it to be a petition
of the highest integrity that could possibly be presented to any people in a land of democracy—a petition that is just in every respect. . . . This change will not only exemplify courage and dignity in
our approach in meeting the challenges that lie ahead, but it will also
speak out in a resounding voice, say to the nation that we, the citizens of Thomasville, have the courage, dedication and determination
to deal adequately with all local problems.[18]

In support of Washington Virgil's and Elijah Hill's campaigns, an
aggressive voter registration drive was mounted in the black community
by civil rights advocates. Of the 5,858 registered voters eligible to vote
in the upcoming election, it was estimated by election officials that
more than 2,000 were Negroes. On Election Day, December 7, 1965,
the *Thomasville Times-Enterprise* reported "Early City Vote Unusually
Heavy." In the field of three candidates for post number four on the
Thomas County Board of County Commissioners, C. W. McKinnon
won with 1,753 votes, while Elijah Hill received 990 votes, thereby
losing the election. Among the five candidates seeking the three open
seats on the board of education, Washington Virgil came in last place,
receiving 980 votes for his efforts.

The day following the election, the *Thomasville Times-Enterprise*
asked the question, "Why So Many 'Voids' in Tuesday's Vote?" The
article stated: "As it turned out, a total of 1,163 'voids' were reported by
election officials. This was more than a third of the record turnout of
3,378 voters." Election officials justified such a high number of disqual-
ified ballots by placing the blame squarely on voters' incompetence and
their "carelessness or ignorance" of the voting procedures. At this late
date, it is extremely difficult to determine exactly what happened during that election and whether or not procedural improprieties and voter
suppression occurred. However, it is known that both Elijah Hill's and
Washington Virgil's candidacies were seriously disadvantaged due to
the countywide, or at-large, voting system used in local elections.

In Thomas County, there are six towns and unincorporated villages
in addition to Thomasville, the county seat. In 1965, the total popula-

tion was around twenty thousand people, and most blacks lived in Thomasville. In local elections, county commissioners and members of the board of education were elected by a countywide voting system rather than by a district voting system. This meant that if you ran for office from Thomasville, you had to get a majority of the votes cast in Thomas County as a whole, and not just a majority in Thomasville itself. Therefore, because candidates for office had to depend on support from the surrounding areas in the county, where registered white voters vastly outnumbered Negro voters, the countywide system diluted the strength of the black vote. This could be construed as racial discrimination, but the reverse was also true: if you were from one of the smaller towns or villages in the county, you needed strong support from voters in Thomasville in order to win an elected position.

Some Thomasvillians, therefore, simple viewed the countywide voting system as inherently unfair, regardless of any possible racial bias, and sought to change the system. That is why, in 1966, a group of white citizens living in Thomasville filed a federal lawsuit, *Davis v. Thomas County, Georgia, et al.*, claiming "invidious discrimination."[19] The court ruled against them. Later, in 1978, the NAACP would attempt to get the countywide voting system thrown out by filing a similar lawsuit, claiming racial discrimination instead, and again, a federal court ruled against the plaintiff. Nonetheless, the outcome of the local 1965 election was decided, and black Thomasvillians continued to have no political representation in governmental affairs.

Following that election, the issue of school desegregation continued to dominate the sociopolitical climate of Thomasville. Token desegregation in the form of the grade-a-year strategy was no longer acceptable to the Office of Education. Therefore, the Thomasville Board of Education had to come up with another plan for full school desegregation and put forth a "good faith" effort in order to stave off the risk of defunding. A new threat was looming also—the possibility of a federal takeover of the local school system. As outlined in the Office of Education Statement of Policies, the board of education had to adopt one of three proposals: the Freedom of Choice plan, geographic attendance, or a combination of both. On behalf of the Thomasville city school district, the superintendent and board submitted a desegregation plan calling for Freedom of Choice, in compliance with federal guidelines.

∘ ∘ ∘

In April 1965, a new superintendent of Thomasville City Schools, Charles McDaniel, along with nine other educators from Georgia, met in Washington, D.C., with officials from the Office of Education to discuss problems in implementing the Statement of Polices guidelines. The superintendent told the *Thomasville Times-Enterprise* that he believed that some of the guidelines "are impractical, arbitrary and impossible to implement." He specifically pointed out the transfer of 8 percent of the Negro student population to white schools; placing Negro and white teachers in desegregated schools regardless of whether they wanted to make the change; and the lack of criteria for determining when a racially dual school was eliminated.

Regardless of his concerns, following that meeting, McDaniel submitted a school desegregation plan that complied with federal requirements, and it received approval. It is noteworthy that Thomasville's Freedom of Choice plan for school desegregation was the only one approved by federal officials out of the fifty-one plans submitted from local school districts in Georgia for the 1965–1966 school term. "The Thomasville plan calls for desegregation of all grades this fall with students granted the opportunity to sign for any school they want."[20] Thus Thomasville's Freedom of Choice plan became a model for other local districts to follow.

In anticipation of federal approval, as required by the Office of Education, the Thomasville Board of Education announced the "Notice of School Desegregation Plan under Title VI of the Civil Rights Act of 1964" in the *Thomasville Times-Enterprise* on April 29, 1965. The Freedom of Choice plan called for the parents or guardians of the student to select which one of Thomasville's schools they wanted their children to attend. The plan laid out in detail the process for enrolling students and the school choices that were available. Explanatory letters and school choice forms were sent out to parents and guardians at the end of May 1965 to be returned to the board of education within thirty days.

The Negro community was abuzz. The Freedom of Choice plan for school desegregation hinged on Negro parents' and guardians' decisions. White parents and guardians were also required to select a school, but local educational officials anticipated that whites would not voluntarily choose to enroll their children in an all-black school, and they proved correct in their assessment. However, officials did not anticipate the decisions made by Negro parents and guardians.

Under the Freedom of Choice plan, Madea had the power to decide which school my sister and I would attend, but there was really no decision to be made. We would all remain in the Douglass schools: Madea as a second-grade schoolteacher, my sister as an eighth grader, and I as a fifth grader. For the vast majority of Negro parents and guardians in Thomasville, which had more than two thousand school-age children, this decision was a no-brainer. Given the option to choose, they would not send their children to white school. Like Madea, their choice rested on two important considerations: the historical attachment and pride they had vested in their Negro schools and the possibility that their children would be in a hostile learning environment because of forced racial mixing. Negro parents were not prepared to expose their children to a possibly dangerous situation, and they were not convinced that sending their children to another school simply because the teachers and students were white was the better or best choice to make.

Many black Thomasvillians supported ending Jim Crow segregation but not necessarily school desegregation. There were parents who made different choices, in spite of real concerns for the safety and well-being of their children, because they believed that school desegregation was a critical step in moving race relations forward in Thomasville. During the 1965–1966 school term, under the Freedom of Choice plan, eighty-eight Negro students were registered to attend six white schools in Thomasville—forty-five in elementary schools, thirty-three in junior high schools, and ten in the only white high school. Most, but by no means all, of the parents who sent their children to white schools were from Thomasville's small black middle class—many of whom were teachers or leaders in the civil rights movement.[21]

Their children were trailblazers, charting the course for others to follow in the process of desegregating public education. They were the ones who tested the boundaries and defined the complexities of what it meant to be black in white-dominated space; they were the first to meet the challenges that came with this dramatic change in race relations in Thomasville. This first group of desegregated Negro students was seemingly better able to confront the fear, anger, and hatred that came with racial otherness than those of us who would later follow in their footsteps. Maybe growing up in middle-class homes with higher socioeconomic status had something to do with how well they could, or would, adjust to the dominant behavioral norms in structured white social space. One must ask, in a racially charged environment, does economic class somehow neutralize or provide a buttress against racial animus?

The lessons of history strongly suggest that merely occupying the same previously exclusive social space is simply not enough to bring about meaningful racial change. One's mere presence does not alter power or race relations. It is what actually happens in that space that colors the contours and shapes the character of significant change. The first Negro students to attend white schools entered spaces created to serve the needs and interests of white students, and the presence of black students did not radically alter that reality. To the contrary, most were seen and treated as intruders into that privileged space. Many felt isolated, especially the ten Negro students attending Thomasville High School. They were the only black students among nearly nine hundred white students. The burden of change rested on their shoulders. They were expected to fit in, assimilate, and ultimately gain acceptance and status among their white peers.

Now Negro and white students occupied the same social space— sitting in the same classrooms, eating in the same lunchroom, sharing the same bathrooms and water fountains, playing on the same sports teams, and pledging allegiance to the same American flag at student assemblies. Would these tiny acts begin to break down the walls of racial intolerance? Would children hold the key to fostering meaningful change for the future of race relations? Or would history require much more? In four years, the rest of us—almost two thousand Negro students—would be added to this experiment and be expected to emulate the behaviors of those who went before us. Would we have to abandon our history, traditions, and identities to accommodate being educated in white social space?

Whatever that transition held for us, it would have to wait. Our parents and guardians had made their choices. We returned to the process of learning at the Frederick Douglass and Susie H. Dunlap schools. I was an average student, and the academic subjects—even though more depth and sophistication was added each year—were fairly easy to grasp; I received decent grades for my efforts. I cannot recall any major problems with classroom learning. Generally, I was polite and respectful to teachers, addressing them as Mrs., Miss, or Mr. and using the formal Southern "yes, ma'am," "no, ma'am," or "no, sir," as the case dictated. Other than the constant complaints by my teachers that I was not applying myself to my studies, I did not have any unusual difficulties in the classroom.

I had more difficulty in grasping the unpredictability and nuances of change, especially those changes that were occurring inside myself. As I matured, I realized that something was shifting at my school. Because of the advent of desegregation, I felt the loss of several childhood friends, who were now seemingly in another world. Not only did some students disappear from my life, but also a few teachers, as the vortex of school desegregation began to swirl around me. One day, without fanfare or introduction, several white faces simply appeared in the venerable hallways and classrooms of Douglass High, Junior High, and Elementary Schools. Five white teachers were hired to desegregate the faculty. The swirling seemed to quicken with the passage of time; promotion from grade to grade, alterations in physical appearances, and shifts in attitudes and behaviors all contributed to my feeling of loss. I was not unique; change began to envelop the experiences of my fellow students as well.

Seemingly overnight, we had developed into teenagers. My fellow students and I were questioning who we were and who we might become. We were adopting the attitudes of youth, moving away from the passivity of childhood toward becoming audacious and arrogant adolescents. Increasingly, we were growing sick and tired of what seemed to us to be accommodations to white privilege and Negro subordination. We had difficulty grasping the reasons that white people's thoughts and actions seemed to matter more in the scheme of things than what Negroes felt and did. Why it was incumbent on us to prove to whites that we were not lesser beings? As human beings, why weren't we simply good enough, as we were, to be accepted as equal? We were growing angry over those things that justifiably, we should have been angry about: right and wrong, fair and unfair, and the just and unjust ways we were seen and treated by whites. We were growing strident in our intolerance and righteous in our indignation.

In this vortex of change that was enveloping us, we began to reject our Negro racial identity. To be a Negro failed to capture our increasing angst: our anxiety, apprehensions, insecurity, and anger were spilling out all over the place, but especially inside of ourselves. We would no longer be complicit in our own racial oppression or give unearned deference to white opinions and actions. We firmly rejected our expected roles of "Aunt Tomasina" and "Uncle Tom."

"Black" was no longer a dirty word to us, a slur added to demonize and demean. Instead, our cultural icons were telling us that black was a noun; that "Black is beautiful." For us, the *B* in Black was now capitalized. "Black" rolled off our tongues as James Brown instructed us to "Say it loud, I'm Black and I'm proud"; as Nina Simone affirmed that we were "young, gifted, and Black"; as Stokely Carmichael commanded us to assert "Black Power"; and as Tommie Smith and John Carlos saluted the power that lay within the boldness of our Black selves to an international audience on the medal stand at the 1968 Olympics. We readily swayed to the newly found rhythms that flowed from the drumbeats of blackness while the older generation clung to its identity of Negro.

A revolution was occurring in our minds and hearts: a radical change that was not only transforming how we saw ourselves but also how we viewed others. What it meant to be black was embodied in our individual and collective attitudes and actions.

At Frederick Douglass High School, the transformation came to a head in 1968, when one of the white teachers, Mr. Underwood, called a student in his class a nigger. Whether true or not, the word spread like wildfire down the hallways and into the classrooms. The campus grounds quickly filled with black faces. In protest, we walked out of school and refused to return to class until Mr. Underwood was fired. He and one or two of the other white teachers left. Shortly thereafter, the superintendent, Mr. McDaniel, announced that Thomasville's schools would soon be fully desegregated. So starting in the fall of 1968, we would be forced to trek across town to Thomasville High School, because although Douglass High was good enough for us, it was not deemed good enough for white students. Through our newly formed Black-with-a capital-*B* lens, however, we saw this as yet another step in the process of accommodating white interests.

Federal officials were placing pressures on the Thomasville Board of Education to fully desegregate the schools. The Freedom of Choice desegregation plan ran headlong into a major political snag. In March 1968, federal officials informed the superintendent that the school district had not made substantial progress toward full desegregation.[22] This meant that the district stood to lose federal funding. But regardless of whether funding would be withheld, the district had to comply with federal guidelines or court action would be taken; it was possible that the federal government would assume control of the school system. Federal officials made it quite clear to the board of education that nothing short of total desegregation of Thomasville schools would do. The board's back was up against the wall, and it was scrambling to avoid a federal action.

Under the Freedom of Choice plan, the board had anticipated that desegregation would be phased in over time, regardless of the fact that the Office of Education had established 1967 as the deadline for ending segregation in public schools. The board did not anticipate that the Office of Education would reject its plan for the upcoming 1968–1969 academic year.

With more than 4,500 students in the district and only six schools in which to place them—Frederick Douglass High School was excluded as a viable option—the logistics of immediately consolidating students was a major problem. Figuring out what to do with high-school students was particularly a concern—almost 1,700 students from ninth to twelfth grades were attending high school. Consolidating the two student bodies at Thomasville High School would result in enormous overcrowding, thereby adding potential chaos to the already complicated efforts of full desegregation.

In an attempt to mitigate the situation, the board of education proposed the construction of a new high school. This meant that both resources and a location had to be found in a short period of time, as the federal clock was ticking.

Unaware of these concerns, we happily returned to our beloved Frederick Douglass High School for the start of the 1968–1969 school term.

☼ ☼ ☼

It is often hard for me to decipher the true nature of change and its lasting effect on my life while in the midst of it. There are moments in my life when time seems suspended—when events are too large and overwhelming for me to fully grasp—when I am stupefied, not knowing exactly what to say or do because any response seems grossly inadequate to the occasion at hand. Even in such moments, I know that life continues on regardless of the events that shape it.

On Thursday, April 4, 1968, Dr. Martin Luther King was fatally wounded on the balcony of the Lorraine Hotel in Memphis, Tennessee. He was dead, and like most black Americans, I was absolutely stunned, hurt, and angry over the killing. Madea had a particularly bad time of it—she was dying from cancer and was in a lot of pain that day, so I had stayed home from school to care for her. We were watching the evening news when Walter Cronkite announced Dr. King's assassination and then President Johnson expressed his disbelief and called on the nation to reject violence. Madea said nothing, but her tears flowed freely. For me, the horror of that moment seemed to make time stand still.

Immediately following Dr. King's assassination, Black Power activist Stokely Carmichael held a news conference and told black America to take to the streets in retaliation.[23] Whether heeding his command or through their own initiative, blacks set aflame cities across the nation, and smoke bellowed from black communities near and far. Black Thomasvillians offered a different response to Dr. King's death; even though pain, frustration, and anger seemed omnipresent, our reaction was peaceful. Religious leaders took control of the situation—an interracial ministerial alliance was formed, and within days it had organized several public functions to commemorate Dr. King. These included a motorcade processional of about 150 cars; an interracial and interdenominational service that was held at the all-white First Presbyterian Church; and, on the Sunday following Dr. King's death, a large community memorial service at the Negro Varnedoe Stadium that was attended by hundreds of people.[24]

To highlight the significance of this interracial collaboration, for the first time the *Thomasville Times-Enterprise* printed a guest opinion piece written by a Negro. On August 9, 1968, author Frank Martin III wrote a piece titled "Race Relations in Thomasville a Two-Way Street." He asked the question: "Why hasn't Thomasville had a major racial outbreak?" The conclusion he drew was: "Local leaders of both races have used remarkable foresight and frankness—even when the truth hurt at times—to provide Negroes with good jobs and schools, and a chance to be a definite part of the community. . . . Constructive yet frank discussions, not fire bombs, bricks, and bloody riots are keeping Thomasville ever-progressive, and yet peaceful. . . . Thomasville may not be a model city of racial harmony. But it soon might be if Christians—not militants and Klan—lead the way."

I think that at the time, many Thomasvillians—both black and white, but especially those cloaked in strong Christian faith—wanted to believe that what Martin said was absolutely the case. The conclusions he drew were not necessarily right or wrong but rather an idealistic distortion of the facts. It is true that the voluntary, collaborative mourning of Dr. King's death undeniably suggested a meaningful and significant shift in racial attitudes and behaviors, particularly among some white Thomasvillians, for such interactions had never happened before. But it was premature to say that a peaceful and progressive state of affairs existed in Thomasville's race relations in 1968. The everyday reality of life for blacks was that white supremacy and racial injustice continued to dominate and undermine our lives. Yet viewed within the overall context of what was happening in other places around the nation, Martin's assessment of race and race relations in Thomasville could be seen as a logical conclusion.

Taking a broader view, however, 1968 was a watershed moment in our nation's history. Political chaos and violence gnawed away at the very foundation of the nation as many, especially youths, called for radical changes and challenged the established order of things. Those calls for fundamental changes in the status quo represented deep ideological divisions, but more important, they represented alternative ways of identifying who we were and who we were becoming. The sociopolitical conflicts of that year unfolded new social identities that would influence political interests and politics for years to come. Individually and collectively, no matter what our ideological differences might have been, we could not avoid or be unaffected by the political upheavals of 1968. As a nation, we shared those unavoidable conflicts in one way or another, and so did my hometown, the isolated and rural community of Thomasville.

During 1968, the *Thomasville Times-Enterprise* reported that the long, undeclared war in Vietnam had escalated; that the number of dead and wounded on both sides of the conflict had risen; how student demonstrators protested and occupied buildings on college campuses across the country; that Robert Kennedy, who was seeking the Democratic nomination for president, was assassinated at the Ambassador Hotel in San Francisco; about Richard Nixon receiving the Republican Party's nomination for president; and, finally, about all hell breaking loose as street battles between protesters and police ensued during the Democratic National Convention in Chicago.

Following the race riots (many blacks called them rebellions) held in the immediate aftermath of Dr. King's murder, Reverend Ralph Abernathy, his successor, established "Resurrection City" on the Mall in Washington, D.C. More than 2,500 poor people lived in the encampment. Parents in Brooklyn, the largest black community in the country, sought total community control over schools as white teachers went on strike in protest; police and law enforcement officers killed three students and wounded thirty-seven others at South Carolina State College; Charlene Mitchell became the first black woman to run for president, as the Communist Party nominee; Shirley Chisholm occupied a seat as the first black woman in the US House of Representatives; and the undeclared war between the Federal Bureau of Investigation (FBI) and the Black Panther Party and other black radical groups left death and destruction in its wake.

The summer of 1968 was long, dry, and hot in Thomasville. By the fall, it seemed as if everyone was dripping in sweat and exhausted. In late August, nearly eight hundred black students returned to Douglass High School in the sweltering heat as the board of education, under fire from federal officials, scrambled to avoid a takeover of the Thomasville school system. In an attempt to ameliorate the looming crisis, the Georgia Department of Education stepped in with a million-dollar grant to help construct a new high school to facilitate consolidating the two existing schools. This grant was by no means enough; other steps were desperately needed to acquire resources.

Under Thomasville's city charter, the board of education had the authority to levy property taxes, and even though the county commission strongly disagreed with the move, there was nothing it could do about it. A school bond referendum was placed on the ballot for the 1969 local election; it proposed an 8 percent property tax increase. Additionally, the board of education requested from the county commission forty acres of land designated by the US Department of Housing and Urban Development (HUD) for restoration, to be used as the new campus site. The *Thomasville Times-Enterprise* reported on November 14, 1969, that: "Many homeowners, in a predominantly Negro residential area designated for a proposed new Thomasville High School complex, are expressing their opposition to the plan that would wipe out their home sites." In the article, the paper reprinted a joint letter signed by many of the homeowners addressed to the city manager, it said:

> We, the homeowners in this Renewal Area, met in discussion concerning our homes. We arrived at the conclusion that we do not want to sell our homes, as we have worked very hard down through the years to pay for them. We are happy in our homes and do not wish to change. Some of us have lived in this area for over 51 years. We hope that if you were in our places, you would feel the same as we do.

The proposed campus site consisted of 125 housing units and several local businesses; if granted site usage, those buildings would have to be torn down. In a small town with limited housing stock, particularly for poor blacks, this was large acreage to acquire through eminent domain.

Constructing a new high school required significant changes to the sociopolitical infrastructure of Thomasville. In the absence of those changes, what was particularly burdensome was the fact that some white students would be forced to attend Frederick Douglass High School, and if this did not happen, school officials risked federal intervention in the school district. But could Thomasvillians, especially white property owners, take on the financial burden of building a new high school? The *Thomasville Times-Enterprise* addressed concerns that many voters faced in a March 7, 1969, editorial titled "Conversation Centers on How to Finance New School," by stating:

> A MAJOR TOPIC of conversation at this time is the problem of how to finance the city's share of building a $1,500,000 high school complex. This is right and proper because the proposed new school building program has many angles, any one of which could seriously affect the kind of education that will be available to the children of this community.
>
> The school situation has become more complex as the guidelines set by the Department of Health, Education and Welfare are being

brought into play with desegregation rulings, and forced racial mixing. . . .

The plan for a new and larger high school building to take care of
students of both races has been outlined by the school authorities. It
has also been stated that unless the new high school complex is
provided then colored students would be bussed to the existing white
high school building and white students would then be bussed across
the city to the present Douglass High School building, all to the end
that any imbalance in racial lines shall be changed. . . .

The voters are asked to help the official bodies make a vital decision and it is desired that the burden of new school costs shall be as
widely distributed as possible. Heretofore the burden has been
borne largely by property owners. This group now feels there should
be a better plan for sharing the cost of educating the children of the
community. This is right and proper.

Despite the paper's subtle encouragement to voters to vote against
the school bond referendum, it passed. The county commission received HUD's approval to use the proposed building site and declared
eminent domain over the proposed forty-acre location for the new high
school. Having acquired the needed resources, the board of education
turned its attention to planning and constructing a new campus. The
school would take at least two years to complete and at the earliest
would not be ready for students until the academic year of 1971–1972.
The immediate issue confronting the Thomasville Board of Education
was whether federal officials would approve the new school desegregation plan for consolidation.

❋ ❋ ❋

Amid the political upheavals created by assassinations, widespread race
riots, antiwar protests, and massive street demonstrations in 1968, Richard M. Nixon was narrowly elected as the thirty-seventh president of
the United States. Many white southerners supported the archsegrega-
tionist George Wallace as an independent presidential candidate, but as
a Republican, Richard Nixon was also seen as a welcome relief from a
Democratic administration.

Southern whites who anticipated a more sympathetic political environment about the issue of school desegregation under a Republican

administration were not disappointed. Within months of taking office, President Nixon radically altered federal school desegregation policies. Most notably, the federal Office of Education began to ease up on the timetable for completing full desegregation by providing extensions to local school districts; forestall defunding decisions for those districts that were out of compliance; and give local districts more discretion in decision making regarding desegregation. These were welcomed changes because during the 1968–1969 academic year, only 20 percent of Thomasville schools and 10 percent of Thomas County schools were desegregated.

These administrative shifts in school desegregation policies ran into a major legal obstacle, however. In 1969, the US Supreme Court case of *Alexander v. Holmes County Board of Education*, a legal case that arose from Mississippi's slowness to desegregate its schools, gave definition to the doctrine of "all deliberate speed."[25]

In this case, for the first time, the federal government sided with the school district. The US attorney general's office argued that to proceed with full school desegregation in a hostile community would only create confusion and setbacks for local school districts. Government attorneys asked the court to slow down the pace of school desegregation by delaying federal penalties and federal intervention for noncompliance. Ultimately, however, the Supreme Court rejected the government's argument and ruled that "the obligation of every school district is to terminate dual school systems at once and to operate now and hereafter only unitary schools."[26] In other words, the Supreme Court held that public schools had to desegregate *immediately*. By implication, the Freedom of Choice plan as the main avenue for accomplishing full school desegregation ceased to be an option.

In a November 3, 1969, editorial, the *Thomasville Times-Enterprise* expressed its outrage over the Supreme Court's decision:

> The action of the US Supreme Court in demanding immediate desegregation in the schools of the South, and elimination of the dual school system now raises the question: "will the US Court rulings finally destroy the public school system of the nation?"
>
> So far as we know, there is no parallel in history, for conditions now posed by court decisions forcing racial mixing along the lines set forth by the court. If desegregation is going to destroy or seriously damage our public educational system, the nation ultimately will be

faced with a choice, "either desegregate and damage the educational system," or "preserve the education system by refusing to be a part of destroying the schools."

President Nixon himself is quoted as expressing the opinion that in Mississippi "satisfactory progress is being made in the integration program." But it isn't fast enough for the court, which has now taken a very dictatorial stand in demanding full compliance immediately, regardless.

There appears to be a rising tide of resentment and opposition to the high Court's efforts to remake the country in a manner that will conform to the sociological ideologies of Judges who not only have assumed the law-making prerogatives of the Congress, but who now demand that people individually and collectively must do as the court demands.

Others feel it has now become obsessed with power and like individual dictators doesn't care whom it crushes and runs over, if in the doing thereof they have their way.

In January 1970, the Thomasville Board of Education received a fateful letter from federal officials that said: "We cannot accept your plan which extends beyond the beginning of the 1970–1971 school year. We now have no alternative but to require the complete desegregation of Thomasville City schools by September 1970."[27] Caught off guard by the Supreme Court's decision, local education officials were thrown into a state of turmoil. The sudden resignations of Superintendent McDaniel and the principal of Thomasville High School only complicated an already difficult situation.

Scrambling to avoid federal intervention, the board of education hired thirty-six-year-old Garfield Wilson as the next superintendent of schools. Upon his appointment, Wilson strongly encouraged the board to comply with the Supreme Court's decision and immediately desegregate Thomasville's schools by the start of the 1970–1971 term. The board supported Wilson's recommendation, and within two weeks of receiving the letter of rejection, a new plan was submitted to federal officials. This plan was in compliance and received federal approval. Essential to that approval was the board's commitment to totally desegregate the school system by the fall of 1970, even though it had only five months to develop and implement a plan.[28]

Building a new high school was no longer an immediate priority; there was not enough time to finish it before desegregation had to take place. Instead, Superintendent Wilson turned his attention to meeting with parents, teachers, and students to discuss the unanticipated and dramatic change that would occur in the elementary and secondary schools at the start of the upcoming academic year. Many white parents expressed concern about the possibility that their children would travel out of their neighborhood to attend their designated school, but underlying this concern was the fact that some white children now had no choice but to attend schools in the black community. This was especially the case for white parents whose children were attending the elementary and junior high schools, because under the newest plan, in order to ensure an even racial balance Susie H. Dunlap Elementary School would house all of the sixth graders in the system, and Douglass Junior High School would be used for all seventh and eighth graders. Douglass High School was deemed unfit to be used, leaving only Thomasville High School to hold all ninth- through twelfth-grade students. [29]

Again, on March 3, 1970, the *Thomasville Times-Enterprise* expressed its problem with "The School Situation Here":

> The people of Thomasville are justifiably and unhappily concerned with the suggestion that children in grades five and up will be shuttled about arbitrarily from one section of the city to another.
>
> Under the proposed plan white pupils would be required to travel to Susie Dunlap School 3 miles or so distant out on Lester Street, and Douglass High [campus] at Alexandria Street.
>
> By the same order Negro pupils would be required to commute the same distance, in order to get into the now predominantly white schools.
>
> This is for the purpose of attaining racial balance under the desegregation and integration plan laid down by the courts.
>
> Many will agree that efforts to integrate the races are disintegrating the nation's public school system. If "Rule or Ruin" is to be the policy of the High Court, then it appears we are now near "ruin" so far as our public schools are concerned. . . .
>
> It is apparent that the nine man, judicial tribunal in Washington doesn't know and understand the feelings of the people and now somewhat power-mad they issue directives in wanton disregard of

the will and wishes of the people. They are too far removed from the
masses to understand the problem of the school classes.

Regardless of the strong sentiments expressed by the paper, the new
school superintendent moved ahead with a full desegregation plan. His
priority was to speak with parents and lay out what was expected in the
upcoming academic year. When he spoke with black parents of high-
school students, the superintendent—but more important, the new
principal—of Thomasville High School stressed the need for strict discipline. He told parents: "A firm policy on discipline will be established
and strictly enforced. No student will be permitted to interfere with the
right of another student to learn. If a student cannot behave in school,
he will be sent home to the parents. He will not be permitted to return
to school until the parents can give assurance that the son or daughter
will not interfere with the orderly operation of the school."[30] To ensure
a heavy hand in handling disciplinary problems, Wilson had recommended that the board of education hire thirty-three-year-old Thomas
Strealdorf to head Thomasville High School. The *Thomasville Times-
Enterprise* reported that Wilson called Strealdorf "a strong disciplinar-
ian, having served for two years as assistant principal in a high school of
about 2,000 students with a major responsibility of maintaining student
discipline."

For us, there was a series of orientation sessions designed to introduce Douglass High School students to Thomasville High School, with
an emphasis on discipline and behavioral codes of conduct.

Mr. Varner, who had been the principal of Douglass High since
1953, was seriously ill during this time period. It was left to Mr. Hopkins, a former student and math teacher at Douglass High School, to
assume Mr. Varner's duties as acting principal. He was responsible for
guiding us through this transitional process, and we looked to him for
leadership. As part of that leadership effort, each Douglass High School
student received a booklet outlining the code of conduct that we were
expected to follow once we got to Thomasville High School. Because
many of us had never actually been there and knew only that Thomasville High School was located somewhere in the white part of town, we
were shuttled back and forth to the school to get acquainted with the
facilities. Initially, they took us to the school cafeteria, where Mr.

Strealdorf laid out the rules and told us what to expect once school started in the fall.

To further prepare us, the black students and teachers who had disappeared from my life when they went to Thomasville High School magically reappeared to talk to us about their success in negotiating desegregation. But these were no longer friendly faces to us; through our newly formed black lenses, they were considered accommodationists, full-fledged "Aunt Tomasinas" and "Uncle Toms"—Goody Two-shoes, bowing to the expectations of whites and making no demands. We were expected to emulate them by adjusting and going along with whatever was put before us to complete the goal of full school desegregation. But unlike the few blacks who went to Thomasville High School before us, we were too plentiful—there were nearly eight hundred of us—to simply lurk in the shadows of this white space. Our presence there would surely be seen as well as felt.

The only question that I recall anyone asking during those orientation sessions was, "What is going to happen to our teachers and Douglass?"

° ° °

By the fall of 1970, I was dizzy from the changes swirling around me. Madea had died, leaving me vulnerable, lonely, and yearning for a stable presence in my life. My mother wanted me to come to Miami. It would have been a welcome invitation years before, when I was much younger and in need of her comfort, but then, even in such a tender state, it just did not seem like the right thing to do. It was too late. I really wanted to stay in Thomasville; somehow, the familiarity of that place was my anchor.

I went to stay with Madea's married sister, my aunt, and her husband. Even though as a child I had occasionally spent weekends with them, living with them full-time as a teenager required major adjustments. Experience thus far had taught me that at its most basic level, survival was accommodating and learning to live with things you cannot avoid or change. My aunt, similar to her sister, was a giving person; but dissimilar to Madea, she was overly concerned with middle-class Negro standards and respectability. Her concerns about proper behavior and what would impress others were a source of ongoing tension between the two sisters that I inherited.

My aunt was a secretary for the Afro-American Life Insurance Company, and my uncle worked as a waterman for the Seaboard Coast Line Railroad. They, like most people in my community, were hard-working people. For the first time in my life, I had a room all to myself, but I had to be careful as I moved about the house because my aunt was protective of her things. With no children of her own, my aunt focused her attention on home improvements and acquiring objects to beautify her house. She was particular about the things she purchased and, as a result, in constant debt. No matter how many times her friends visited her house, they were always greeted with a grand tour that showcased the latest piece of furniture or the new whatnots. This was for inspection but also, more important, to garner their admiration. The tour always ended with the hostess and her guests sitting on plastic-covered furniture, amid the flowers and doodads that adorned the living room. This was by no means a ritual that was all her own; when my aunt visited friends, she was expected to engage in the very same ritual of house touring. Like Madea, I had other things on my mind and was uninterested in such pretentious nonsense.

Beyond advice on how to act in public, my aunt provided little guidance, especially about how to negotiate the tricky terrain of school desegregation. In fact, she expressed little, if any, interest in that process or, for that matter, my education. I knew, or at least I thought I knew, that if Madea were alive, she would surely have shepherded me through that difficult process. In her absence, I was lost and virtually left to raise myself. Unencumbered by strict adult supervision, the only people I could turn to at the time were those who were equally as lost, my friends. The ignorance and arrogance of youth was the bulwark that sustained and guided us as we guardedly trudged down the rocky path of school desegregation.

In the fall of 1970, my fellow students and I entered Thomasville High School, sixteen years following the landmark decision of *Brown v. Board of Education*. School desegregation, as a legal and procedural matter in Thomasville, was complete. It was our new reality, and we had to survive as best we could in white space. The only lingering issue was whether or not it would work out.

Total strangers greeted us as we stepped through the doors of Thomasville High School, and we eyed one another with the utmost of suspicion. We were all on guard in anticipation of the slightest insult or inappropriate behavior. In one way or another, it had been thoroughly conveyed what was expected of us, yet it never seemed to have dawned on anyone—except for ourselves—that we, too, had expectations. We expected to hold equal shares in determining how this new social space, created through the consolidation of black and white realities, would be structured in meeting our needs and interests. Our expectations centered on what we considered to be issues of fundamental fairness. Forced to attend Thomasville High School, we fully expected that the two schools would be consolidated—not just the people, but also the history, culture, and traditions of Douglass High School. In retrospect, we were naïve, but it was this rich cultural heritage that had sustained us throughout the generations.

With no accommodation to our needs and interests in place (after all, what more could we possibly want or deserve than the legal right to occupy white social space?), we immediately decided to present a list of our demands to the all-white school administration. Foremost on that list was the hiring of black school administrators. Mr. Varner, our principal when we attended Douglass High, had died. Rumor had it that if he had lived, he was slated to become the head of the all-black janitorial services at Thomasville High. In fact, if he had lived, he was to become something called the "public relations administrator" for the Thomasville Board of Education. We felt this was a waste of his experience, as he had been a supervising principal of the Negro school system and affiliated with Douglass High School for more than thirty years.

In place of Mr. Varner, we demanded that Mr. Hopkins be appointed as assistant principal. For whatever reason, this was unacceptable, and to placate us, the board of education hired a Mr. Conyers. He had been a Negro elementary school principal with the Thomas County school system for three years. Not knowing much about him, we assumed that he was just another "Uncle Tom" and gave him no respect.

Furthermore, we demanded that Douglass High School's history and traditions merited continuing acknowledgment in the cultural life of Thomasville High. Seemingly frivolous, yet very important to us, were the twin issues of the school's colors and mascot. Thomasville High's mascot was a bulldog, and its colors were red and black. Naturally, this clashed with Douglass High's mighty lion and its colors of blue and gold. We wanted Thomasville High to change its mascot to a lion and its school colors to the blue and gold. If our request was granted, we felt that, at least symbolically, the public identity of the school would be altered to include some presence of Douglass High School. In an attempt to compromise, Principal Strealdorf agreed to change one of the school colors from black to gold. Everything else remained the same; none of the symbols that reminded us of Douglass High appeared at Thomasville High. Not only the mascot and school colors disappeared; so did the athletic and academic trophies, the pictures of notable alumni, our school anthem and motto, and all reminders of student awards or recognition. In one fell swoop, evidence of our ever having attended Douglass High was summarily discarded, and subsequently, our school identity was stripped away.

With each rejection by the white school administrators, our frustration grew. However, it was the more subtle insults that many of us received from our white teachers that quickly brought everything to a boiling point. I experienced the degree to which some white teachers imposed their positional power to mask racial prejudice from Mrs. Stowers. No matter how high or how persistently I raised my hand in response her questions, I was never called on. I spent inordinate amounts of time carefully writing essays that were worthy of As, but that grade was never forthcoming. To her, if you were black, you were invisible in this white space.

On Monday, September 14, 1970, two weeks after the start of school, black students gathered in the school auditorium. Prior to this, both the superintendent and principal met with several of us to once again discuss our demands and grievances. Dissatisfied with their response, we went back to the auditorium and reported the conversation to our friends. Angered by the administration's response, we decided to walk out of Thomasville High School in protest and took note of Thomasville's police—dressed in riot gear—surrounding the school. We gathered beneath the tall Georgian pine trees that dotted the campus as we tried to figure out what to do next. The administration sent Mr. Conyers to persuade us to return to class, but we ignored him. We did, however, listen to several of the black teachers, most notably among them Mr. Hopkins. He advised us to seek a promise from the superintendent that no disciplinary action would be taken against any of the protesters, and this we secured. In reporting the walkout, the *Thomas-ville Times-Enterprise* noted, "Dr. Wilson promised no disciplinary action would be taken if all students returned to classes immediately."

On September 15, The *Thomasville Times-Enterprise* also ran a front-page article entitled "Black Students Hold THS Walkout, List Demands." Also on the front page it printed an editorial that said, in part: "School authorities are trying desperately to solve the problems and to anticipate others that might occur." The editor of the paper wanted to help ease the racial tension at the school, so he decided to take a stand by saying: "We cannot help but feel that to publish news of every incident would be tantamount to fanning the flames of hatred." In other words, the paper would stop reporting on racial incidents at Thomasville High. However, the paper gave a column to a white mother of five children and former president of the PTA to voice her concerns and opinions of the "problems caused by school desegregation." Furthermore, it published letters to the editor on a weekly basis under the byline of "Parents Should Know Truth about School Incidents," usually written by unsigned white Thomasvillians and expressing concerns and opinions about what was happening at the high school. The overriding issue expressed in both the column and the letters to the editor centered on the lack of discipline, particularly of black students, as was promised by the superintendent and principal.[31]

Taking issue with the editorial decision to stop reporting on racial incidents at Thomasville High, one concerned citizen wrote to the *Thomasville Times-Enterprise* saying: "If students are being forced to attend schools where the atmosphere of violence and physical harm threatens, then the parents of the entire community should know. Parents could decide for themselves whether or not to continue sending their children to public schools. Are you willing to wait until someone's child is murdered in the hall of a public school before you let the citizens of this town know just how serious and potentially explosive the situation really is? I will not be counted among the silent majority any longer."

Another nameless citizen wrote: "Why were the Negro students who disrupted classes at Thomasville High, left the campus and went to Central (the county high school) in an attempt to gain support from students there, allowed to return to classes without fear of punishment? How can it be justified? It can't! The Negroes have told us often enough that they want the same things white people do and that they are the same as white people except for the color of their skins. They demand the same rewards as whites. They deserve the same punishment, too!" Also, a letter sent to President Nixon from a concerned citizen was reprinted by the *Thomasville Time-Enterprise*. It said, in part: "These Negro Children are not prepared intellectually, culturally or socially to be integrated. . . . The Negro teachers are not educated or prepared enough to teach the white children. . . . Integration, on the basis that is being forced on us now, is being endured, but believe me, it is Not working."

The *Thomasville Times-Enterprise* also printed two noteworthy opinions, offering different views on what was happening at the high school. One, from a black student, A. C. McIntyre, who was "willing to speak openly," said: "As a senior of Thomasville High, but from Douglass High, I think it's about time to get a few things off my chest. Let me say I was one of the Blacks to walk out and would do it again if necessary. . . . I say we as a race have waited too long. For those who say 'Negroes have achieved integration,' let me say integration doesn't mean anything to me because it would have suited me fine to attend Douglass. What I want is 'equal rights' and Respect . . . so let me say, slavery is over and there are no days of sitting and waiting, because Blacks today are outspoken."

The other letter was from "A White Anglo-Saxon," who specifically addressed the many anonymous concerned citizens who had written to the editor by saying:

> What you don't realize (or don't want to admit), Mr. Citizen, is that because you and those other millions like you either did not for years believe in equal education for the Negroes or, in any event, did not believe in it strongly enough to provide it. The Negroes did not, in fact, receive equal education. Now we are paying the price for our years of "benign neglect."
>
> It is entirely possible that an entire generation of white school children will be sacrificed before the Negro children are brought up to their level, education-wise. Furthermore, you had better believe that the Negroes are perfectly willing to sacrifice the education of their own children, as well as the white children, in order to achieve integration.

You see, Mr. Citizen, when we speak of the Negroes we are speaking of over 20 million people. They are not going away, and the sooner we assimilate them into the economy and the culture, the better off the South will be.

✦ ✦ ✦

In those early days, weeks, and months of desegregation at Thomasville High, there were ongoing protests by black students. Black Mondays were our favorites, when many of us boycotted classes altogether. We would just hang out at somebody's home, listening to music and engaging in a new recreational activity, smoking marijuana. Back at school, there was a lot of name-calling and many fistfights between black and white students, but I do not recall anyone being seriously hurt or injured. Usually the black participants were expelled. Many simply lost interest in going to school altogether and dropped out; for those of us who continued on, we waited for the next racial incident to occur.

We were organized. We were determined to use our black presence to pierce white social space; we took over the student government with our vote, where three out of four elected class officers were black, including myself. We elected the first black homecoming queen. En masse, we joined student clubs and participated in other extracurricular activities, such as band, chorus, cheerleading, football, basketball, and track and field. The 1970–1971 yearbook reveals pages upon pages of black and white smiling faces that mask the racial tensions lurking down the hallways and in the classrooms of Thomasville High.

It is often difficult to decipher the true meaning of change, let alone the consequences, while engaging in change itself. Having no choice but to participate in this racial drama, as expected, we gradually adjusted our behaviors, even as we altered the social space that had once been completely denied to us. Were we simply deluding ourselves into thinking that the shifts in the customary ways of doing things in Thomasville brought about by desegregation were producing meaningful changes in race and race relations? Clearly, the mere fact that we stepped into white social space brought about change, not only in our social environment but also, importantly, within ourselves. At the time, little did we realize that we were embarking on a journey through a desegregated landscape that would carry us down paths that would slowly lead us into racial gray zones. Many of us, having achieved the best that formal education had to offer, would be forced to confront who we had become in social space that was no longer exclusively black or white but gray, an area created in a reconfigured, multiracial society in a new millennium.

On graduation, I could not wait to leave Thomasville High School, and especially the town of Thomasville itself. Even though it was my anchor, the weight had become too heavy for me to drag around, and I felt myself slowly sinking into the abyss. I had completed all of the requirements and graduated a year early, and I wanted to go to college, but I did not know exactly how that was going to happen. My grades, at best, were only average; Cs dotted my transcript, but somehow, I could score fairly high on standardized tests. I had no guidance or money. I applied to several historically black colleges in Georgia and was accepted—but who would pay the tuition, room, and board?

Then I received a fateful telephone call from my sister, who told me to come to Minnesota and go to school there. I relished the opportunity of reuniting with her but was intimidated by the possibility. Minnesota! With my new, golden American Tourister luggage given to me as a graduation gift from my aunt and uncle, and dressed in a cloth winter coat, I landed in the white, frigid terrain of the Twin Cities, St. Paul and Minneapolis, Minnesota.

As I was leaving Georgia, in an attempt to ease if not erase racial tension, the Thomasville Board of Education tore down Douglass High School and discarded all that was encased within its halls and classrooms, without notification to the black community.

4

ARE WE A PART OF EACH OTHER?

Integration and Inclusion

White is one of my favorite colors, though some may consider white to be neutral, lacking the vibrancy of other hues in the color palette. I wear it often. For me, its crispness accentuates and adds visibility to black, brown, red, yellow, and other darker shades. Yet white also readily reveals spots, blemishes, and flaws that darker colors can more easily hide. If one does not recognize the distinctions between the fine gradations of white—cream white, pearl white, or snow—then one can easily fail to recognize that different shades of whiteness can sometime clash when worn together.

I never really gave much thought to the color white or recognized the variations in shadings until I landed in the Twin Cities of St. Paul and Minneapolis, Minnesota. It was in January 1973, when the snow was already hardened and piled high along the icy Minnesota landscape. With my neatly coifed Afro hairdo leaving little doubt of my newly found black identity, I stepped out of the plane and into a land of white space. I was far removed from all that I knew. In the Minnesota winter, everything appeared to be colored white: the air I breathed, the frigid cold that seeped into the very core of my being, the icy lakes and fields, and especially the people with their funny ways of talking and doing things. Minnesota white was far removed from the vibrant displays of local color in the rural South. I was inundated by the different shades of whiteness that faded into a singular hue, revealing the truth of my aunt's adage: this was a whole new world made from things that I did not know.

When I arrived, my sister was attending her last year of college at Macalester College and lived off campus in the Summit-University community of St. Paul. Summit Avenue was particularly well known for its large and elaborate Victorian mansions, built by industrial magnates between 1890 and 1920. It was also known as the former residential area of two famous authors, F. Scott Fitzgerald and Sinclair Lewis. University Avenue, about fifteen blocks away, wound its way from downtown St. Paul through the University of Minnesota Twin Cities campus to downtown Minneapolis. Between the two, about two blocks over from Summit Avenue, was Holly Avenue, where my sister and I lived. The Summit-University community was listed as a National Historic Landmark site, but such a prestigious designation was not based on my sister's and my tiny, dilapidated, one-bedroom apartment, with its shabby furnishings. Although lacking in comforts, it had the well-lived coziness of home for two young adults starting out in life.

The Summit-University community was also home to most blacks living in St. Paul during the early 1970s. Prior to this, the black community had been centered on Rondo Avenue, where blacks migrating from the South to escape Jim Crow segregation and poverty during the 1920s and 1930s had resettled.[1] In the early 1960s, when the city imposed eminent domain and constructed Interstate 94, hundreds of blacks living in the Rondo community were forced to leave their homes. Given discriminatory housing practices, most resettled not far away in the Summit-University area. Unlike other northern areas in the 1920s and 1930s, Minnesota did not attract blacks in droves during the great black migration. So when I arrived in St. Paul, they comprised less than 0.5 percent of the total population.

The notion of being part of a community, of belonging, took on added importance in this white environment. I felt a strong desire to connect with other blacks, but among them, I always felt a little out of kilter. I never felt really secure in this new black space; something always seemed to be missing. My sister fitted in quite nicely among her circle of fellow black college friends, but I brought my self-consciousness and shyness with me from Georgia. My backwoods upbringing and country awkwardness made me stand out among this more worldly and sophisticated collegiate crowd, and I mistakenly assumed that they were all smarter than I. The fact that they were all attending an elite private college, Macalester College, made me feel even more self-conscious and inadequate.

Yet my sister made me feel welcome and was ever encouraging me to participate. Feeling out of place, I trudged along with her to lectures at the college and parties at the Black House on campus. It was painfully clear, at least to me, that I was not really a part of her crowd. However, I also really did not have time to sit around and bemoan whether I fitted in or not; I had other pressing matters to attend to. I could not expect my sister to take care of me. I had to carry my own weight. Broke, I had to find a job, and quickly—not only to survive but to maintain my sanity in this new environment.

With no particular skills, I found a job that anybody could do—cleaning up after others. Four blocks over from Holly Avenue, I found work at a nursing home. Like my mother, I became a maid of sorts—a cleaning woman—mopping floors and cleaning toilets while the heavy aroma of disinfectant filled my nostrils. It was most peculiar to me that all of the other cleaning women at the nursing home were white. It had never really dawned on me that white women, too, could be cleaning women; that they, too, could do hard, shitty work for little pay; or that they faced similar challenges in life, had similar opinions about the world, and had similar dreams of something better. Mostly, it had never before occurred to me that because of those similarities, the possibility of becoming a part of one another's lives—even friends—existed.

The white cleaning women were completely different from my sister's black college crowd; I felt that we occupied a common ground that allowed for mutual sharing. But why did I find that I had more in common with the cleaning women? How was I to make sense of the apparent contradiction between my interactions with the educationally privileged yet racially disadvantaged black college students and the working-class, yet racially privileged white cleaning women?

* * *

Ten years of living in Minnesota taught me the distinction between inclusion and belonging. It is a distinction that is only realized in the ways we acknowledge and accept one another's differences. At first glance, inclusion and belonging can, on the surface, appear to be the same thing; sometimes, I even confuse the two myself. In reality, though, if one looks just beneath the surface, they are by no means the same. In my mind, it is the role that power plays in any given situation—the way that it is applied to others—that clearly differentiates inclusion from belonging.

To me, inclusion suggests to me some degree of mutual sharing regarding one's sociopolitical needs and aspirations. Yet my experiences have taught me that if those coming together share the power unevenly to make and implement important decisions about mutual needs and aspirations, then inclusion can become the mere presence of a body in the politics at hand. In those situations, inclusion can be largely tokenistic in effect. Tokenism, even when a person asserts agency, is not mutual sharing, because others impose their will on your fate.

Further complicating the reality of inclusion is the notion of difference, because it has a tendency to emphasize those needs and aspirations that are dissimilar and can thereby limit meaningful access into seemingly inclusive space. When this happens, those having the power to decide a person's fate sometimes give special consideration to differences, especially if the circumstances force them to or if there are advantages to be gained in so doing. Inclusion due to differences is still largely tokenistic and can carry the burden of stigma, which labels an individual as "not good enough" or "less than" the others, even while he or she is included and may fully participate in the same sociopolitical space.

Balancing on the racial tightrope in my ten-year sojourn in Minnesota, my footing often slipped on the tensions, dilemmas, and particularly the contradictions that inclusion held for me. That was due to my desire to be part of the whole rather than being forced to stand outside, looking in. To be part of something, to be included in the whole—even in white space—is quite seductive. But that inclusion must not be confused with belonging. Belonging occurs when there is an acceptance of full humanity—embodying both strengths and weaknesses—and attachments are born out of a mutually beneficial dependency. Such attachments require a sharing that contributes to the well-being of not only oneself but of others as well. Belonging then becomes a bridge, rather than a barrier, that leads toward future possibilities—even improbable historical moments.

However, the process of belonging is not easy. There are still hardships, frustrations, crises, or conflicts when seeking to respond to individual as well as collective needs and aspirations. It simply means that in the midst of those things, a mutual and respectful understanding exists—on which meaningful relations are forged—that considers our similarities and differences as sources of strength rather than weaknesses, which binds us individually and collectively to one another.

You may ask why this distinction between inclusion and belonging is important to an understanding of how we, as a nation, arrived at the age of Obama. I say this distinction introduces another historical layer, another important step along the racial tightrope that is revealed in the strategies and struggles to affirmatively admit African Americans' entry into the formal body of politics in our democracy. In spite of significant differences, African Americans claim a space of belonging.

* * *

The attempt to include people marginalized because of racial differences in our democracy was never more evident than in the concerted efforts of one of Minnesota's most notable sons, Hubert Horatio Humphrey Jr.

In 1945, as the newly elected mayor of Minneapolis, Minnesota, Humphrey chose to take affirmative steps across the wobbly tightrope of racial politics, and many Minnesotans followed in his footsteps. In taking those steps, he became instrumental in shifting the body politic of race relations in Minnesota and later in the nation. Humphrey's rise to political prominence was rooted in a new liberalism, which called for a more inclusive democracy, one built on active citizen engagement, fair elections, and equal application of legal processes. Fundamental to Humphrey's political stance was an antiracist agenda that increasingly focused on black disenfranchisement and the responsibility of the government to ensure equal rights. Now, in a state where racial minorities as a whole made up less than 1 percent of the total population in the 1940s, why would Hubert H. Humphrey stake his political career on including blacks and other minorities? Obviously, these groups had limited political influence, both in the state and nationally, in the formal processes of democracy. Why not take full advantage of the prevailing sociopolitical climate of exclusion, especially in the Democratic Party?

In comparison to other states, the history of Minnesota politics is atypical, which provides a partial explanation as to why Humphrey took the steps he did on the racial tightrope. As in other states, a two-party system—Democrats and Republicans—dominated the mainstream of electoral politics in Minnesota. But, as Jennifer Delton details in her book *Making Minnesota Liberal: Civil Rights and the Transformation of the Democratic Party*, earlier in the state's history the dominance of those parties was highly dependent on independent political alliances. By the 1940s, such alliances were forged with the more progressive forces of organized labor and farmers.

The Great Depression of the 1930s, which swept across the country, bringing economic deprivation in its wake, had devastating effects on urban laborers and small-time, rural farmers. This spurred a wave of political activism based on leftist ideology—influenced by Marxist anti-capitalist thought—that threatened the economic foundation of the country. Long before the economic depression hit the state of Minnesota, many residents had a long history of skepticism toward mainstream political parties that seemed to favor big businesses rather than the needs and aspirations of working people. As a result, they formed their own independent political parties and alliances. Documenting some of those attempts, Delton notes:

> Since statehood in 1858, Minnesota had been home to a variety of self-consciously anti-party, sometimes radical third parties and farmers' movements, including the Anti-Monopoly party, the Greenback party, the Peoples' party, the Prohibition party, any number of Socialist parties, and the Nonpartisan League.[2]

Two significant factors contributed to this independent political spirit that many Minnesotans adopted:

> First, nineteenth-century Minnesota was almost completely rural. Sixty-six percent of the population lived in rural areas in the 1880s. The issues that concerned most people in Minnesota were agricultural issues. Second, the Republican party dominated state politics. This was in part due to the Civil War, which had branded the Democratic party the party of treason, but the Minnesota Republican party was powerful in its own right. . . . The Democrats, on the other hand, were dominated by a despised Irish Catholic minority. They posed no threat to the Republicans. The power of the Republican Party and

the irrelevance of the Democratic Party meant that the only political avenues open to discontented farmers were the great agrarian, anti-party protest movements of the late-nineteenth century.[3]

In the 1920s, the Working People's Non-partisan League and the Farmers' Non-partisan Leagues were making significant inroads into electoral politics. More often, these nonpartisan political leagues ran their candidates on the more liberal Republican ticket in an attempt to advance their own political agendas. To stop these leagues from using the Republican Party solely as a political pass-through for their candidates, the Republicans passed legislation banning the practice in 1921. Forming a political alliance among themselves, the two leagues created the Minnesota Farmer-Labor Party. It was established as an influential and thriving third party in the state of Minnesota, so influential that it could change the outcome of an election.

But there were sharp ideological divisions that developed within this new political party that threatened its long-term viability. By the early 1940s, those differences included such issues as anticommunism, anti-Semitism, isolationism, internationalism, and imperialism. The thread running through this tangle was the looming prospect of the United States entering another world war. The situation reached a boiling point, and talks of a possible political merger between the Democratic Party—which had gained national strength and prominence with the election of President Franklin D. Roosevelt and his left-leaning New Deal agenda—and the Farmer-Labor Party began to emerge within the state.

Meanwhile, at the University of Minnesota, Hubert H. Humphrey was pursuing a doctoral degree in political science. He was also working to support his young family under President Roosevelt's Works Progress Administration (WPA), a New Deal program, and this brought him into contact with labor unions. He was a dynamic speaker and enthusiastic about the New Deal agenda. In 1943, his academic colleagues and the Minneapolis Central Labor Union asked him to run for mayor of Minneapolis; he accepted the invitation. Humphrey was seen as politically progressive and as someone who could bridge the ideological schism between liberal Democrats and the more leftist farmers and labor constituents. A new political party was formed—the Minnesota Democratic-Farmer-Labor Party (DFL). During the fall election of

1944, Humphrey won the mayoral seat in Minneapolis, and other candidates on the DFL ticket were elected to mayoral offices in St. Paul and St. Louis Park. DFL candidates also won two congressional seats.

Humphrey was firmly committed to the idea that government must play a central role in helping to meet the fundamental needs and aspirations of the people and that aggressive political participation by citizens was essential to this endeavor. Having lived through and witnessed the devastation wrought by economic depression, Humphrey prioritized the use of government authority to develop and expand economic opportunities for all. He also recognized that this was a useful political path on which both liberals and the left could tread. Such thinking was occurring at a time when racial discrimination and prejudice were fermenting, especially among white ethnic groups in Minnesota, as World War II loomed on the horizon.

Prior to World War II, racial tensions and conflicts in Minnesota largely occurred between white ethnic groups.[4] During this period of time, popular ideas about race were not too dissimilar from those held in Europe, particularly in Nazi Germany. Spurred on by the racist fallacies of the eugenics movement, racial theories were based on pseudo-scientific methods, which led some fanatics to focus on finding a biological determinant for race in which they might separate "inferior" from "superior" races.[5] Based on arbitrary classification, not all white ethnic groups were seen as fully "white," and they were thereby determined to be inferior. Thus, some white ethnic groups were denied the privileged status that whiteness afforded in their search for the American dream.

Minnesota's racial tensions and conflicts, according to Delton, were largely played out between the "Germans, Swedes, and Norwegians, with significant enclaves of Danes, and then a diverse mix of Finns, eastern European Jews, Irish, Croatians, Slovenians, Poles, and Italians."

Above all, Delton notes, racial antagonism in Minnesota targeted the Jews, apparently because they seemed more different in appearance and culture from other white ethnic groups. As she says:

> Minneapolis Jews were barred from country clubs, restaurants, and neighborhoods. Civic organizations like the Rotary, the Kiwanis, the Lions Clubs, and the Minneapolis Automobile Club refused to accept Jews. Crosses were burned on the lawns of Jews who moved into certain restricted neighborhoods. The Jewish population was

concentrated in the slums of north Minneapolis in neighborhoods adjoining the black areas. Jews were involved in state politics, particularly the Farmer-Labor party, and this led to the overt use of anti-Jewish tactics in the Farmer-Labor primary and the general election in 1938. In a 1946 article, Left-wing activist and journalist Carey McWilliams called Minneapolis "the capital of anti-Semitism in the United States."[6]

During the mayoral campaign of 1944, Jewish youths were routinely attacked. The police were often unsympathetic to such incidents. Jewish leaders called for a mass meeting to address the issue of anti-Semitism in the Minneapolis area; in response, 2,000 people attended. Mayor Marvin Kline, running for reelection, pledged to provide more police protection to the Jewish community to prevent future violence. But his political opponent, Hubert H. Humphrey, went a step further in his response to anti-Semitism, asserting:

> This tragic display of intolerance requires more than the superficial treatment of additional police personnel. It requires a unified community program based on the recognition of the true ideals of democracy, wherein every person is accepted as a human being regardless of race, creed, or color.[7]

With the start of World War II, a shift began to occur within the sociopolitical context of race and race relations regarding white ethnicity. Ideas about what constituted whiteness as a distinct racial category were gradually redefined and broadened to include those—even, begrudgingly, Jews—who were once seen as not being fully white. According to racial standards based on physical appearance, some white ethnicities, especially those with darker skin complexions and kinkier hair, were not fully white. Although society was beginning to broaden its definition of "white" to include many different ethnicities, African Americans regardless of their appearance—light-skinned with straight hair, for instance—still occupied a distinct racial classification of their own.

This finely chiseled distinction between fully white and nonwhite was largely in the eyes of the beholder, yet it could determine many of one's life circumstances. The privileged status of whiteness not only afforded one more opportunities to advance economically and politically but also embodied the very meaning of normalcy, thereby forming the baseline against which nonwhites could be judged as different. By allowing many more white ethnic groups to assimilate into this very rigidly defined racial hierarchy, this baseline shifted.

This shift in racial attitudes was partially influenced by the need to mobilize and unify the nation in order to meet wartime needs, but it was also supported by governmental policies designed to provide economic stability following the war. The nation needed a growing, white middle class on which a solid political buffer could be built between the wealthy and impoverished classes.

To grow this middle class, white ethnic groups were absorbed into the larger cultural and social norms of American society.[8] Successful absorption involved embracing racial norms, values, and expectations that governed attitudes and behaviors regarding those whose physical appearance and character were antithetical to a white sociopolitical identity. By this standard, the group that differed the most was, of course, blacks. Both Minnesota's white liberals and progressives could agree on this point.

No longer seen as the racial other after World War II, white ethnics were now firmly ensconced as a part of America's white mainstream. Concomitantly, Native Americans, Asians, Latinos, and particularly African Americans became the racial other. Deemed to be physically and culturally different, their nonwhite status embodied a new ideological meaning of race, and the sociopolitical conditions of their lives would come to form a new reference point for what constituted racial issues and racial problems.

By the late 1940s in Minnesota, white ethnic groups shared a more racially homogeneous community, and discrimination based on race was no longer seen as an issue. Instead, many liberals and progressives in this community coalesced around antiracist strategies used to respond to the needs and aspirations of the "persecuted" nonwhite races. There was a tacit understanding between the two political groups that the more egregious incidents of racial violence and discrimination involved African Americans. Gunnar Myrdal, in his book *An American Dilemma: The Negro Problem and Modern Democracy*, calls blacks the weakest link in the chain for national unity.[9] Hence, more energy needed to be expended on the black problem.

As the newly elected mayor of Minneapolis, Hubert H. Humphrey hit the ground running with his antiracist agenda in hand. His efforts to respond to the sociopolitical exclusion of blacks and Jews were at the top of his list. Timothy Thurber, in his book *The Politics of Equality: Hubert H. Humphrey and the African American Freedom Struggle*, points out that Humphrey's political beliefs enabled him to envision "a community in which all citizens willingly treated each other with dignity and enjoyed equal social and economic opportunity, not one in which the majority accepted minorities grudgingly under the threat of legal sanction."[10]

At Humphrey's inaugural address, says Thurber, he called for establishing the first municipal Fair Employment Practices Commission (FEPC) in the country to "eradicate intolerance and discrimination wherever they may be found." Humphrey did not stop there: he tried to expand job opportunities, end racially discriminatory service in public places, and reform the police department. He expected police officers to be more respectful and responsive to the concerns of minority communities.

Humphrey was well aware that deep-seated attitudes and behaviors toward racial minorities could not simply be legislated away. Positive, meaningful inroads into race relations necessitated partnering legislation with aggressive community outreach programs and education strategies. Utilizing outreach and education, Humphrey believed that "change in white attitudes and actions toward minorities was not impossible," and therefore he created the Council on Human Relations to carry out this endeavor. The primary purpose of the council was to reduce tension and conflict against racial and religious minorities and advance the cause of civil rights. Community outreach and education were the cornerstones in accomplishing this mission.

Under the auspices of the mayor's office, one of the first things that the Council on Human Relations did was to administer what was called the Community Self-Survey. Developed by Charles Johnson, an eminent sociologist at the all-black Fisk University in Nashville, Tennessee, the survey

> involved local citizen volunteers investigating aspects of minority life and offering solutions to the problems uncovered. Johnson believed that most citizens lacked experience with discrimination and minority concerns, and because they doubted there was a serious problem

they could not be easily rallied to address it. . . . Johnson openly expressed his goal of deepening citizens' sensitivity to racial matters. [11]

Administering the survey was a massive undertaking; more than five hundred people trudged through the cold and snow to document minority life in the city. Of course, this survey was largely conducted by white citizens, who were "removed from the ravages of racial prejudice." Humphrey believed that "the economic, political, and social injustices suffered by blacks and Jews stemmed from the failure of the white majority to live up to the democratic ideals." [12] Under the guise of research, which he felt would be a "hands-on, eye-opening educational" process, Humphrey thought that white Minnesotans would be "more effecting in inspiring action than pamphlets and statistics." [13] Humphrey believed that the way to build political momentum and citizen activism about civil rights was through the process of direct community engagement and experiential learning. His intent was to bring those who had been excluded fully into the fold of participatory democracy.

As the 1940s waned, black veterans, having fought for freedom and democracy abroad, returned to the realities of Jim Crow segregation. Around the country, organized efforts to advance the struggle for civil rights began to take on added momentum. The racial orthodoxy championed by southern white politicians had to be challenged especially within the Democratic Party if fundamental changes were to be advanced in the party structure. Representing the liberal wing of the party, Hubert H. Humphrey was ideally suited to take on that task.

Humphrey was gradually gaining a national reputation and establishing a position of leadership within the Democratic Party by speaking to audiences around the country on civil rights and by promoting his antiracist political agenda as mayor. These efforts were not based solely on a moral imperative—they were political maneuvers as well. He needed political allies to help convince party leaders of the importance of liberalizing the Democratic Party. That meant standing up to the southern Democrats. Humphrey knew that political leadership in the South, dominated by loyal Democratic segregationists, wielded enormous power; he took calculated steps and used the civil rights political platform to force segregationists out of the Democratic Party. Humphrey believed that segregationists had to move out of the way if liberalism was to gain a solid footing in the Democratic Party. Committed to the broader inclusion of minorities into the formalities of democracy, Humphrey advanced a civil rights agenda as a means toward an end to gain significant political power over the future direction of the Democratic Party.

In 1948, during his second term as mayor of Minneapolis, Humphrey announced his candidacy for the US Senate. At the Democratic National Convention in Philadelphia, as the head of the Minnesota delegation he led the liberal faction of the party on insisting that the federal government protect the rights of racial minorities. This was contrary to the beliefs of southern Democrats, who insisted on maintaining states' rights when making decisions regarding racial matters. These opposing views were fought out over a proposal to include the development of a federal fair employment commission into the party's platform. During a highly contentious platform debate, southern segregationists threatened to walk out of the convention. If southern Democrats abandoned their traditional support of the party, there was a possibility that the Democratic Party would lose the upcoming presidential election. After twenty years of being in control of the White House, the political stakes were high; however, Humphrey refused to back down. In a short but strident speech before the full convention, he said:

> Our demands for democratic practices in other lands will be no more effective than the guarantees of those practiced in our own country. . . . I do not believe that there can be any compromise of the guarantees of civil rights, which I have mentioned. In spite of my desire for unanimous agreement on the platform there are some matters, which I think must be stated without qualification. There can be no hedging—no watering down. There are those who say to you "we are rushing the issue of civil rights." I say we are 172 years late. There are those who say, "this issue of civil rights is an infringement on state rights." The time has arrived for the Democratic party to get out of the shadow of states' rights and walk forthrightly into the bright sunshine of human rights. [14]

Humphrey's impassioned appeal won support from the majority of convention members. Southern Democrats, true to their words, walked out, but Harry S. Truman nonetheless won the presidential election. This fight at the 1948 Democratic National Convention would come to represent a seminal moment in racial politics, marking the precise time and place when southern whites began to shift their political allegiance away from the Democratic Party and toward the Republican Party. This prophetic shift on the racial tightrope came to play a critical role in future presidential elections.

Humphrey was no different from other crafty politicians in his attempts to gain political power and advantages over his opponents. Clearly, he was opportunistic in his racial stance and gained political currency within the Democratic Party as a result. However, his political ambitions do not, by any means, diminish his moral stance and the steps he took down the road toward greater inclusion for all in our democracy. He was unwavering in his commitment to social equity and justice, and for him, inclusion meant "equality for all—no exceptions, no 'yes, buts,' no asterisked footnotes imposing limits."[15] The fight over racial inclusion only deepened Humphrey's resolve and the liberal political ideas that spawned it. His commitment and tenaciousness rested on the trust that white Americans would ultimately live up to their democratic ideals of "human dignity, personal expression and fulfillment, justice, freedom." He refused to accept anything less from them.

Little did I know in 1974 that I would utilize Hubert H. Humphrey's legacy and become entangled in this nation's attempts to define what racial inclusion actually meant. More specifically, I encountered affirmative action—federally imposed proactive strategies that addressed and attempted to remedy past social inequalities due to racial exclusion. In this encounter, I moved away from the racial orthodoxy that defined my experience growing up in the rural South and toward racial liberalism. As a young black woman living in Minnesota, I experienced the tensions, dilemmas, and most interesting, the contradictions inherent in liberals' attempts to include the black presence in their white space.

* * *

What did it mean to be eighteen years old in 1974? This was a question that never really entered my mind. With the certainty and arrogance of youth, I was absolutely sure that much of my life lay ahead rather than behind me, so at that particular time, age simply did not matter. The question that did make a difference concerned what it meant to be a young black woman during this period of time.

As I was getting used to feeling my way along the racial tightrope in Minnesota, I stumbled. Unbeknown to me, the reality of my gender, of being a woman, made me lose my balance, and teetering, I almost fell off the rope. What did this new gendered reality mean to me? My political identity was no longer centered solely on just being black; womanhood began to slap me in my black face. Not only is my race gendered, but also my gender is racialized, and vice versa. Thus, in Minnesota, my race and gender merged into an inseparable reality. At the time, it did not matter whether I was ignorant of this fact, vigilant in my understanding, or a little of both—the reality was that I occupied a dual sociopolitical space. My inseparable identities of race and gender—of being black and female—held untold consequences for my youthful life.

About a year after I landed in Minnesota, my sister completed the requirements for a degree in early childhood education and was ready to leave. She moved to the East Coast, to Connecticut. I remained in St. Paul, living in my dingy apartment and working at the nursing home. By this time, the nuances of my new community were becoming more familiar to me. Whatever I needed could be found on or around Selby Avenue, the heartbeat of the black community in the Summit-University neighborhood. It was black space. Everything seemed to be located there—within a ten-block radius, there was a bar, dance hall, liquor store, grocery store, Chinese and soul food restaurants, pool hall, clothing store, hair salons, and barbershops. The Inner City Youth League, the St. Paul Urban League, four black churches, and the Hallie Q. Brown Community Center that housed the Penumbra Theatre Company. All of this was within walking distance of my small apartment on Holly Avenue.

However, walking even a short distance in my community was not a safe endeavor, no matter where you were going, especially if you were a young black woman. White men penetrated that black space. They would cruise the streets throughout the day and night in search of black women who would have sex with them. They simply assumed that if you were black and female, you were nothing more than a whore, and they acted accordingly, tooting their car horns to announce their presence. It really did not matter to them what you looked like or how you dressed or presented yourself; they blew their horns and beckoned with their white hands, demanding that you come to them. Having no frame of reference for these actions, the first time this happened to me, I was stunned, afraid of what might happen, and instinctively started to run. Angered by such presumptuousness, I would tell them, "Motherfucker, I hope you go to the deepest part of hell!" The more aggressive ones dismissed my anger, however; undeterred, they would continue to follow and beckon in anticipation that I would get into their car.

I had no choice but to walk the four blocks to and from my cleaning job at the nursing home, usually working each weekday and every other weekend. Increasingly, the job was growing tiresome, but I needed the money. I had to pay rent to my sleazy landlord on the first of the month—he would come to pick up the rent money, and I would hand him the cash through the crack of my chain-locked door. On occasion, he tried to force his way into my apartment, but the meager door chain kept him at bay. Then, with no other options in mind, one Saturday I quit my job.

There was only one black patient at the nursing home, a blind woman. As I mopped her floor and cleaned her toilet, I could tell that she was despondent. This was nothing particularly new because all of the patients seemed to be shrouded in a veil of sadness and helplessness. However, one fateful Saturday, she decided there was nothing more to live for and somehow managed to open the window of her second-floor room. She jumped! Blind, she could not see that just beneath her window was an air-conditioning shaft. Rather than breaking her neck, she managed to break only her pelvis. Right then and there, I could no longer stand to work at the nursing home, enveloped by the gloom and doom that it presented, so I quit. At the time, I really did not understand such a deep sense of hopelessness or about having reasons so powerful that one would want to kill oneself.

Clearly, my decision to quit my job only created a much bigger problem for me to solve: how was I going to pay my rent? Looking for an answer, I turned to the St. Paul Urban League for help. There, seemingly for the first time since arriving in Minnesota, I was presented with options. They helped me get a job under the Comprehensive Employment and Training Act, a CETA job, at an insurance company in downtown St. Paul, as a filing clerk. It was just another one of those anybody-can-do-this, minimum-wage jobs, but it covered my rent, and for this I was thankful. The Urban League also presented me with a long-term option that completely met my aspirations—the prospect of going to college. After all, that was my main reason for being in Minnesota in the first place.

Hanging onto Madea's words of wisdom, I knew that I would indeed be nothing without an education. Deciding whether or not to go to college was a no-brainer; I jumped at the opportunity. I followed the standard routine that all students follow in order to get into college— filled out the application, requested my high-school transcript and letters of recommendation, and took a college entrance exam. Weighing my odds of admission, I knew that my grades were only average at best, which could be a hindrance, but I always seemed to score fairly well on standardized tests, which could be in my favor, so I felt I had a chance of getting in.

I was admitted. In the fall of 1974, I enrolled at the University of Minnesota (the U) as a full-time student and got my tuition and most of my living expenses paid in the process, through a combination of grants and student loans. I had followed the usual process that most students follow in applying for college, yet my acceptance was by no means usual. I now know that my admission to the U was not based solely on my abilities to read, write, and think and the likelihood of academic success due to these qualities; rather, my inclusion was owed to affirmative action. At the time, I did not even know that there was such a thing as affirmative action—legislated proactive strategies designed to increase the number of racial and gender (female) minority students' admission into higher education. Others, however, were fully informed of its importance, and that is what mattered.

Once again, I stepped into a whole new world. The main campus of the University of Minnesota is located on the east and west banks of the venerable Mississippi River, not far from downtown Minneapolis, with a smaller campus in St. Paul. The simplest way to describe the Twin Cities campus is to say that it is humongous, with the sixth-largest student body in the nation. It is a city unto itself, with its borders being Minneapolis and St. Paul. On each side of the sprawling Mississippi River are buildings; the East Bank houses the older structures, with their pillars and staircases, and the West Bank is interspersed with more modern architectural designs. The East Bank, where the vast Northrop Mall was built, is where most of the fifty thousand students take classes. The campus buildings are connected by an elaborate underground tunnel system to ward off the brutal Minnesota winters.

✿ ✿ ✿

The writer Zora Neale Hurston once said that going back to school did something for her soul. For me, the U renewed my spirit. My only reason for being in Minnesota was to get an education, and finally I was a college student. I was exactly where I was supposed to be at that particular time and place in my life. And, like Zora, I was determined to "wrassle me up a future or die trying." [16]

When I stepped onto the University of Minnesota's campus in the fall of 1974, there were maybe two hundred black students scattered among the population of fifty thousand pupils. This meant that there might be one other black student in the large lecture hall—which held four hundred or more students—taking some type of introductory course with me. Or I might see a colored face here or there on Northrop Mall, darting in and out of classes. Mostly, the brilliant glare of this white space rendered black, brown, red, and yellow almost invisible, including me. However, like flower buds in springtime, the darker hues gradually began to unfold in the rays of sunlight to reveal their leafy presence, and accordingly, I adjusted my eyesight to the new realities of seeing colors amid the illumination of brilliant white space.

Adjusting one's eyesight can be a very difficult endeavor, especially if one is trying to read something in a glare. Squinting, I came across a new term that described how I was seen through the eyes of others— the college administrators, the faculty, and my peers—it was the word "minority." I first encountered it while reading an article printed in the *Minnesota Daily*, the campus newspaper. I quickly learned that "minority" referred to me, the few other black students on campus, Latinos, Native Americans, and Asian students who were enrolled at the U. Labeling nonwhite students as minorities not only bestowed a new racial identity on us but also positioned our academic needs and aspirations differently from those of our white classmates. It was a difference built out of skepticism about our learning capabilities and our individual worth. What made us special? Why were we different from the others, who were just like us? What impact did these questions of difference make?

As minority students, many factors gave meaning to our racial otherness on campus; most notable were the college administration's policies and practices designed to include nonwhite students in the academic life of the university. Concurrently, black students insisting on meaningful, rather than tokenistic, inclusion. On the surface, both appeared to express a similar intent—greater inclusion; beneath the surface, however, the critical question of how to achieve that shared intent was quite a different matter.

The issue of balancing similarities with differences, of balancing majority needs and aspirations with those of the minority, was of utmost concern; it created a difficult balancing act on the racial tightrope. Decisions about what would be sacrificed, what would be gained, and what would be forever changed in the progress toward greater racial inclusion had to be made. How could race relations at the U be reconfigured in ways that simultaneously recognized common as well as divergent interests, especially when weighing those of a tiny minority against those of a much larger majority? If the shift toward greater inclusion extended beyond mere token attempts, then steps toward doing so had to be negotiated. With institutional authority on one side of the bargaining table and only the sheer determination of a handful of black students on the other side, how would power ever be balanced in order to yield meaningful change?

I did not know that prior to my attendance at the U, in 1969, sixty or so black students took over Morrill Hall, an administrative building, demanding that the U become more responsive to their concerns.[17] It was during the Black Power era, when black students across the country, particularly at predominantly white universities, insisted on changing the racial status quo on campuses. Their demands took on added impetus in the immediate aftermath of Martin Luther King's assassination. At the University of Minnesota, foremost among the students' demands for change were the calls for increased black enrollment, full financial support, naming the new West Bank library in honor of Dr. King, and greater representation of black students on all university policy committees. But it was their demand to create a black studies department that captured most of the attention from the administration and faculty alike.

Rose Freeman, Marie Braddock, and Horace Huntley formed the leadership of the Afro-American Action Committee (AAAC), which spearheaded black student activism on campus, including the January 1969 takeover of Morrill Hall. It was the first time that any student group had ever occupied a building at the University of Minnesota. Like the civil rights movement beforehand, students used the only power available to them in demanding changes to the status quo—political activism in the form of collective protests and disruptive actions. Most notable were the widespread antiwar demonstrations, such as the ones organized by the Students for a Democratic Society (SDS) that engulfed almost every aspect of campus life. Into this political fray and climate of protest, black students—transcending regional, class, and gender difference—actively began to press their demands for changes in race relations on college campuses.

The fundamental difference between black and white students' campus protests in the late 1960s was largely one of focus. The antiwar protesters directed their activism toward the warmongering policies and actions of the Nixon administration with the goal of ending the US military engagement in Vietnam. Black students turned their attention to the policies and actions of the college administration with the aim of ensuring racial equity and fairness. In Minnesota, both forms of campus activism occurred in the politically liberal climate. Thanks to Hubert H. Humphrey's championship, the state had a political history that fostered active citizen engagement and tolerance. When it came to attempts at negotiating race relations, this legacy made a difference. The U touted a particularly liberal disposition toward racial responsiveness; for instance, immediately following the assassination of Dr. King, the following was printed:

> The Minnesota Student Association (MSA) began organizing to set up a fund to provide free tuition to poor students. . . . Similarly, an ad hoc faculty group calling themselves The Committee of Fifty met to set up a Memorial Fund following the assassination. . . . Another group of professors created a proposal much like the MSA's which requested free tuition for poor people. Furthermore, University President Malcolm Moos asked Vice President Paul Cashman to set up a task force on human rights. Many groups responded to the assassination showing a disposition for improving race relations on campus.[18]

Thus, in the wake of these good-faith efforts to respond to the needs and interests of black students, the college community was completely stunned and caught off guard when Morrill Hall was taken over in protest of racial grievances.

Prior to the occupation, well-meaning efforts by the administrators and faculty had yielded few, if any, tangible results. AAAC had presented President Moos with its own list of demands for more effective inclusion in campus life. In order to press those demands, the leadership of AAAC agreed to participate in a series of meetings with the Task Force on Human Rights in an attempt to help shape recommendations to be submitted to the president for concerted action. But given the particular ebb and flow of academic life, where momentum is often lost due to graduation and the long summer vacations, the task force's progress in addressing black students' concerns lagged. When classes resumed in the fall of 1968, black students found change had indeed occurred, but not the change they had expected.

Over the summer, the U had actively recruited about 550 black students, yet the administration had raised enough money to partially support the financial needs of only about 300 students. Many of those students, anticipating grants to cover tuition and housing expenses, discovered to their dismay that their financial aid was largely composed of loans, which they had to repay. Adding fuel to their ire, rather than a black studies department, the task force had proposed the creation of an interdisciplinary graduate program in comparative racial and ethnic studies. Not only was the focus of this program unacceptable to AAAC, but the fact that the proposal was for a graduate program excluded most of the black students on campus from taking courses in the program because they were largely undergraduates. In the face of these frustrations and disappointments, the anger of the black students regained momentum and became an avalanche.

Jared E. Leighton describes what happened at a meeting between the college president and the leadership of the AAAC and during the subsequent takeover of Morrill Hall in "A Small Revolution: The Role of a Black Power Revolt in Creating and Sustaining a Black Studies Department at the University of Minnesota."

Leighton writes, "On January 13, 1969, seven black representatives of the AAAC at the University of Minnesota entered the Office of the President to meet with him." Freeman, the president of the AAAC, immediately sat in Moos's chair and refused to move, as a way of letting the president and the other administrators know who was in charge of the meeting. The AAAC wanted a clear "yes" or "no" to each of their demands. President Moos said "no" to all of the demands, and the meeting came to an abrupt end after about twenty minutes, with the different parties going their separate ways. Following that fateful meeting, President Moos left campus to attend another meeting in St. Paul, and AAAC members went to the bursar and to the Admissions and Records Offices to take up occupation.[19]

During the occupation, a series of meetings was held between the AAAC's leadership and college administrators to address concerns and hammer out a plan for ending the takeover. Through those negotiations, an agreement was reached that created an Afro-American Studies Department, which included undergraduate courses; a Martin Luther King Jr. Scholarship Fund, with seven of the fourteen governing seats reserved for people in the black community; and a conference titled "Which Way Black Students? The Role of Black Students in the White University," with half the expenses covered by the U.

These agreements came at a heavy price, for both the college administration and AAAC's leadership alike. Not only was there an immediate backlash from state politicians, who threatened to withhold funds for the new department, but there was also a public outcry over the agreements. As Leighton documented: "Citizens flooded the University of Minnesota with letters responding to the takeover and the administration's decisions. One letter quoted in the *Minneapolis Tribune* said, 'Dr. Moos: You have lost our respect by kissing the boots of a disgusting, belligerent minority.'"[20]

In this acrimonious political climate, and as a result of their actions, AAAC's leaders—Freeman, Huntley, and Tucker, as well as Richard Roe and Jane Doe—were indicted by a grand jury for aggravated criminal damage to property and unlawful assembly. Their arrests galvanized both black and white student activists to protest. At the trial, no legal proof was presented that directly linked the three named leaders to the actual occupation of Morrill Hall. Eventually, Tucker was acquitted of all charges; Freeman and Huntley were convicted of misdemeanors for unlawful assembly. Both received ninety-day suspended sentences and were placed on probation by the judge.

By the time I arrived at the University of Minnesota in 1974, most of the black student activists that took part in the Morrill Hall occupation had left the campus, either through graduating or by simply dropping out. But the AAAC's student organization remained in existence, and its legacy of disruptive protest continued to inspire other marginalized student groups who were also seeking greater inclusion in campus life. When I arrived on campus, Native Americans, Latinos, Asians, gays, and lesbians were all practicing their own unique brand of protests and calling for changes in the status quo. Among those groups of activists, the white women's rights group was noteworthy in its determination to gain full equality of the sexes. They had a steely resolve to obtain their goal, as it was called for under affirmative-action policies barring discrimination against women. With that resolve, they ran headlong into the difficulties in their interactions with nonwhite women as they tried to form a collective sisterhood in order to advance gender equality.

◦ ◦ ◦

The racial shifts that occurred in higher education as a result of black student activism during the late 1960s produced important changes in academic life. By insisting on inclusion and refusing to accept the racial status quo as a given, black activists opened up opportunities for greater access to knowledge. I would not otherwise have gained an opportunity to learn from the vast intellectual traditions in the social sciences and humanities. Black scholarship might have been completely lost to me if there had been no one willing to step up and insist on black inclusion in the canons of knowledge.

As an undergraduate, some of my most exciting classes at the U were in the newly formed and struggling Afro-American Studies Department. It was there that I developed a sense of belonging, even though I was surrounded by white space. In particular, I credit Professor Anita Tucker's series of classes on black women writers with opening up a whole new world for me to explore. Prior to those classes, I had never read a book authored by a black woman; it simply never dawned on me that such books existed. In thinking back, how could I have ever missed such an obvious endeavor to pursue? But, as the saying goes, "You don't know what you don't know." Professor Tucker introduced me to the literature and poetry of black women writers such as Louise Meriwether, Ann Petry, Margaret Walker, Nella Larsen, and of course, the irrepressible Zora Neale Hurston. Toni Morrison, Alice Walker, Ntozake

Shange, and the otherworldly writings of Octavia Butler were also presented in her courses.

Such an obvious oversight of these and other black women authors was not mine alone. Regardless of when they were first published, many black authors' books were just beginning to be commonly available in print in the mid-1970s. There the black stories were, comfortably resting on the pages between the dustcovers. Their words were intellectual treasure troves, with more to come. The lives of black women were at the centers of their storytellings—their hopes, dreams, fantasies, and triumphs were all on display, along with the worries, miseries, sadnesses, and all the joy and the cruelty that life has to offer. I was absolutely enthralled and claimed their writings for myself. Their prose and poetry helped me to see, and more important, they helped me to appreciate the complexities of the other side of blackness, the other story. The feminine story that only black women in all their similar and different voices could uniquely tell. Or so I thought.

I would come to learn there were others who thought differently, who thought that they were better positioned to tell not only black women's stories but all women's stories. Mistakenly, they believed the stories were essentially one and the same. They believed that men, using dominance, defined the circumstances and the limitation by which women lived their lives, regardless of their race. Following this logic, all women were thought to share a common reality—a reality binding them in gender oppression and subsequently binding them in sisterhood, regardless of their differences.

It was precisely this issue of differences that undermined gender solidarity among women during the mid-1970s. To lay claim to a universal sisterhood—based solely on gender relations—the importance of racial differences, in particular, had to be diminished, thereby rendering the color of one's skin and experiences derived as a result largely invisible and unimportant. Race, then, was seen as a neutral factor when considering the real issues challenging women's lives. The women's rights movement at the time adopted a seemingly color-blind stance toward gender inequality amid the omnipresence of race.

Through my eyes, the mostly white, middle-class women forming the leadership and actively participating in the movement were the embodiment of the difference of racial privilege. Their whiteness allowed them to assume that they could speak for all women. This was a problem. But this attitude could not be sustained because of the rancorous and loud shouts of dissenting voices whose racial makeup made a critical difference in life.

Many white women in the movement tried to avoid the stark reality of American life, but nonetheless, they could not refrain from taking steps on the racial tightrope. This created conflict because whether they acknowledged it or not, their gender was inexorably linked to their racial identity. They erroneously assumed that their privileges allowed them to mask their racial identity. In a stratified society such as ours, different values are placed on human life, depending on how one is positioned on the sociopolitical hierarchy; those values afford both advantages and disadvantages. One can be positioned in such a way that both advantages and disadvantages exist simultaneously. For instance, if a person is a woman, her gender places her at the bottom of those privileges reserved for men. In spite of this, if a person is white, then regardless of gender, he or she has access to privileges based on the value given to whiteness in our society.

Disadvantaged yet advantaged, white women step into this paradoxical sociopolitical space. It is their white-skinned status, even if limited in its scope, that gives them the idea that they can assume an authoritative voice when speaking for those less privileged. Being neither white nor male offers little advantage in our society, and it is in this position that many nonwhite women often find themselves. This creates an imbalance of power in relations between the two groups, and that is why enormous political tensions, dilemmas, and contradictions arose between the groups of white and black women involved in the women's rights movement during the 1970s.

Across college campuses, many white female students were taking on the new gender identity of feminists and adopting a radical insistence on women's rights. At the University of Minnesota, like the black students before them, white women were actively seeking to establish a Women's Studies Department. Their list of demands also included more women faculty, the university hospital offering a full range of gynecological and obstetrical services, including abortion, and establishing a child-care center.

At the time, I did not consider myself to be a feminist, black or otherwise. However, as I read black women's literature and engaged in discussion groups about their writings, I was developing a more female-focused consciousness that sharpened my gaze on the world. But, like most blacks on campus, whether females or males, I viewed feminism as a white women's thing and had little desire to become involved in their campus movement.

This is not to suggest that I was not politically active on campus—on the contrary, as a member of the AAAC, I had many issues to consider. For one thing, the Afro-American Studies Department was under attack. Along with the existing six full-time faculty members, the administrators—over our objections—appointed five adjunct faculty (four of whom were white), and unlike other academic departments, these new members had full voting rights on personnel and policy decisions within the department. Then there was our demand that the Martin Luther King program be divided into four separate student centers to accommodate the four distinct minorities (black, Native American, Latino, and Asian), which the administration refused to do.

There were also protests and demonstrations that required our attention. We supported the lettuce boycott led by Latino students and the United Farm Workers; demonstrated at the university's board of regents meetings, demanding that the university divest itself of its thirty-five-million-dollar corporate holdings in stocks, bonds, and other securities from companies operating in South Africa, as called for by InCAR (International Committee against Racism); and confronted the likes of Arthur Jensen, an eminent psychologist from the University of California, Berkeley, who was brought to campus by the Institute of Child Development to give a series of lectures expounding the racist belief that blacks are genetically less intelligent and therefore inferior to whites.

In this climate of activism on campus, the leadership of the women's movement approached a small group of us, wanting to discuss the possibility that we would support their efforts to establish a Women's Studies Department. We were wary of their intent yet intrigued, so we agreed to meet. In preparation, we developed our own plan for a more inclusive Women's Studies Department.

With our plan firmly in hand, we arrived at a dimly lit office where three white women greeted us. Immediately, the vibrant and colorful posters draping the office walls took me aback. They were of black, brown, red, and yellow women, especially those living in "revolutionary situations," such as in Angola. One of them portrayed a black woman dressed in colorful African garb with a child on her back and a rifle in her arms. I could not figure out what such images symbolized to the three white women sitting across the table from us. Did they see these marginalized women as heroines? Did the photos represent a feeling of solidarity with the strength and courage of "third-world" women? Were they an attempt to appropriate these women's experiences? Or did they represent something altogether different? Whatever the reasoning, the posters were imposing: they held my fascination, and my eyes kept wandering back to the images during most of the meeting. Then all hell broke loose.

Erroneously, the feminists at the meeting assumed that we would eagerly jump at the opportunity to collaborate with them, but using their agenda and on their terms. It seemed that it had never dawned on them that we would have ideas of our own about the Women's Studies Department. They took umbrage at the fact that we wanted our full share in determining the focus and direction of the department. In return for our active participation, we, at the very least, expected that such a department would include black, brown, red, and yellow female faculty members as well as a racially diverse curriculum. They rejected our plan in no uncertain terms and accused us of trying to take over their efforts.

In doing so, they accused us of "Mau-Mauing" them: a blatantly racist and pejorative term that only stirred our passion.[21] The 1952 revolt against the colonial rule of Great Britain by the Kikuyu people of Kenya is what is often referred to as the Mau Mau Rebellion. The British used the racially offensive term "Mau-Mau" as propaganda to discredit the rebellion. They covered up the massive human rights violations of murder, torture, and internment of the Kikuyu. We took tremendous offense at being referred to as Mau Maus. In retort, we cussed the women out by calling them white racists and left the meeting in a huff.

One of the most important lessons I learned from this meeting was that racial differences are much easier to accept if they are symbolically portrayed as images, as pictures on a wall. Pictures, no matter how dramatic they are, are passive images. Even when the portrayal appears obvious, there is still room for interpretation because images, whether literal or figurative in presentation, do not open their mouths to speak for themselves. When the figure embodying racial difference is actually standing right in front of you speaking her mind, then the image loses its passivity, and the interpretation becomes a completely different matter.

The problem of racial difference in the development of women's studies was the problem of racial privileging: "White middle-class women had converted their reality into the currency of universal womanhood, a conversion itself which was only possible by virtue of privilege."[22] In assuming racial privilege, white women undermined the development of women's studies. Unfortunately, while at the U, I never took a class in women's studies. I wonder what the Women's Studies Department would look like today if we, with all of our differences and similarities, had worked together to determine a more inclusive academic focus and direction. The avoidance of racial concerns continues to plague many women's studies programs across the country.

Clearly, back then, we were all strident and dogmatic in the stances we took. That was only heightened by our profound mistrust of each other's motivation to work together. The racial dynamics of our particular meeting was not a unique occurrence; variations of the tensions, dilemmas, and contradictions between black and white women feminists were played out in different racial circumstances throughout the 1970s. Given the deep acrimony that developed between the two groups, there seemed little room for compromise, even though there were mutually beneficial issues on which we readily agreed.

Many black women did join the women's movement, but I cannot claim to have been one of them. Inclusion and how racial differences are acknowledged and responded to remain a significant tripping point for me on the racial tightrope. I especially dislike it when others assume the authority to speak for black women. For myself, it is an authority that I am determined never to relinquish to others. As bell hooks pointed out, if black women do not claim the right to speak for themselves, then "we risk a more insidious and dangerous form of erasure. We become the objects of a feminist privileged discourse on race and gender which actively silences our voices."[23] My determination not to relinquish that right grew out of the hard lessons that I learned from my own inseparable racial and gender experiences.

At the University of Minnesota, I learned things outside of the classroom that I never could have dreamt. In 1978, I completed the formal requirements for a bachelor of arts degree in child psychology from the

Institute on Child Development—yes, the very same institute that brought Arthur Jensen to campus to tell black students that genetically, they were racially inferior and there was absolutely nothing that could be done to reverse this scientific certainty.

With a sense of pride, I walked alongside hundreds, if not thousands, of other graduates donned in academic regalia to accept my college degree. In the beaming white lights of Northrop Hall Auditorium I received my cherished diploma, but there were no family members to bear witness to my accomplishment. Nonetheless, like always, their presence was firmly rooted within me. The weight of their determination to simply survive guided each step I took across Northrop's vast stage. I inherited that determination; I was entrusted with the knowledge of their sacrifices, which made my steps and the opportunities leading up to that moment possible.

◦ ◦ ◦

But what was I supposed to do with a BA degree in child psychology? I had no particular career goal in mind, and I was definitely not interested in working directly with young children in a child-care center or anything of that sort, so what were my options?

One day, while browsing through the psychology stacks at Wilson Library, I came across the book *Prejudice and Your Child*, written by Kenneth Clark. Who was this man? In my two years of study at the Institute for Child Development, I had never heard of Kenneth or his wife, Mamie Clark. Thumbing through the pages, I discovered that they were two of the best-known black child psychologists in the country because of the instrumental role they had played in the civil rights movement. Their research immediately piqued my interest—their most famous study about black children was the "doll test." This study was designed to document racial perception and the ravages of racism on black children's psychological development.

I was fascinated by their work. Using black and white diaper-clad baby dolls, identical except for the color of their skin, they documented young children's attitudes toward race. Almost all of the children in their study, ranging from three to seven years of age, could readily identify the race of the dolls. But more astounding, these young children, when asked which doll they preferred, overwhelmingly selected the white doll and gave positive attributes to that skin color. Most of the children gave negative impressions about the black doll. The Clarks concluded that "prejudice, discrimination, and segregation" gave black children a sense of inferiority and self-hatred. As expert witnesses in the landmark *Brown v. Board of Education* case, their findings proved to be absolutely critical in influencing the Supreme Court's ruling, as noted by Chief Justice Earl Warren, when he said in the ruling: "To separate them [Negro children] from others of similar age and qualifications solely because of their race generates a feeling of inferiority as to their status in the community that may affect their hearts and minds in a way unlikely to ever be undone."[24] Voila!

After reading *Prejudice and Your Child*, I was clearer about what I wanted to do. I was intrigued by how public policy imposes its own reality on the everyday lives of black children; by how laws are crafted by public institutions, implemented by administrators, and interpreted by judges; and by the role those actions play in creating opportunities that allow humans to either flourish or diminish. I wanted to know more. So I decided to continue to pursue formal education. I applied to the Hubert H. Humphrey Institute of Public Affairs at the U.

To my utter amazement, I was accepted as a graduate student. I was thoroughly intimidated because academically, I knew I was underprepared for this opportunity. Going from studying psychology to public policy was a major leap because of the fact that I did not have the necessary academic prerequisites. The sticking point for me was the quantitative focus of the course work. Even though I had struggled through statistics as an undergraduate, I did not have a strong background in math, let alone a mastery of the calculus that was essential for succeeding in the program. I questioned why I was accepted. This question loomed even larger when I found out that in my class of about twenty-five students, there was only one other black student accepted besides myself. To the best of my knowledge, we were the first black students admitted to the Humphrey Institute.

Although I do not know for sure, I believe that my acceptance to the Humphrey Institute was once again owing to affirmative-action policies. During the mid-1970s, the federal government, through the department of Health, Education, and Welfare (HEW), began to impose stringent guidelines in an effort to increase racial minority students and faculty in higher education.[25] A key component of those guidelines required that "annual goals" be set to reduce disparity between the proportion of black and white, as well as female and male, students, particularly at state educational institutions. Additionally, the guidelines called for hiring goals for racial minorities and women faculty where they were "underutilized." The 1964 Civil Rights Act barred racial and gender discrimination in major public institutions, including colleges and universities. Although the focus of the federal government's attention on higher education during the 1970s was largely targeted at southern white colleges and universities, the guidelines were national in scope, and northern white educational institutions had to comply as well.

The issue of establishing goals for greater racial and gender inclusion, or what many considered to be "quotas," was a major bone of contention about affirmative-action policies in higher education. The claims of opponents were a variation on the same argument: predetermined quotas—numerical set-asides—especially for racial minorities meant limiting opportunities for white males, even if they were considered the most qualified applicants. But seldom throughout the rancorous debate over affirmative action was there any questioning of the sociopolitical privileges that white males as a group enjoyed in our society. Or, as Julian Bond, the noted civil rights activist, said:

> Argument over affirmative action reminds him of a football game that's in the fourth quarter. The white team is leading the black team 145–3. The white team owns the stadium, the ball and the referees, wrote the rules and has been cheating since the beginning of the game. Now, with two minutes to go, the new quarterback of the white team says, "let's play fair."[26]

The new quarterback for the white male team was a thirty-three-year-old former student of the University of Minnesota named Alan Bakke. In 1973, Bakke applied to medical school at the University of California, Davis. He was denied admission. He reapplied for the next academic year and again was rejected. But the second time, he discovered that the medical school had a dual admission policy, where sixteen student slots out of a total of one hundred had been reserved for black and Latino applicants. Bakke filed a lawsuit against the governing board, the Regents of the University of California system, and charged the medical school with reverse discrimination—discriminating against him because he was white and male.

Bakke argued that the medical school's admission policy violated Title VI of the Civil Rights Act of 1964 and the Fourteenth Amendment to the US Constitution's Equal Protection Clause. The Regents of the University of California lost the case against Bakke in the state court but appealed to the US Supreme Court on constitutional grounds. Ruling on one of the most celebrated legal challenges to affirmative action, in a sharply divided split decision with Justice Lewis Powell casting the deciding vote, the court held in favor of Bakke. The majority opinion concluded that:

> The medical school racially discriminated against whites because it excluded them from 16 out of 100 spots solely by virtue of their race. The fact that blacks have historically been discriminated against more than whites was irrelevant to this case, because racial quota systems, whether applied against whites or blacks, are always odious to a free people whose institutions are founded upon the doctrine of equality.[27]

Meanwhile, as the Bakke case was working its way up to the Supreme Court, the U's administration required each academic department to develop an affirmative-action plan in compliance with federal guidelines. Lillian Williams, the director of the Office of Equal Opportunity (OEO), which was responsible for meeting those guidelines, oversaw this process. According to the *Minnesota Daily*, under her direction, department chairs were required to submit action plans that included the following elements: "a work force analysis, a utilization analysis, and goals and timetables including specific and detailed action-oriented programs."[28] Williams told the campus newspaper that "more effort is needed to recruit women and minority group members into graduate programs in which very few presently are enrolled." I believe I was the beneficiary of that effort.

In the fall of 1978, having won acceptance through the Supreme Court's decision, Alan Bakke entered his first year of medical school. Through affirmative action, I entered the Hubert H. Humphrey Institute of Public Affairs as a graduate student. Formerly the School of Public Affairs, the Hubert H. Humphrey Institute was established in 1977 to honor Hubert Humphrey, the statesman. It was not done because he was an unflinching advocate for equality and justice, or in memory of his steps along the racial tightrope; to the contrary, John Adams, the dean of the institute at the time, told the *Minnesota Daily* that "the Institute will not be a bastion for Humphrey polemics simply because it is named for him."[29] In the two years that I studied there, Adams's words proved prophetic. The institute's focus was on developing policy analysts, with little, if any, consideration of the sociopolitical contexts that influenced public policies.

It was precisely Humphrey's polemics, rather than the training to become basically a technician, that I was interested in. His steps on the racial tightrope—now largely forgotten, overshadowed, or dismissed—helped to shift our nation away from a posture of absolute racial intolerance to a begrudging inclusion of racial minorities in our democracy. Humphrey wholeheartedly championed the importance of citizen engagement in the process of change, even when he took an unpopular stance about the war in Vietnam. Humphrey's steps helped widen the space for inclusion. As we continued to teeter toward the age of Obama, those who followed in his footsteps on the racial tightrope played critical roles in moving us, as a nation, a step forward to a more inclusive democracy.

In 1978, the year I entered the institute, Hubert H. Humphrey died of cancer. I believe Humphrey's death symbolically marked the waning of white liberalism. As liberal ideas began to die a slow and painful death, we as a nation began to take backward steps on the racial tightrope. Retreating, we wavered on the rope as we stepped back into old fears, hatred, and anger of/at other races and reneged on our commitments to racial equality and justice. These steps were largely reactionary, taken in retaliation against liberal efforts that had pushed too fast for greater racial inclusion in our democracy. By the 1980s, we as a nation had entered another dark era as a result.

However, the new era of race and race relations was different from the past. Our social institutions were gradually reconfiguring race relations and adjusting to a new reality of inclusion. Blatant exclusion and marginalizing practices of the past were no longer as obvious and straightforward as before. In adjusting and reconfiguring our social institutions to meet the new challenges of this new era, the rigidity of racial exclusion became more blurred in its import, as the day-to-day effect of race and race relations continued to have a major influence on life chances.

Having graduated from the Humphrey Institute and accomplished my goal of getting a formal education, it was time for me to leave Minnesota. I had learned the hard lessons of the distinction between inclusion and belonging. I had no sense of belonging in Minnesota, although I was included in that white space. But go where? Once again, my sister came to the rescue by encouraging me to come to New York City and stay with her. Starting over, how would I balance on the racial tightrope in a nation that was moving backward while I was trying to move forward? This would indeed become a tricky feat that began in 1984, when I moved to New York City.

5

ARE WE DIFFERENT YET THE SAME?

A Multicultural World

I have tried, but I really cannot imagine a world without human differences, where there are no special qualities that uniquely distinguish individuals, cultures, or nations one from another in some form or fashion.

People tend to embrace their differences and often expect others to recognize how their special, unique, and extraordinary particularities set them apart from one another. How boring life would be if we were all exactly the same. If there were no obvious distinctions, if we were completely homogeneous, what would the world look like? How would that sameness change the way we interact with one another? Would there be harmony—none of the contempt, conflicts, or chaos that differences sometimes engender, because we would look, think, and act in the same ways? Taken to the absolute extreme, what would be the thread binding humanity? What would allow us to care about the well-being of others as much as we care about ourselves if we were all the same? With such musings, the world could be structured much differently. But what we have to work with is our given reality—a reality composed of differences. In turn, those differences give meaning to the value—or lack thereof—that we place on human life.

In 1984, I moved to New York City, the most culturally diverse city on the planet. New York is a world unto itself; it thrives on the very essence of differences, almost to the point of a collective narcissism.

The city prides itself on being the cultural capital of the nation and on setting trends and styles for other cities to emulate. It evokes fascination; others look to New York for ideas, inspirations, and motivation. Eyes near and far are always peering to see what is going on in the city.

Seen from afar, many New Yorkers appear to hold to the mantra that asserting one's unique identity is crucial. Nothing seems to be out of bounds as New Yorkers create and re-create their identities, especially as such identities are wrapped up in an excess of creativity. Perhaps it is precisely that boundless creativity that has made New York City the financial, fashion, media, arts and entertainment, fine dining, and publishing capital of the nation and arguably the world. Daily, people are drawn to the city to experience the fantasy of something different.

Seen up close, however, New York offers an altogether different appearance. Underneath the veneer of fantasy, there are realities where differences are feared and shunned rather than embraced and admired. In those realities, racial differences matter; the boundaries, real or imagined, are clearly drawn and gated accordingly. Looking beyond the fantasy of difference, the black experience readily emerges.

The black experience in the city is not a singular reality, where all blacks look, think, and act in the same way; to the contrary, there are significant sociopolitical differences composed of many disparate parts. What holds those different parts together is a black identity: an identity that is self-defined, culturally imposed, and shaped by the continuous yet ever-changing political realities of race and race relations. No matter how different they appear, blacks do not step too far away from their racial identity, even when other identities are equally significant in defining their day-to-day experiences. Those other identities may be overshadowed by a racial signifier that is often added to highlight an even greater degree of identification. In a society where racial differences matter, we are never simply free to be women, men, or children. Our race further defines our experiences as black women, black men, and black children.

During the 1980s and well into the 2000s, a gray haze appeared on the racial tightrope. This zone added complexity to an already treacherous balancing act, and it took enormous strength not to fall off the rope. The gray zone was intentionally created by the conservative right through regressive sociopolitical policies that endangered the lives of many, particularly the socially and economically vulnerable in our society, as a backlash against the liberal shifts that had occurred during the 1960s and 1970s. That backlash was largely in response to the more progressive shifts in race relations. Conservatives introduced a punitive gray haze on the racial tightrope that would have a direr impact, especially on the lives of poor blacks, for years to come. In the paradoxical world of New York City, where fantasy and reality intermingle, the gray zone clouded visibility and made our steps on the rope even more hazardous as we attempted to move forward.

The gray zone was an ambiguous space where racial differences appeared not to matter yet, in hindsight, mattered more than anything else. Confronting this gray mass on the rope, critical choices were made under precarious, race-specific conditions—conditions that were not of one's own making but systemically imposed. They always involved compromise. When confronted by this gray mass on the rope, one could not simply stand still or else one would fall off; the situation demanded action of some sort. This action involved making choices, whether wittingly or not, that added to or lessened the burden of the already treacherous steps one had to take in order to continue forward.

In the gray area, one could easily become color-blind and disoriented by the depths of the dense haze appearing on the rope. Still, some were able to step right through this obscure gray matter with no problems; others became completely discombobulated altogether and lost their footing. Some pretended not to see this treacherous gray mass, even as they clumsily felt their way through the hazardous haze; while others, more sure footed, carefully weighed each step they took. Like most, in response to these added challenges that appeared on the already treacherous racial tightrope, my steps embodied different reactions at different times. It was how we as a nation moved through this gray zone that crafted our future decisions and actions, which helped us move a bit closer to the age of Obama.

I entered a new phase of my life when I moved to New York City. Leaving behind the mostly white space of Minnesota, I stepped into the multicultural world of the city, where bright colors dominated the cultural cityscape. In the midst of this rainbow of vibrant colors, unbeknown to me, I was stepping into the gray zone on the racial tightrope.

* * *

During my lifetime, for whatever reasons, I have traveled around this country and others, often finding myself among people and in places that I could never have imagined. This has allowed me to experience and really come to understand the essence of my aunt's long-ago admonition—a whole new world could be made from the things I did not know. I am thoroughly intrigued by the fact that human beings are so culturally different in the ways that they look, think, and act yet are very similar to one another in their basic human needs and aspirations.

As a sociologist, I know, theoretically, that human culture is composed of all thoughts, modes of behaviors, and material items that are passed down from one generation to the next through various processes of communication. More than anything else, it is culture that distinguishes one group of people from another. But culture is highly malleable; we can simultaneously embrace and reject aspects of our cultural heritage or create subcultures that produce an altogether different worldview and lifestyle within the framework of a given culture.

Regardless of what particular form it takes, culture does not exist in isolation. It is not somehow set apart from the established norms, values, and traditions of the broader society that influence how we engage one another. Shaped by history, culture and society are intertwined. As a result, we are simultaneously cultural and social beings. We embody our cultural and social identities, and in turn they shape the meaning of our lives: culture and society influence how we interpret our world, how we see ourselves within it, and how we interact with others accordingly. This says that our cultural and social identities provide critical reference points for the value—or lack thereof—that is placed on our individual and collective lives.

When I moved to New York in 1984, I was indeed thoroughly intrigued by the multicultural environment of the city. I enjoyed seeing people and experiencing places that I had never dreamt existed. Simultaneously, I entered the gray zone and was almost immediately sucked into the fantasy world of the city—the party world that was created by the use of illicit drugs. Drug use quickly spawned the destructive and deadly effects of drug addiction. Unbeknown to me, I was quickly being dragged into the culture wars—not the euphemistic war of right-wing conservatives that was being waged on social issues, but the multilayered war emanating from the crack cocaine drug culture that was in the early stages of ravaging the black community.

I lived with my sister and three-year-old niece in the Bronx—the Marble Hill section directly across the bridge from Manhattan. In anticipation of my move to the city, my sister found an apartment large enough for all three of us. It was on the second floor of a two-story duplex; a Latino family with a three-year-old son lived beneath us.

I had tried to plan for this move by selling my car and all my furnishings and by putting away a little in a savings account. I thought I had enough money to last for at least six months. I also thought that a master's degree from the highly ranked Hubert H. Humphrey Institute of Public Affairs would surely aid me in getting a professional job of some sort in the city. But, as was usually the case when I tried to plan my life, the unpredictability of life came crashing down on me.

Dutifully, each Sunday morning I would walk to Broadway to pick up the *New York Times*. I would go over the employment section with a fine-tooth comb, looking for any job possibilities, and then send out résumés in response. In response to my efforts, I received what I called "we don't want you" form letters. Starting over in life in a new place, among new people, was harder than I thought, especially because my resources were limited. I did not realize at the time how critical professional networks are to getting a job in the city. Who did I know that could help open doors for my initial interview? The only people whom I knew in the city were my sister and niece.

Divorced, my sister was working in the actuarial department at an insurance company in Manhattan. As I have mentioned before, my sister is much more outgoing than myself. When I arrived in the city, she had already developed a network of friends from work, and they liked to party. Occasionally, because we lived in a large duplex, my sister and I would have dance parties, complete with plenty of alcohol and marijuana smoke fogging the air. Personally, I had given up drugs and smoking dope—but not cigarettes—years before, because I found it incompatible with my attempts to be a serious student. Little did I know that since we shared a bank account, my sister was using my meager savings to underwrite those house parties.

Meantime, I was still unemployed, but babysitting my niece was often a joy. I learned to negotiate the cityscape by taking daylong outings with her and the child of the neighbor who lived below us.

One of the things that I love about young children is that they are always up for an adventure, particularly if it is entertaining. Given their boundless energy, a day trip is a good way of tiring them completely out. With our lunch packed, we would spend a day at the Bronx Zoo; or ride the 1 train to the South Ferry station in Manhattan and then hop on the ferry to visit Lady Liberty; or take the bus to Van Cortlandt Park to have a picnic and play catch; or simply go on long walks throughout the community. The good thing about having very young companions in an adventure is that they do not care about where they are going or about getting lost along the way. Their sheer curiosity sustains them and keeps you alert in the process by answering an inordinate number of "why," "what," and "how come" questions.

I think it is terribly wrong that the structure of our educational system takes alert and inquisitive young minds and, often by the time children enter the fourth grade, turns them into dulled rote learners. It forces children to abandon important parts of themselves with the aim of educating them—but with what skills and toward what purpose? What is the relevance, I wonder, of formal education, when we force children to abandon their curiosity, fascination, creativity, and the simple joy that comes with learning something new? Why are we surprised, then, that in their frustration and disappointment, many choose to drop out of school, particularly many black youth? The process of educating children deserves its own narrative in the complex balancing act on the racial tightrope; however, in giving voice to my frustration, I digress.

The narrative that follows is extremely painful to reflect on, but nonetheless, let me return to the story at hand. Even though my days were full babysitting my niece, I was unemployed and needed more adult interaction. I was also beginning to notice unsettling changes in my sister's behavior. Although she went to work every day, she developed a pattern of hanging out with her friends and colleagues after hours and was prioritizing them above all else.

Little did I know that she had become addicted to crack cocaine. Her increasing need to get high began to take over our lives and drained our finances. Suddenly, we could no longer buy food or pay rent, and we argued all the time. We had to move. I needed to get out of this situation, and fast. Desperate and determined to find employment, I dumbed down my résumé and went looking for a job in Manhattan. I applied for a cashier or clerk job in every bookstore I could find. Immediately, I found a job working the evening shift, from four to eleven o'clock. A friend of my sister's was moving in with her boyfriend and agreed to let me illegally sublet her Upper West Side apartment. The rent took up about 80 percent of my meager pay, but the bookstore was within walking distance, so I could save on expenses. My sister and niece moved in with my sister's boyfriend, and in my anger, we stopped having contact with each other for some time.

My fellow bookstore employees were writers, artists, or students, and we enjoyed each other's company, holding many interesting conversations about the arts and books. Still, I wanted to use my hard-earned skills, so I continued to actively look for a professional job. Finally, after about six months of working at the bookstore, the Community Service Society (CSS), one of the oldest nonprofit agencies in the city, hired me. Its mission was "empowering the poor." Initially, my job was to provide technical support to community-based organizations in the areas of planning, program development, feasibility studies, board development, and general administrative operations. The good thing about the job was that it introduced me to the people and communities of the city. With my activist spirit, I liked the fact that they were all people trying to make the services in their communities more responsive to the needs of the people they served.

When I received a promotion at CSS, I became the child welfare policy analyst for the agency. This promotion was a turning point for me because it introduced me to the ugly underbelly of the city—the drug culture of the crack cocaine epidemic that was tearing through the poorer communities like an unstoppable, raging cyclone, leaving total destruction in its wake. As a researcher and analyst during the mid-1980s, I took on the task of trying to explain the unexpected and rapid increase of black and brown children entering New York City's foster care system and how the city was responding to it.

Hence I entered the bizarre culture of the entrenched city bureaucracy—in the form of the Child Welfare Administration (CWA)—as it responded to the illicit drug culture that was stimulated by the crack cocaine epidemic. These two realities were linked together by the presence of poor, often black, mothers and their children. I found that the CWA often questioned the maternal adequacy of poor mothers and could legally separate some of them from their children forever. I also found medically vulnerable and often addicted infants languishing in the baby wards of city hospitals or in infant orphanages entitled Congregate Care Facilities for Babies. There was a glaring absence of touching and loving hands in the lives of many of these children.

In this drug-infected culture, I witnessed the effect of physical and emotional abuse—sometimes including total abandonment—that drug-addicted mothers inflicted on their own children. This abuse was largely fueled by their insatiable drug addiction. Not only were babies abandoned in city hospital wards immediately on birth, but young children were also left on street corners or in homes to fend for themselves while their mothers fed their drug habits.

In addition to being absolutely horrified by what was happening to children as a result of the crack epidemic, I was equally dismayed by what was happening to their mothers. I saw the effects of physical and sexual abuse, criminal activities, and the exploitation of women involved in the crack cocaine drug culture. Sex in exchange for drugs was rampant; women traded the only thing they had to offer—their bodies—for a quick hit on a five-dollar vial of crack cocaine. For many, unbeknown to them, the HIV virus and other sexually transmitted diseases (STDs) were moving through their bodies as a result of unprotected sex. What was happening to black life in the city—and beyond—due to this raging epidemic? The gray haze on the racial tightrope was becoming denser; many were falling off the rope and destroying their lives. Noted public health researchers Becky Watkins, Robert Fullilove, and Mindy Fullilove documented the inability of many to negotiate through this thick haze when they said:

> Crack use typically occurs during binges which may last for days at a time, that is, until the user is forced to stop because of exhaustion or lack of the financial wherewithal to continue. During the binge, the need to procure and use crack overwhelms all other demands that might face the user. By necessity, kinship, work, and social duties are neglected. As one woman told an interviewer in describing the ways in which she had failed her children, "It hurts, it really hurts because you really want to do it. You really want to take care of your children and everything, but the drug is just constantly like a monkey on your back. I want it, I want it, I want it."[1]

During the mid-1980s and on into the 1990s, crack clogged the air like a dangerous pollutant hanging over many of the black and poor communities in New York City. There were only a few residential drug treatment facilities in the city. More often than not, the therapeutic models for intervention were usually geared toward men's, rather than women's, needs and experiences. To top it off, there was only one facility that would admit pregnant women or mothers and children together into its program.

Meanwhile, I missed my niece, and I decided to swallow my anger at my sister and visit her. I could not believe what I found—I have no words to adequately express the severity of the pain and angst I felt on entering their run-down apartment in Harlem and seeing my sister and niece living in such squalid conditions. I immediately focused on my niece, who had been sleeping in a filthy closet. I told my sister that she had a choice—either I would take my niece away from that environment that very moment, or I would immediately report her to CWA for child abuse, endangerment, and neglect. She could decide which option I would take, but my niece was leaving, one way or another, right then and there. She decided to let me take my niece. In that painful moment, all of our hearts broke into tiny pieces.

Taking my niece back to my apartment, I called her father, who was in another state, to explain what had happened. I did not have a good relationship with him, but I knew he loved his daughter deeply. To his credit, he wanted her to come and live with him and his family. I kept my niece with me for about a week in an attempt to reintroduce her to the joys and fantasies of childhood. It was extremely difficult to watch her leave with her father, but it was for the best.

Even though my sister's life was marred by an addiction that was facilitated by an enabling drug culture, I was not going to abandon her. I was determined to save my sister's life. She was one of the loves of my life, and I cared deeply about what was happening to her. Little did I know what I was dealing with—love and caring are not enough when confronting drug addiction.

I contacted the director of a community-based addiction treatment referral program, one which I had provided technical assistance to, looking for a residential treatment program for my sister. He was able to find a spot in a treatment program for her, but in order for her to get into the facility, she had to be declared "officially homeless" so that the program could be financially reimbursed through a third-party payment arrangement. She had to be declared indigent to meet the program's eligibility requirements. After convincing my sister to enter the addiction recovery program, we went to the city's homeless services to get her declared homeless. We sat in the crowded waiting room for hours while the bureaucrats determined her eligibility and finally got the necessarily documentation attesting to her homelessness. Here was a woman who had a sharp and agile mind and had gone to one of the most prestigious colleges in the United States. She had always been there for me when I needed her, and I had largely followed in her footsteps. Then she had to join the official ranks of the hundreds of thousands of indistinguishable faces of New York City's homeless people. I was, in a word, devastated.

My sister joined a twelve-step program, which required residents to work toward becoming healthy by earning privileges. It was a rigorous, step-by-step process. She lasted for three days and then went back to the streets again, to be with her drug-addicted friends. This became routine—she would go in and out of drug treatment programs, never staying more than a few days. When she was in really dire straits, she would come to my office, reeking of crack cocaine and looking for money. I never gave her money—I was not going to support her drug habit—but I always bought her whatever she lacked in order to fulfill her basic needs.

One day she hobbled into my office on a broken foot. She and another addict had tried to retrieve a quarter that had fallen beneath an iron street grate; the grate was too heavy for them to hold up, and it had dropped on my sister's foot. For whatever reason, she had managed to take the cast off and was limping badly on an unhealed foot. She looked so thin and worn out and was so incoherent that I wondered whether she had finally hit rock bottom.

At the moment nothing seemed to make sense to me, either. My sister was dying in front of my eyes, and there was absolutely nothing more I could do to help her. I could not save my sister's life, but how could I walk away from her, even when there were plenty of good reasons for doing so? She was so much a part of my being, as much as the air I breathed. She needed me, yet this truth only made the decision I had to make even harder to bear. My decision to let go went against every human instinct I had, but I knew that there are times when I cannot do anything to alter fate except pray. That was one of those times.

That day we had a long talk. I confronted her with the hard truth of her life: she had lost her daughter and everything that was once important to her; the only thing that she had left was her mind; and now she was losing that. I told her how much I loved and cared about her but that I would not watch her die. She had to find the courage to save her own life.

She did. Soon thereafter, without any prompting or help from me, for the first time she went into drug treatment of her own accord. She stuck with it and has been clean and sober for more than twenty years. She continued to pick up the broken pieces and moved on with her life, taking it one step and one day at a time.

To this day she credits that conversation in my office with giving her the courage, strength, and motivation to take the steps she needed in order to change. She continues to be one of the kindest and funniest people in my life, and I value our friendship. Above all else, I believe that her strength and courage in waging her battle against the odds are owed to the goodness of her heart and in the obligations we share to those who made our lives possible.

✿ ✿ ✿

The appearance of the gray zone on the racial tightrope was by no means limited to New Yorkers. A haze began to show up around the rope at about the mid-1970s, and as it grew denser and more hazardous, it affected the steps of people throughout the nation. It emerged in opposition to the liberal shifts that introduced social reforms, particularly regarding race and gender relations, during the 1960s and 1970s.

The gray zone took shape as blacks, as a group, became a legally protected class. Under affirmative-action policies, they had constitutional protection against racial discrimination. Given the nation's history of race and race relations, this was indeed an enormous accomplishment; in just over a twenty-year period, blacks moved from a state of absolute exclusion to procedural inclusion in our democracy. These liberal shifts altered the social standing of blacks in society by increasing their access to societal resources and by opening up opportunities that they were once denied. However, there was no executive, legislative, or judicial protection of any kind against systemic racism. This created the gray zone.

As the United States continued its journey along the racial tightrope, many white conservatives began to see these liberal shifts as an unwelcome altering of the racial status quo in race and race relations. Even by those who seemingly had little at stake or who had few meaningful interactions with blacks, perceived racial equity, even if largely procedural, was seen as diminishing the greatness of the nation and eroding the social standing of whites. Specifically, the conservative New Right movement, which sought to restore the United States to its greatness after being compromised by decades of liberal reforms, sought outlets of expression for these simmering resentments. Initially, the main target of conservative white resentment during the mid-1970s was affirmative-action policies.

The majority of blacks were living in racialized poverty during the mid-1970s, enduring a series of public policies that challenged the implementation of liberal reforms; but the harsh reality that affirmative action had surely fallen short of its goals for blacks did not seem to matter to its opponents. Their concerns were not simply about the success or failure of affirmative-action policies; the core of the matter rested with what those policies represented: the decline of the country's greatness and concurrent erosion in the privileged status of whites—especially middle-class males.

The American concept of affirmative action rests on the underlying premise that diversity should not justify inequality. Presumably, having white skin should be given no greater nor lesser value than having black skin, for instance. In reality, even with this concept firmly in mind, in a diverse, stratified society, there are many ways in which power is unequally distributed. What many conservatives fail to acknowledge is how whites, as a group, benefit from this arrangement. Herein lies a critical contradiction: conservatives want to enjoy unfettered white racial privileges yet deny that such privileges even exist by extolling victimization. This is akin to having one's cake and eating it, too.

This contradictory viewpoint was labeled "reverse discrimination," and no group exemplified it better in the United States than white males.[2] Historically, even if white male privileges were not readily extended to or reflected in an individual's daily struggles, as a group they were the sociopolitically privileged class of our society. Thus, this group formed the powerful normative standard in US society on which others are judged, and it follows that under affirmative-action policies, white males were particularly excluded as a protected class.

○ ○ ○

Many white conservatives want to focus on the racial qualities of others as they engage race relations but seek to omit the sociopolitical realities that shed light on the advantages of having white skin in our society. In other words, they become color-blind to the power of a white normative standard in our society. But that color blindness lasts only until that standard becomes breached and, hence, acknowledged. Affirmative-action policies breached that normative standard; as a result, many conservatives harbored resentment over white male exclusion under affirmative action. It was viewed as a diminishment of their racial superiority, as illustrated by the landmark reverse discrimination case of Alan Bakke.

White women, on the other hand, took full advantage of affirmative-action policies in order to further their individual and collective efforts to gain societal privileges and power.[3] Under affirmative action, white women radicals often flaunted established rules of participation and challenged the authority of social and cultural institutions. After gaining procedural inclusion into once-restricted gender spaces, many white women aggressively pursued their self-defined needs and aspirations; in so doing, they asserted their different ways of being into those spaces. In redefining what inclusion meant, their definitions did not necessarily conform to the gender status quo—to traditional societal values and norms.

White conservative resentment over affirmative action was not necessarily expressed overtly as racial and gender animus or in blatantly racist and sexist terms.[4] Conservatives took note of the political climate of the country, and increasingly their resentment became coded and wrapped in a new political framing. By the mid-1970s, that framing was revealed in the guise of the "culture wars": an oblique attack on liberal principles and policies. The term "culture wars" was used in a euphemistic and ambiguous way. In political debates of that era, it could mean many different things, depending on the particular conservative actors involved, ideologies advanced, and social and moral issues targeted for attack.

A new conservative movement—the New Right—began to emerge on a sociopolitical landscape that reflected all of these divisions.[5] What brought the New Right coalition together, with its different actors, ideologies, and issues, was the fundamental idea that racial and gender differences compromised American values by undermining the core ethics, norms, and traditions on which the nation was founded. From the perspective of New Right advocates, only a realignment of white racial and gender standings could accomplish their aim of restoring the country to its former glory. That would involve returning white males to their "proper status" in society. By the mid-1970s, the battle lines were clearly drawn; diversity, whether racial, gender, and/or cultural, was under attack. White conservative warriors and a few of their black allies were aggressively mobilizing to mount all-out attacks on many liberal principles and policies. The New Right was gaining momentum.

Initially, the New Right was largely composed of a loose network of single-issue groups. In "Coalition and Conflict among Women of the New Right," Rebecca Klatch maps out some of the actors and organizations at play in this movement. She states:

> While no consensus exists on the exact boundaries of the New Right, generally the phrase is used to delineate a network of people and organizations that came into prominence in the mid-1970s, including conservative politicians such as Jesse Helms, Orrin Hatch, and Jack Kemp; conservative think tanks such as the Heritage Foundation; general purpose organizations such as the Conservative Caucus, the National Conservative Political Action Committee, and the Committee for the Survival of a Free Congress; as well as the religious sector, including prime-time preachers, the Moral Majority, and groups working against such issues as abortion, gay rights, and pornography.[6]

Klatch divides the New Right warriors into two main ideological camps: social conservatives and laissez-faire conservatives. The theoretical roots of their ideology differ: the views of social conservatives are largely based on biblical interpretations, while laissez-faire conservatives embrace notions of unfettered capitalism. Contrasting the ideological differences, Klatch contends that the two camps see

America as a morally decaying country in which the basic unit of society is crumbling. The social conservative activist's special mission, then, is to restore America to health; to regenerate religious belief; to renew faith, morality, and decency; and to return America to the righteousness of the founding fathers. . . . Laissez-faire conservatives, in contrast, view the world through the lens of liberty, particularly the economic liberty of the free market and the political liberty based on the minimal state. Laissez-faire belief is rooted in the classical liberalism associated with Adam Smith, John Locke, and John Stuart Mill. Hence, the concept of liberty is inextricably bound to the concept of the individual. . . . Laissez-faire conservatives view humans as beings endowed with free will, initiative, and self-reliance. . . . The erosion of liberty, rather than moral decay, however, is their utmost concern.[7]

Clearly, there was a contradiction between the worldviews of social and laissez-faire conservatives. Yet both camps readily agreed on one main point: they deplored the liberal direction in which the United States was moving. On reaching this consensus, by the late 1970s the New Right was poised to attack the political excesses of liberalism. Having considerable resources, a variety of expertise, and dedicated members (including financiers, politicians, and grassroots activists), the movement came to have extensive political reach. Its influence was seen on issues as diverse as education, family, religion, immigration, crime, taxes, corporate deregulation, labor relations, environmental protection, defense spending, and foreign policy.

For blacks, especially those who were poor, this conservative influence had devastating consequences in their daily lives. When debating, conservatives took the stance that poverty among blacks evolved from their particular culture. Black poverty, they argued was endemic and pathological, a product of black culture; hence, there was little need to offer targeted public policies or social programs to respond to it. No amount of liberal sociopolitical engineering could change the situation; it was up to blacks to assume responsibility for changing the nature of their culture.

Joel Olson argues in "Whiteness and the Polarization of American Politics" that by emphasizing the degenerative nature of black culture as the main font of their poverty, conservatives attempted to neutralize the causal effects of systemic racism by providing an alternative rationale for actions or inactions. As he said, in using culture as a proxy for race, they muddled issues such as

> chronic unemployment, illegitimate children, poverty, crime, and welfare dependency and contrasted this with "traditional values" that extolled work, male-headed nuclear families, sexual restraint, law and order, and personal responsibility. . . . Out of these articulations of values came a set of debates (over welfare policy, crime, family, anticommunism, and abortion) that superficially appeared to have nothing to do with race but in fact revolved around the perceived pathologies of the black poor and the implicit virtues of the normalized white middle.[8]

Apparently, conservatives were mindful of the fact that they could no longer launch a direct frontal assault on blacks and simultaneously succeed in mobilizing broad-based support for their political agenda. But their indirect attacks had the same effects. They wanted to avoid creating the perception that conservatives were racist and liberals were antiracist. Thus, they began to strategically disguise their stance on vital issues by using political rhetoric that became increasingly coded. Their indirect attacks had the same effects but used different words.

In 1981, Lee Atwater became one of the main architects of this coded political language. He was a conservative political operative and later chairman of the Republican National Committee. Reflecting on the strategic importance of using coded language when discussing blacks, Atwater bluntly says:

> You start in 1954 by saying "Nigger, nigger, nigger." By 1968 you can't say "Nigger." That hurts you. It backfires. So you say stuff like forced busing, states rights and all that stuff and you get so abstract. Now you talk about cutting taxes and these things you're talking about are totally economic things and a byproduct of them is, blacks get hurt worse than whites. And subconsciously maybe that's part of it. I'm not saying that. But I'm saying that if it is getting that abstract and that coded, we are doing away with the racial problem one way or the other. Obviously sitting around saying we want to cut taxes and we want this, is a lot more abstract than even the busing thing and a hell of a lot more abstract than "nigger nigger."[9]

Speaking in code does not change the fact that when one is told that an issue is not about race, usually race lies at the heart of the matter. Conservatives used this coding of political language along with symbolic imagery to verbally attack blacks; they were as a threat to the values, norms, and traditions of white Americans. The solution, although never bluntly articulated by conservatives, was to impose greater social control over black life, particularly over those who were politically vulnerable by virtue of being poor.

To exert those controls, however, the New Right needed political power to advance an agenda based on conservative principles and policies. Democrats had used the power of the White House, Congress, and the judiciary to institutionalize liberal principles and policies during the 1960s and 1970s; to reverse that trend, New Right advocates turned to the Republican Party for a political home. The Republican Party proved to be fertile political ground for the New Right's principles, mobilizing white resentment and establishing a permanent conservative voting base. Allies of the movement were already ensconced in the party; they had not stood idly by watching as the New Right gained political momentum.

Though moderate Republicans attempted to maintain a solid bloc of support in the party, by the mid-1970s, they were beginning to lose power and were being pulled to the right on issues. Olson notes, for instance, that moderates of the party had, in principle, accepted "legal equality but opposed policies or programs designed to overcome the sedimented effects of racial discrimination." To the more fundamental conservative, racial equity was unacceptable even as a principle. These fundamentalists included those southern conservatives who were once Democrats but who, after being deposed by Hubert H. Humphrey's liberal faction, left the Democratic Party.

By 1976, social and fiscal conservatives had made tremendous inroads into the Republican Party, and their influence was shifting the party's political thrust away from a moderate stance toward an archconservative focus. As the Republican Party became increasingly more conservative following the civil rights era, its voter base also became increasingly white, male, and southern. Joe Feagin, in "White Party, White Government," argues:

The Party of Abraham Lincoln, which had supported civil rights for African Americans, was becoming not only whiter but also the party of former segregationists. A fair number of members of the white southern elite were moving into the resurgent racially and socially conservative Republican Party. Moving into the party, for example, former Democratic senator Strom Thurmond helped it capture politically much of the white South, and neither he nor most other Republican Party leaders seem to have viewed his former rabidly segregationist role as problematical. . . .

It was not just some older white segregationist leaders and voters who were moving in ever larger numbers to the Republican Party in the 1970s and later; many younger white conservative leaders and voters in the growing white-collar (for example, clerical, professional, managerial) groups in the rapidly expanding suburbs of the southern cities were also joining the ranks of those opposed to the racial and other social programs of the Great Society era. . . .

In addition, intensive opposition to racial desegregation and Great Society programs was also led by important conservative segments of the white elite and affluent middle-class groups in northern and western areas.[10]

This demographic shift in the Republican Party would have fateful consequences for future electoral politics, as white conservative southerners, northerners, and westerners would come to dominate the leadership and the voting base of the party. The shift, however, was not limited to the Republican Party—the Democratic Party was changing as well. Its leadership and members were becoming increasingly diverse, reflecting racially, gendered, and economic differences. The significance of these revisions did not seem to matter to white conservatives; after all, most elections—no matter how politically divisive—were won on the strength of the white vote.

In 1976, the conservative right wing, with a solid political base in the Republican Party, was ready to mount an all-out campaign to gain national and local political power. The prize, of course, was to win the 1976 presidential election; but first conservatives had to win the Republican Party's nomination for their candidate, Ronald Wilson Reagan.

The frontrunner for the 1976 Republican nomination was the moderate incumbent president, Gerald Ford, and his vice-presidential running mate, Senator Robert (Bob) Dole. The conservative wing of the Republican Party wholeheartedly threw its support behind its leader,

Ronald Reagan, former governor of California. By the time the Republican convention rolled round, the party's nomination was up for grabs. A bitter floor fight ensued between moderates and conservatives for delegates. Because the initial roll-call vote was too close to predict, Ronald Reagan, the conservative sector's candidate, narrowly lost to Ford, but Ford was politically weakened by their arguments. They blamed him for his role in compromising the country's reputation. During his tenure, President Ford ended the conflict in Vietnam, which the United States lost; signed the Helsinki Accords, an agreement designed to reduce tensions between the Soviet Union and Western-Bloc countries; and agreed to give Panama dominion over the US-built Panama Canal. President Ford's biggest vulnerability, however, was on the domestic front—he pardoned former president Richard Nixon for Nixon's crimes during the Watergate scandal without providing any explanation to the public as to why.

President Ford's rival for the Democratic presidential nomination was the little-known former governor of Georgia, James (Jimmy) Earl Carter. Jimmy Carter positioned himself as a Washington outsider and moderate social reformer to win the Democratic nomination. He selected Minnesota senator Walter Mondale, a protégé of Hubert Humphrey, as his vice-presidential running mate. Carter faced enormous challenges during the Democratic primaries, not only from other candidates running for the nomination but also from a group of liberal Democrats who called themselves the Anybody but Carter (ABC) movement. Members of this group were highly skeptical of Carter's southern political roots.[11] Nonetheless, Democrats were determined to present a united front coming out of their national convention in New York City. Congresswoman Barbara Jordan, the first African American to deliver a keynote address at a major party convention, was instrumental in uniting the Democrats behind Jimmy Carter's nomination.

Jordan's speech focused on the importance of an inclusive "national community." As she said:

> We are a people in a quandary about the present. We are a people in search of our future. We are a people in search of a national community. We are a people trying not only to solve the problems of the present—unemployment, inflation—but we are attempting on a larger scale to fulfill the promise of America. We are attempting to

fulfill our national purpose, to create and sustain a society in which
all of us are equal.[12]

At the end of her speech, she reiterated the call for an inclusive
national community "in which every last one of us participates" and
quoted Abraham Lincoln in her final words: "As I would not be a slave,
so I would not be a master. This expresses my idea of Democracy.
Whatever differs from this, to the extent of the difference, is no Democracy."

Surprisingly, Jimmy Carter won the 1976 presidential election over
the incumbent Gerald Ford by a narrow popular vote. The New Right
had not anticipated that Carter—a southerner—would win; but, even
more stunningly, it had not expected the Democratic candidate to
sweep the former Confederate states of the South. It would be the last
time a Democratic presidential candidate would accomplish this feat
for many years.

Right-wing Republicans were undaunted by this presidential defeat.
Their conservative supporters were increasing in number, giving them
the momentum to continue their efforts to construct the gray zone on
the racial tightrope—to gain the political power necessary to take back
the United States from both liberals and moderates. When it came to
blacks, they were even more adamant in their efforts—dismantling affirmative-action programs remained at the top of their political agenda.
Greater inclusion was to be replaced with greater social controls over
black life.

They lost their chance to win the White House in 1976 but through
the process gained a champion for conservative principles and policies—Ronald Wilson Reagan. His style and presentation captured the
imagination of many white Americans; the perfect man to reverse liberal trends, pull the country solidly to the right, and restore American
white manhood to its proper place.

That opportunity to impose their conservative ideals on the nation
came on January 20, 1981, when Ronald Reagan was sworn in as the
fortieth president of the United States. Using the power of that office,
he advanced a conservative agenda that had a devastating effect, especially on poor blacks. This political climate loomed over New York City
and reverberated throughout the country. Struggling to keep our balance on an already wavering racial tightrope, the nation had to find

ways of moving through this gray zone if we were to continue toward the age of Obama.

* * *

Adopting a hard-line stance on foreign affairs, President Reagan sought to restore the United States' stature as the preeminent political, economic, and military power in the world. Reagan was a Cold War warrior—under his administration, the United States assumed a "zero option" foreign policy toward the Soviet Union. In the midst of an economic recession and high unemployment, his administration increased the Department of Defense budget and launched a nuclear arms build-up in order to mount a strategic offensive against what he considered to be the main "evil in the modern world"—the worldwide spread of communism.

Almost immediately after assuming office, President Reagan sent an anticommunist signal to the world. Flexing the United States' military might, Reagan was determined to stop communist incursions into the Western Hemisphere. He invaded the tiny black Caribbean island nation of Grenada that was ruled by the leftist New JEWEL Movement. That invasion was meant to send a message; under the "Reagan doctrine," military intervention rather than diplomacy was the guiding principle of the US posture toward international affairs. During Reagan's second term in office, the fall of the Berlin Wall helped President Reagan negotiate an end to the Cold War.

Meanwhile, President Reagan also took a hard-line approach when addressing domestic issues. He aggressively assaulted the liberal welfare state while attempting to reinvigorate a stagnant economy. His economic policies emphasized unrestrained market competition with limited government oversight and enforcement. Widely known as supply-side economics, or Reaganomics, his policies called for lower federal taxes, increased savings, greater investments, and stronger work incentives to stimulate the economy. In order to induce a favorable corporate climate and to put the United States back on the road to economic prosperity, the burden of Reagan's economic recovery policies was placed on the backs of the poor. Although his economic strategies were not specific to race, the results were disproportionately borne by poor blacks. As I outline in my book *Through Our Eyes*, the Reagan administration imposed draconian budget cuts on liberal social welfare programs:

> The Reagan administration quickly moved to end or reduce social programs specifically aimed at the poor, and slashed the budgets of Medicaid, Medicare, and Food Stamps; terminated the Comprehensive Employment and Training Act (CETA); and placed stringent eligibility requirements on Aid to Families with Dependent Children (AFDC).[13]

In addition to eliminating or reducing many entitlement programs that served as a safety net for the nation's poor and infirm, President Reagan declared a war on drugs. He proposed comprehensive legislation to stop illegal drug trafficking and illicit drug use in the country. This "war on drugs" program received solid bipartisan support from Democrats and Republicans alike with the passage of the noted Anti-Drug Abuse Act of 1986.[14]

The overall intent of the Anti-Drug Abuse Act was to eradicate illicit substance abuse by destroying the networks used for distribution and illegal sales, but the force and violence that followed was equal to a military assault. Similar to the invasion of Grenada, this war was intended to send a strong message, particularly to blacks.

Like all wars, it required strategies and resources. It also demanded an identifiable enemy. Internationally, the battles were waged against drug cartels and kingpins largely in South America. On the home front, the drug war was fought in inner-city communities, and black, low-level drug dealers and addicts were the primary target. In *The New Jim Crow*, Michelle Alexander argues that in the buildup to the war:

> The Reagan administration hired staff to publicize the emergence of crack cocaine in 1985 as part of a strategic effort to build public and legislative support for the war. The media campaign was an extraordinary success. Almost overnight, the media was saturated with images of black "crack whores," "crack dealers," and "crack babies"— images that seemed to confirm the worst negative racial stereotypes about impoverished inner-city residents. The media bonanza surround the "new demon drug" helped to catapult the War on Drugs from an ambitious federal policy to an actual war.[15]

The 1986 Anti-Drug Abuse Act appropriated $1.7 billion to fight the "war on drugs" at home. Major allocations included: $97 million to build new prisons, $200 million for drug education, and $241 million for addiction treatment. The centerpiece of this legislation, which had a decisive impact and long-term implications for the black community, was the mandatory sentencing guidelines imposed on convicted drug offenders. Such guidelines eliminated judicial discretion and established a "mandatory minimum" sentencing requirement for drug violations. Congress deliberately made a distinction between crack and powdered cocaine in this legislation.

Both crack and powder cocaine are derived from the leaves of the coca plant. Crack cocaine is usually produced through the simple process of heating powdered cocaine in water with baking soda until it forms a hard, waxy form of cocaine, which is broken up into small, rocklike pieces. Crack cocaine is smoked, while powdered cocaine is snorted. Through this process, cocaine becomes a matter of form rather than content. The substance of the drug is exactly the same.

By establishing a gross sentencing disparity between the two, Congress introduced two obvious questions: why did they do so; and, more important, what role did race play in crafting those distinctions?

Supposedly, the overall intent of the mandatory guidelines was to impose severe penalties on international drug "kingpins," "big-time drug traffickers," and "mid-level dealers" who were moving large volumes of illegal narcotics into and around the country. However, because the conversion from powdered to crack cocaine takes place at the end of the distribution chain rather than at the beginning, it was usually done by local dealers. Low-level street dealers, who were selling small quantities of crack cocaine mainly to people in their communities, were receiving harsher sentences than the major drug traffickers who were trading in large quantities of drugs.

In his analysis in "Cocaine, Race, and Equal Protection," David A. Sklansky carefully documents the different sentencing thresholds established under the "mandatory minimum" guidelines. As he says:

> For defendants caught with quantities of narcotics above or below the thresholds for five- and ten-year mandatory minimum sentences, the Guidelines prescribe sentences extrapolated from those required by the Anti-Drug Abuse Act. Thus with no aggravating or mitigating circumstances, a defendant would be sentenced to ten to sixteen

months for trafficking in twenty-five grams of powder cocaine or only a fourth of a gram of crack, seventy-eight to ninety-seven months for two kilograms of powder cocaine or twenty grams of crack, and thirty years to life for 1500 kilograms of powder cocaine or fifteen kilograms of crack. At every quantity level federal defendants convicted of trafficking in crack cocaine receive the same sentences as defendants convicted of trafficking in one hundred times as much powder cocaine. [16]

Sklansky argues convincingly that the gross sentencing disparities between crack cocaine offenses and powdered cocaine had everything to do with race. Crack distribution and use were concentrated in poor, inner-city black communities, due largely to the fact that crack could be cheaply made and obtained—it was usually purchased for five dollars a vial. Because of this situation, the popular image of drug pushers and menacing drug addicts was associated with black space. In noting the historical tradition of associating illicit drugs with racialized space, Sklansky points out that

Crack is the most recent in a series of drugs that at various times have come to symbolize, to a greater or lesser extent, the entire problem of illicit narcotics in America. A similar role was played by smokable opium in the late nineteenth century, powder cocaine in the early twentieth century, marijuana in the 1920s and 1930s, and heroin in the 1950s. In each case, the drug of primary concern was strongly associated in the white public mind with a particular racial minority: opium in the late nineteenth century with Chinese immigrants on the west coast, powder cocaine in the early twentieth century with southern blacks, marijuana in the 1920s and 1930s with Mexican Americans in the southwest, and heroin in the 1950s with urban blacks. In each case, moreover, much of the public anxiety about the feared narcotic stemmed from a concern that use of the drug was spreading beyond the confines of the minority group with which it traditionally had been associated. [17]

Furthermore, Sklansky argues that: "not only did crack do most of its damage in the ghetto, or at least most of its visible damage, but crack vendors were widely understood to be, for the most part, black men. . . . What was coming was not just a drug—it was a black drug, sold by black men." The possibility of a black drug spreading into the white space of the US middle class had to be contained. The war on drugs, with its legally sanctioned strategies, militaristic resources, and above all else, a clearly identifiable domestic enemy, provided the perfect vehicle for this containment. Similar to the historical periods of slavery and Jim Crow segregation, the war on drugs also introduced new and defining patterns of social controls on black life. In its contemporary form on the racial tightrope, those patterns have led to mass prison incarcerations.

At the time, there was little criticism from the black community, given the growing devastation and suffering that crack was wreaking on black lives. Many thought that something had to be done to halt the crack epidemic, and the long-term and devastating effects of sentencing disparities were unforeseeable.

Under slavery and Jim Crow segregation, systems of social controls criminalized the mere presence of the black body. But with the liberal sociopolitical shifts in our society regarding race and race relations, the totalizing effects of those distinct systems were passé by the 1980s. Society had moved beyond the more blatant institutional structures of black exploitation and racial segregation to a more complex and ambiguous system of social controls. Constraints were rearticulated in response to the changing sociopolitical circumstances of contemporary times. New and defining patterns of social controls were established through the linking of crime and drugs to black space. The war on drugs became the dominant means of signifying that rearticulation.

* * *

The crack cocaine epidemic raging through poverty-stricken black communities was a political gift to the conservative right wing. Its political attacks against blacks could be legally coded and socially masked as an appropriate response to illegal wrongdoing. After all, blacks' criminal activity was widely seen as being the culprit that created the crisis in the first place, and given the political climate created by the New Right movement, conservatives were especially opportunistic in imposing a "law and order" response. Stopping criminal activities and punishing wrongdoers provided a legitimate legal rationale for increased social control. The fact that some blacks were indeed complicit by their involvement with the drug culture, through distribution and use, provided ample evidence of their wrongdoing to policy makers; legal justifications for increased racial surveillance, profiling, stop and frisk, arrests, convictions, and, importantly, imprisonment were firmly established by law.

During the Reagan years, conservatives readily pointed to the irresponsible behavior of blacks to rationalize imposing increased social controls on their lives, generally though draconian social policies. During the 1980s and 1990s, as the nation shifted further and further to the conservative right, the ambiguous yet hazardous gray zone appearing on the racial tightrope became denser, making steps even more treacherous. Many blacks on the rope, especially the poor, became trapped in this dangerous gray space. For some, their decisions and actions in the gray zone were complicit in reproducing practices that jeopardized and devalued the lives of others and, in turn, threatened their own lives as well.

Besides my sister and myself, my youngest brother became trapped in the destructive gray zone. As a drug addict and dealer, he was very much a part of the crack cocaine drug culture. We did not grow up together but nonetheless had a close relationship. When my mother was searching for adoptive homes for her children, she placed my youngest brother with his paternal grandmother; when his grandmother died, my brother went to live with our mother. When I visited my mother during summer vacations as a child, my brother and I spent time together; but as we grew older, our lives diverged sharply. During his teenage years, he dropped out of school and ran the streets with his friends. He was always into trouble with the law and was often locked up in juvenile detention. Unfortunately, this became the pattern of his adult life as well.

I do not know what came first—his addiction to drugs or his selling—it is the quintessential question of the chicken or the egg. Both vices were ever present during his entire adult life, and he spent more time in prison than out for selling marijuana and, later, crack cocaine.

I made the decision early on to never visit my brother when he was incarcerated because I hated the idea of him locked in a cage. Over the years, when he was confined, he would sometimes call me (collect), but more often, we would write to each other. Even as a struggling college student, I would try to enclose a twenty-dollar money order in my letters to him. His poorly written letters always gave me an update on what he was doing, what he needed (money), when he was getting out, and how he was going to change his life once out of prison. Over the years, I saved all of our correspondence, but there came a point when I was too angry at him for having hurt other people and himself. We no longer corresponded. Then, unexpectedly, I received a letter from him. Little did I know at the time that would be our last written correspondence. In part, his letter said:

> I know you were not looking for me to write you at all. It's been a long time sister that we have not said a word to each other. I want to know why, me and you don't communicate. Maybe it's because I've been locked up most of the time. This is why I am writing you a letter to let you know how I feel. I am making it my job to know why no one cares any more. I know I have not done any thing to no one or said any thing bad about any one. Is it because I have been in trouble most of my life? I never killed any one or badly harmed or robbed any one. Most of the time I come to prison is because I be with or be around the wrong people. I think that you know that I had to get it any way I could because I did not stay in school like you did and make something out of myself. I wish I knew back then like I know now how to live the right way.

In my last letter to him, I wrote:

> I think that it is a good thing that you are now reflecting upon your life, because yours is a life worth reflecting upon. For most of your life you have been locked up either in jail or prison because of your self-destructive behavior. You have never taken responsibility for the life you've led. Even in your letter, you are blaming someone else for the reason you're in prison today. We have all made mistakes. But we must take responsibility for the consequences of those mistakes. Your actions have hurt many people, even if you have never killed anyone. Have you ever thought about the people whose lives you helped ruin by selling them drugs? What about their children's lives? You're sitting in prison now because you sold drugs. And you've caused those who love you the most enormous pain and heartache. Our mother has always been there for you, and you play on her guilt and take advantage of her in any way you can. What about your children? You have never taken responsibility for them. How can you guide them in life from a prison cell or be a role model when your behavior is so self-destructive. And, what about the women in your life who you have physically and emotionally abused when they tried

to help you? I love and care about you, but I will not participate in your destructive behavior. I need those around me to respect me, but you do not respect yourself, so I no longer have that expectation of you. Maybe, if you can find the courage to make some different decisions about your life once you get out of prison, then maybe we can find our way back to each other.

Drugs, alcohol, and hard living finally took a decisive toll on my brother's body. But before he died, my brother's sadness forced me to forgive him so that I could love him more freely. I was able to forgive him for the hurt, harm, and cruelty he had done to others but, more important, to himself. Through the process of forgiveness, I was also able to forgive myself for the extremely hard and painful decisions I made regarding my brother.

For many blacks, including my brother, my sister, and myself, the gray zone that we entered on the racial tightrope became a hazardous area in and of itself. As victims attempted to negotiate their lives in the sociopolitically ambiguous and dangerous space, they may, wittingly or unwittingly, adopt perspectives and practices that reproduce oppressive conditions. Such was the case with the drug culture that evolved from the crack cocaine epidemic in the black community; it was also the reason that those choices were made.

The insidiousness of the gray zone, akin to the insidiousness of racism itself, masked the influences of oppressive structural relations and institutional practices. Blacks, for instance, seemingly asserted their free will over their decisions and actions; many even viewed their choices as normal. That was precisely how they became complicit. Those choices, according to Claudia Card, are by no means static, but rather are fluid and constantly changing, depending on the various social circumstances that confront people. As circumstances change, so too do our decisions and actions, even in the routines of day-to-day life. Those changes are important to note because "all victims do not become or remain complicit. Some resist to the end; many of these do not survive. Nor among those who become complicit is everyone equally so."[18]

Why is it important to acknowledge the complicity of some victims in aiding oppression in the gray zone? The answer is quite simple: they can further endanger the lives of those with whom they are bonded. People who are bonded to others can also abuse them. Those who victimize others are not blameless; the harm and cruelty that they inflict must be acknowledged, even if they did not create the overall circumstances in which their actions took place.

Even as complicit victims, there is a line that must not be crossed because the personal price of doing so is too great. They risk something fundamental in crossing that line, compromising their own sense of human integrity. In Card's words:

> We lose our innocence when we become responsible through our choices for the suffering of others or when we betray their trust, even when we make the best decision open to us under the circumstances. When we fail to live up to the responsibilities we thereby incur, as we inevitably must when we lack the means, our integrity may be compromised. We risk losing self-respect and moral motivation. Once we feel we have crossed the line of participating in the infliction of evil; we may have less to restrain us from more and worse in the future. [19]

Having said this, let me be absolutely clear; even if they contribute to the problem, blame and guilt for oppressive conditions must not be placed on the shoulders of victims. The main culprits in maintaining racial oppression are those who have the power to effectuate inequalities and injustices through their decisions and actions.

These are critical considerations in assigning blame and responsibility for the oppressive conditions on our racial tightrope. Anything less than this understanding only results in blaming the victim; or, as Primo Levi aptly tells us, "an attempt to shift onto others—specifically, the victims—the burden of guilt, so that they [are] deprived of even the solace of innocence."[20]

Those participating in the crack cocaine drug culture, to a greater or lesser extent, were complicit in abusing others as well as themselves. Not only did crack ravage the lives of many in the black community, like my brother and sister, but millions of other black men and women paid dearly for their complicity—they were arrested, convicted, and sentenced to long-term imprisonment as a result. In linking drugs and crime to black space, Ronald Reagan's "war on drugs" criminalized the black community, poor black men and women in particular.

Kenneth B. Nunn contends that this criminalization was neither accidental nor conspiratorial. The war on drugs and the actions that followed were a convenient way of masking the systemic nature of oppression. Or, as Nunn suggests: "In this way, crime can mask racial oppression by allowing it to be represented as a legitimate response to wrongdoing."[21] For example, under the Anti-Drug Abuse Act's mandatory minimum sentencing guidelines, judges are required by law to impose strict sentencing disparities whether they agree or not. This took decision making and implementation out of the hands of judges. This neither accidental nor conspiratorial process is only one example among many too numerous to note that highlights the more systemic and ambiguous nature that has come to define racial oppression in our society.

This situation has resulted in the deliberate, countrywide warehousing of many poor black men and women in prisons and jails in response to their illegal actions. For those convicted of felony offenses, many states deny them a fundamental right of citizenship—the right to vote. This is a rearticulation of the social controls imposed on black bodies and the spaces they occupy.

It is true that people like my brother, my sister, and myself violated drug laws to a greater or lesser extent, but the underlying intent of the crafting and implementation of those drug laws was by no means colorblind. The complicity of some blacks in violating drug laws does not adequately explain the disproportionate rates of black imprisonment or the vast numbers of those who are not incarcerated but instead are trapped under the supervision of the criminal justice system through probation and parole. In fact, most blacks are found guilty, usually through some kind of plea-bargaining agreement or, to a much lesser extent, a trial conviction. The intentional targeting of blacks under the guise of the war on drugs is the only adequate explanation for this.

There is a long history of black incarceration as both a form of social control and labor exploitation, particularly in the South during the era of Jim Crow segregation. Douglas A. Blackmon calls the railroading of blacks into prisons and convict work camps during that period "slavery by another name." The US Department of Justice Office of Justice Programs (OJP) adds credibility to Blackmon's claims in noting: "In 1926 an estimated 45% of all persons admitted to State prisons in the South were black, compared to 18% in the North Central, 14% in the Northeast, and 5% in the West."[22]

By 1986, in the war on drugs, this picture had dramatically changed. The change did not necessarily appear in the South, however, where blacks were an estimated 51 percent of all admissions to state prisons; it was most noteworthy in the rest of the country. At that time, blacks accounted for 56 percent of the admissions in the Northeast, 43 percent of the admissions in the northern central states, and 26 percent in the West.[23] To explain this dramatic turnaround, Michelle Alexander argues convincingly that a restored system of Jim Crow segregation has emerged in the contemporary form of mass incarceration.

During the war on drugs, blacks were not the only race arrested for narcotic possession, yet they were more likely than others to be convicted of the crime. Even though blacks constitute only roughly 13 percent of the total population, "twice as many Whites as Blacks are arrested while seven times as many Blacks as Whites are convicted. Blacks are almost three times more likely than Hispanics and five times more likely than Whites to be in jail . . . Black, non-Hispanic women are five times more likely than White women to be incarcerated. Black minors represent over half of incarcerated young people." Gloria Browne-Marshall points out these facts.[24] If one excludes the very young and the very old from consideration, then the disproportional impact of this intentional targeting is only heightened.

Since Ronald Reagan's declaration of the War on Drugs, numerous scholars and researchers have documented the precipitous growth in the number of blacks imprisoned in correctional facilities. The number of blacks incarcerated due to drug offenses has more than tripled since 1982. As evidence continues to mount, there is little doubt that blacks were targeted as the primary enemy in the war on drugs. Such targeting was a direct result of conservative efforts to impose regressive principles and policies in their attempt to restore the United States to its "proper" place in the world. The war continues to take a tremendous toll on black life.

During the "Reagan Revolution," the conservative right pushed forth its "law and order" political agenda that resulted in the creation of the cloudy gray zone that appeared on the racial tightrope during the 1980s and 1990s. The war on drugs was a guise, a proxy that masked conservative attacks on the most politically vulnerable within the black community—the poor.

Yet even under oppressive conditions, there is always some kind of push back. Growing signs of a moderate push back against conservatism began to appear on the rope. Pragmatists, having been drawn to the moderate right instead of the moderate liberal side of the political spectrum, were cautious in their approach to race and race relations. Their moderation concerning racial politics would prove to strengthen rather than lessen the gray haze that appeared on the racial tightrope.

With this moderate shift afoot on the rope, we began to see new pockets of leadership emerging within the black community, made up of middle-class elected officials and conservative intellectual activists. Even though they held opposing views on many issues, both groups were firmly committed to the idea of a color-blind United States—the notion that individuals should be judged on the content of their character rather than the color of their skin. That color-blindness would draw us deeper into the fogginess of the gray zone rather than illuminating a way out. The pragmatic approach to race and race relations during 1990 through 2000 helped the nation gradually shift away from the conservative right and created a foundation that became instrumental in moving us to the age of Obama.

6

WHO IS INCLUDED AND WHO BELONGS?

Sharing Ambiguous Space

The first time I voted for a president was in 1980. I was living in St. Paul, Minnesota. While standing in the long line outside of our neighborhood school, waiting to vote for the Democratic nominee and fellow Georgian Jimmy Carter, I heard that polls on the East Coast were closed, and Ronald Reagan was presumptively the winner of the presidential election. Disheartened, I cast my vote anyway, for the losing candidate.

Since that day, I have always voted in national elections and often in local contests. I relish the act of stepping into a polling booth, drawing the curtain, and pulling the lever to mark my ballot. Usually, I vote for the Democratic candidate; sometimes, for a third-party or even an independent contestant; but, as I will readily admit, I never vote for the Republican candidate. In most elections, I feel as if I am often confronted with limited choices and wish that there were clear alternatives to the seemingly same old pool of recycled politicians. Why, then, do I bother to vote, especially when the outcome seems so predictable?

In part, I vote because I remember my ancestors. I remember my great-grandparents, Elvie and Caroline Spearman and Isaac and Ellen Spears; their children and grandchildren; and all of those who were denied the simple act of placing an X on a voting ballot because they were of African descent in the United States. I cast my vote in their names, to acknowledge and honor the sacrifices they made to give me the simple right to vote.

Moreover, I vote for myself. By voting, I claim my right of citizenship. The struggles of my African American ancestors bestowed that obligation on me; in my mind there is no other group, except for Native Americans, who are more entitled to claim the national identity of US citizen.

Voting is a fundamental right of every citizen in our democracy that is guaranteed by the Fifteenth Amendment of the US Constitution. Until the landmark passage of the 1965 Voting Rights Act, which was meant to enforce the Fifteenth Amendment by prohibiting discrimination, blacks were largely excluded from participation in the electoral process and thereby denied the opportunity to fully participate as citizens in our democracy.[1] Yet the right to vote has never been freely exercised by blacks, even though it has been constantly demanded. Legislative barriers and legal restrictions have—in one way or another—inhibited black enfranchisement. Unfortunately, today as in the past, voting continues to be a fragile right for many blacks. We continue to see legislative and legal attempts to suppress the black vote. Those dogged attempts at voter suppression are a constant reminder of our nation's dark legacy of slavery and Jim Crow segregation.

Currently, the Brennan Center for Justice at New York University documents the existence of at least 180 pieces of legislation that restrict voting in a total of forty-one states.[2] The recent (2013) decision by the US Supreme Court to strike down the "preclearance clause" of the 1965 Voting Rights Act provides added impetus to the possibility that state legislators of the future will have even more power to restrict voters' rights.[3] Because of this ruling, section 4 of the Voting Rights Act is no longer valid. As a result, states are no longer required to seek approval from the US Department of Justice before changing voter qualifications and voting procedures. Immediately following that decision, Texas moved to impose tighter restrictions on voter participation. Other states, particularly those controlled by Republican officeholders, are currently preparing to follow Texas's lead.

What are we to make of this new legislative and legal assault supporting voter repression in the age of Obama?

Voting is a right of inclusion in our democracy. Whether one wants it or not, US citizens have a say in determining who will represent them in the governance of the nation. I recognize that a single vote appears inconsequential in the overall political scheme of things but that my vote carries weight when cast in conjunction with those who have mutual political interests. I am well aware that my vote will probably wind up on the losing end of things, particularly when considering the sophisticated political machinations based on financing that currently dominate mainstream electoral politics. Yet I continue to vote.

Even amid the political clutter of a seriously flawed electoral system, I continue to believe that voting can play a significant role in helping to shift—I hope in a progressive way—the circumstances of our lives. Those of us who are the most vulnerable to abusive administrative, legislative, and judicial policies that have an implicit, if not explicit, aim of turning back the hands of time on racial progress have a vested interested in voting.

There is no denying that it makes a difference who occupies an elected office and what type of political agenda an elected official chooses to pursue. So I vote, and I encourage others to claim this right of citizenship as well—even amid political frustrations and disappointments. By claiming this right, I also claim my stake in helping to determine the present and future course of our nation. I claim my obligation to participate in holding those who have political power accountable, because they represent "we the people," a phrase in which I am included. However, the lessons of history have taught me well; if I care about social equity and justice, then I should not expect fundamental change to occur solely within the structure of mainstream politics. I consider it a wise act not to put all of my political eggs in the electoral basket.

Instead, over the years, I have joined with others in participating in demonstrations, marches, rallies, political meetings, and movements. My reason for this active political engagement is to push back against encroachments on social equity and justice while at the same time insisting on fundamental fairness in the processes that allow people to flourish. I am ever mindful of the give-and-take process on which electoral politics is built. Thus, I am wary when politicians—especially those whom I supported—place black needs and aspirations on the bargaining table for negotiation or renege on promises altogether as they engage in the art of political compromise.

There is such a thing as fairness. It is at the root of what constitutes the politically right and wrong. My idea of what is fair differs from the popular notion of "political correctness," an idea that rests on words instead of actions. I learned this distinction from my heroes and heroines in their struggles for social change. Their actions have taught me that there are circumstances where deep intellectual contemplation is important, but it is not always necessary when attempting to right something that is clearly wrong. What is necessary is moral courage, against the odds, in seeking to correct injustice. Politically, I continue to be very basic in my fundamental understanding of what is right and wrong: slavery was wrong; Jim Crow segregation was wrong; and the current mass imprisonment of many poor blacks is simply wrong. Usually, when I see human dignity and worth compromised, I have such clarity of thought.

How much should we expect elected officials, once they hold the reins of power, to simply do the right thing? This is a critical question for many, but especially for those within the black community, as more and more black politicians are assuming greater power and the responsibility that goes along with it as they ascend to higher political offices. For most black elected officials, their elections were predicated on the strength of black voter participation, and blacks as a group represent their core constituency. But what is given to that constituency in exchange for electoral support? Specifically, what are the group benefits that are derived from casting the decisive vote in an election? Are those benefits merely symbolic—the euphoria and pride that is taken in the knowledge that one of your own has reached the pinnacles of political power that have heretofore been denied? Or does that power signal the full inclusion in democracy and an end to our struggles on the racial tightrope?

I am mindful of the structural constraints placed on elected officials, black and otherwise, and aware of the pragmatism that often influences the political decisions and actions of an officeholder. Therefore, I know that political compromises and deals are made. But when confronted with issues of race and race relations, what bargains and negotiations will black elected officials make? Will they, too, in their compromises and deals, maintain the racial status quo, or will they make new history in their steps on the racial tightrope?

° ° °

Soon after I arrived in New York City in 1984, I experienced a moment in history that seemed horribly wrong to me. I was watching the morning news when it reported that Eleanor Bumpurs, a sixty-six-year-old black grandmother, had been fatally shot in her public housing apartment by a white police officer, Stephen Sullivan. Mrs. Bumpurs had been withholding her monthly rent, $98.85, for four months to protest long-standing maintenance problems in her apartment. Housing Authority officials labeled her emotionally disturbed and instituted eviction procedures against her. The New York Police Department Emergency Service Unit sent a special squad trained in handling emotionally disturbed people to evict Mrs. Bumpurs. The *New York Times* reported what happened on October 29, 1984, when four white police officers tried to remove her from her home:

> Three officers entered Mrs. Bumpurs' fourth-floor apartment. One carried a Y-shaped metal bar to restrain her. Two other officers, with plastic shields, tried to pin her right hand, which held the knife, against a wall. . . . Officer Sullivan, who was carrying a shotgun, was behind the other officers. . . . Officer Sullivan fired twice, with the shots one to three seconds apart. The first shot is believed to have struck the deceased in the hand (with the knife) but was not sufficient to stop the forward movement of Mrs. Bumpurs.[4]

The Office of the Bronx District Attorney attempted to get a manslaughter indictment against Officer Sullivan for the killing. During the grand jury hearing, the district attorney argued that the first shot fired by Officer Sullivan hit Mrs. Bumpurs's "right hand and shattered a 10-inch knife she was holding." Thus, "it was anatomically impossible for her to hold the knife after the first shot."[5] Additionally, Mrs. Bumpurs was reported to have weighed three hundred pounds and been severely arthritic with a bad heart condition, which would have impeded her forward movement. But, as the *Times* reported, the judge in the case, Vincent A. Vitale, threw out the grand jury indictment on the grounds that Officer Sullivan "followed the existing Police Department guidelines" in shooting Mrs. Bumpurs. The message sent to the public, as expressed by one of Mrs. Bumpurs's daughters, was: "The judge and the police department are saying, if you're poor, if you're black, then there's no justice."

Through my eyes, the killing of Mrs. Bumpurs was clearly wrong. Yet it was only one of several incidents that dominated the racially charged climate in New York City throughout the 1980s.[6] There were other notorious attacks on blacks—in 1982, Willie Turks, a New York City Transit Authority worker, was pulled from his car on a Brooklyn street and beaten to death by a white mob. In 1984, Bernard Goetz shot three black youths who approached him and asked for money while on a subway car. 1986 found Michael Griffith being chased by a mob of white youth onto a Queens highway, where he was struck and killed by a car. His companions, Cedric Sandiford and Curtis Sylvester, were severely beaten by the mob. Finally, in 1989, Yusef Hawkins was shot dead on a Brooklyn street by a mob of twenty to thirty whites lying in wait for any black who came along.

Outrage and protest over these racially charged attacks mounted. Many in the black community held Mayor Edward (Ed) Koch responsible for the tense racial climate looming over the city during the 1980s.

Ed Koch was a three-term mayor.[7] Initially, he was widely perceived as a liberal, a man who had marched for civil rights in the South during the 1960s. In his first term as mayor, Koch inherited a weakened city economy. He was credited with leading the city government back from the brink of bankruptcy and restoring the city's creditworthiness, during the late 1970s. By his second term in office, with the national political climate trending toward conservatism, Koch was moving increasingly to the political right on social issues in order to maintain his political power. With his reelection in 1981, he became the first mayor to be endorsed by both the Democratic and Republican parties, receiving 75 percent of the votes cast. By his third term, many blacks considered him to be solidly conservative in his political stances on social issues, especially regarding race relations.

In the mid-1980s, the Koch administration was plagued with a series of corruption scandals, although Koch himself was never directly accused of any wrongdoing. Amid those scandals, deep animosity was brewing in various advocacy communities, particularly over the issues of the crack cocaine epidemic, growing homelessness, and the spread of HIV and AIDS. As a result of these and other issues facing New Yorkers, the overall quality of life for many in the city was waning, and the lack of effective responses from the city administration in confronting these challenges only heightened advocates' anger.

In this acrimonious political climate, Mayor Koch made several critical decisions that would draw the ire of many in the black community. He closed Sydenham Hospital in Harlem, purged antipoverty programs, and said that "Jews would be crazy" to vote for Jesse Jackson during his 1988 presidential campaign after Jackson had referred to New York City as "Hymietown." In an attempt to appease his black critics, Mayor Koch appointed Benjamin Ward as the first black police commissioner of the city; but it was under Commissioner Ward's watch that the notorious racially motivated attacks against blacks occurred.

The white mob attack on sixteen-year-old Yusef Hawkins occurred just over a month before Koch faced David Dinkins in the 1989 Democratic primary for mayor. Dinkins was the Manhattan borough president and the only black candidate in the race for mayor. In calling the city a "gorgeous mosaic," Dinkins pledged to bring racially divisive New Yorkers together. Winning the Democratic primary over Koch, Dinkins went on to defeat the Republican challenger Rudolph (Rudy) Giuliani, thus becoming the first and only black mayor of New York City.

Many New Yorkers viewed Dinkins as the ideal black political candidate—someone who did not flaunt his blackness by being acrimonious and who was articulate, urbane, and well liked among whites. This was especially noticeable in comparison to Jesse Jackson, who was confrontational on racial issues. For many whites, but particularly those within the Jewish community of the city, Dinkins was the antithesis of the Reverend Jesse Jackson. At the time, Jackson, a former aide to Dr. Martin Luther King and a civil rights leader in his own right, was the best-known black politician in the country, having run twice for the Democratic Party's nomination for president. Even though Dinkins and Jackson were friends, their demeanor differed, especially when it came to responding to issues of race. Dinkins was heralded as someone who could heal the racial schism in the city, and this aided his victory over the incumbent Koch.

Yet this perception was not based on a political agenda in which Dinkins proposed specific policies and strategies for accomplishing such aims. To the contrary, he had no such agenda, only the widely held perception that he was better qualified to heal the city simply because he was black.[8]

In a city where no one racial and/or ethnic group dominates the electoral process, a coalition of support is essential for obtaining a city-wide office such as mayor. After defeating Koch in the Democratic primary, Dinkins turned his attention to the general election and the Republican front-runner, Rudy Giuliani. By 1983, Giuliani had switched from being a Democrat to being an independent, and finally, to being a Republican. This change in political allegiance was instrumental in promoting his career in the Department of Justice. In 1983, Giuliani was appointed as US Attorney for the Southern District of New York, under the Reagan administration. In this position, he gained a national reputation for prosecuting high-profile figures from Wall Street and organized crime as well as drug dealers and corrupt government officials.

In the racially charged climate of New York City, Rudy Giuliani ran for mayor as a crime fighter on a law-and-order political platform. Surprisingly, Giuliani shied away from exploiting one of the most volatile crimes in the city at the time, the Central Park jogger rape case.[9] This incident happened on April 19, 1989, and involved six youths who were accused of brutally attacking and raping a jogger in Central Park. A feature article in *New York Magazine* describes the suspects of this crime and the victim in the following way:

> The victim was white and middle-class and female, a promising young investment banker at Salomon Brothers with a Wellesley-Yale-Phi Beta Kappa pedigree. The suspects were black and Latino and male and much younger, some with dubious school records, some from fractured homes, all from Harlem.[10]

Beyond expressing "outrage at the crime and sympathy for the victim," Rudy Giuliani did not publicly elaborate further on the incident during his entire mayoral campaign. Others readily offered their opinions to the media, however. Political activists Alton Maddox and the Reverend Al Sharpton, who were instrumental in leading marches in Brooklyn and Queens to protest racially motivated attacks, claimed racism in their support of the accused, while Donald Trump, the millionaire real-estate developer, took out full-page ads in all of the major newspapers in New York City at an estimated cost of $85,000, calling for the reinstatement of the death penalty and declaring the alleged perpetrators to be "wild criminals . . . dispensing their own brand of twisted hatred."[11] These responses only heightened the racial tensions over the incident.

But through it all, Giuliani remained silent on the incident. Dinkins, however, freely offered his assessment and told New Yorkers the tragedy "was not racially motivated" but acknowledged it could be perceived as such. His statement reflected a delicate balancing act of simultaneously trying to allay white fears of marauding black teens indiscriminately pouncing on whites while attempting to avoid perpetuating the racial stereotype of the "criminalblackmale" simply because the accused were young, black, and male. The *New York Times* reported Dinkins as saying:

> I want to avoid a situation wherein any young African-American, any young Latino will be seen as threatening by others who happen to be white. . . . If they broke some windows and destroyed valuable artwork, even if they snatched some pocketbooks, that's one thing. . . . We could try to understand it. But for this kind of behavior, there is no justification, no excuse.[12]

Even though Dinkins stressed that this incident was not racially motivated, he did, like many New Yorkers (including myself), assume that the five young African Americans and one Latino male were guilty of this heinous crime. After all, the accused admitted their guilt on videotaped confessions, which were repeatedly shown on news broadcasts throughout the city. We were all proved wrong when the actual rapist admitted to the crime and DNA evidence supported his claim. At the trial, all of the accused "pleaded not guilty and claimed that their videotaped confessions were concocted by the cops. Antron McCray, Kevin Richardson, Raymond Santana, Yusef Salaam, and Kharey Wise served sentences ranging from five to thirteen years."[13] All these years later, we now know that a gross miscarriage of justice was imposed on the lives of these young men as well as on the life of Trisha Meili, the victim of that vicious sexual assault in Central Park.

Although Giuliani did not discuss the Central Park jogger rape incident in public, he was quite vocal when it came to attacking Dinkins. But he was careful in framing his political attacks; he refrained from playing the race card and drawing on racial stereotypes that would undermine Dinkins's competency and suitability for mayor because of his skin color. In a traditionally Democratic city, with a loyal and substantial liberal voting base, Giuliani had to perform a delicate balancing act on racial issues. He had to avoid giving any impression that he was a blatant racist in order to appeal to voters as a Republican.

Thus, he chose to attack Dinkins's character, and not the color of his skin.

Caught off guard by Dinkins's upset victory over Mayor Koch in the Democratic primary, Giuliani's campaign strategists scrambled to find negative images to portray about Dinkins. They had not anticipated, even amid charges of corruption and scandal, that Koch would actually lose the primary. Therefore, their political strategy for the general election was geared toward defeating Koch, not Dinkins.

When it came to Dinkins, there was little in his public record as Manhattan borough president for Giuliani to attack—there was no corruption or scandal. Given the racial climate in the city, Giuliani wanted to avoid a frontal attack on explosive issues such as the Central Park jogger incident to avoid the potential political backlash. So in his attempt to win votes, his attacks on Dinkins's character were more implicit rather than direct. As Wilbur Rich outlines in *David Dinkins and New York City Politics*, Giuliani

> turned to Dinkins' personal finances, particularly to a questionable deal where he transferred stocks to his son. The charge of financial misconduct continued to haunt Dinkins throughout the campaign. . . . The second strategy was to portray Dinkins as a clubhouse politician who was not good with details. This was an attempt to pin the political hack tag on his opponent and raise questions about his competence. . . . [Next he linked] Dinkins to Jesse Jackson.[14]

Dinkins also wanted to avoid becoming embroiled in racial politics during the campaign, albeit for different reasons. He did not discuss his own racial background or issues of concern to the black community. He ran not as a postracial candidate but as a deracial candidate. He did not present himself as a black candidate for mayor, but rather as a person who just happened to be black running for mayor. He wanted to avoid being perceived as a candidate who would represent only the needs and aspirations of blacks to the neglect of all other New Yorkers. To win citywide office, he needed solid interracial support. To get that support, he had to convince skeptical and hesitant white liberal voters, many of whom had never cast a vote favoring a black candidate, that he could represent them, as well.

Dinkins's campaign, owing largely to his campaign manager, William (Bill) Lynch, built a coalition among the Democratic Party loyalty, including the powerful public employee unions, Democratic political clubs, traditional white liberals, and Latinos, along with his political base, black voters. His deracial strategy worked. During the election, he won the support of the more liberal voters in Manhattan, Brooklyn, and the Bronx, while losing the more conservative voters in Staten Island and Queens—areas with large white ethnic groups. Latinos provided solid support, but liberal whites and blacks turned out in record numbers during the general election:

> White Protestants and more secular liberal white Jews stood by Dinkins despite widespread defections. Areas like Chelsea, the Village, SOHO, and Park Slope in Brooklyn all gave Dinkins two-thirds of their votes. Blacks turned out in record numbers for a general election, particularly in the Central Brooklyn areas of Bedford-Stuyvesant and Crown Heights.[15]

Having won the mayoral election largely on the promise of unifying New Yorkers, it was now time for the first and only black mayor to govern this racially divided city.

o o o

As David Dinkins became mayor of New York City on January 1, 1990, his political ally and friend Ruth Messinger also took the oath of office that day, becoming the Manhattan borough president. She had been a city council member for twelve years and was known as a progressive politician on sociopolitical issues. Because of my involvement and political activism on various issues, I had heard of Ruth, but I had not met her. At the time of her campaign, I was no longer working at the Community Service Society. I had returned to graduate school to pursue my doctorate while teaching public administration courses at a small Jesuit college in Jersey City, right across the Hudson River from Manhattan. So I was completely taken by surprise when she recruited me to be part of her new administration.

At the time, working for the city government was the furthest thing from my mind. Diane Morales, the director of policy development, was quite convincing in her attempts to lure me to the Manhattan borough president's office. She told me that it was my time to make policy decisions, my time to develop and implement public policies that addressed social needs instead of merely advocating for them while leaving the decision making in the hands of others. She went on to say that the newly revised city charter extended different authority to the borough presidents' offices regarding the city's budget, services, and land use policies and that the office would have an impact in these areas. For a year, until the new charter revisions went into effect, the borough president would retain significant authority as a voting member on the powerful Board of Estimate and Apportionment, which was responsible for determining budget and land-use decisions for the city.

Diane was assembling a top-notch team of progressive-minded policy analysts to keep the borough president informed and shape the policy directions of the office. She wanted me to be a part of that effort. I was hesitant. I did not know what it would be like to work on the inside of government and make decisions about people's lives rather than advocate from the outside by offering effective policy and programmatic responses to whatever issue is at hand.

I decided to find out what it meant to work for the government and agreed to become the senior policy analyst for human services. Of course, I brought my activist sensibilities with me, and as I saw myself as a progressive activist, my focus was on social change. I wanted to improve the established rules and processes that sometimes limited people's growth and development, not to mention their needs and aspirations, so that they could realize their full potential. Little did I know how difficult and frustrating it was going to be to maintain such lofty aims while working within a government bureaucracy. A plethora of institutional regulations, well-established hierarchies, procedures, programs, and politics had to be considered in order to get things done. If I was to promote change, I had to learn many important lessons about how a government really works.

When I began working with the Manhattan borough president's office, one of the first things I learned was that government structures are composed of two important layers. One layer, the bureaucracy, is made up of civil servants, who implement various programs and monitor compliance with rules and policies. At various ranks, they represent the permanent government, and their jobs and responsibilities largely remain intact, regardless of political changes. The other layer of government constitutes political officeholders and their administrative support staff—staff who are appointed by elected officials to work on their behalf for the duration of the term that they are in office. The main difference between these two layers is that the civil servants are not beholden to a particular politician or constituency, whereas elected officials must seek to address the interests and concerns of their constituency if they wish to be reelected to office. This distinction between the bureaucracy and the elected officials has a direct bearing on what can be accomplished when working inside the government culture.

For instance, one of the first requests I received, shortly after starting work, was from a day-care provider. The playground for the day-care center was located on a lot that was between two high-rise buildings. Each day, before the children could go out to play, day-care staff had to clean up the garbage dropped by the buildings' tenants from their windows onto the playground. Broken glass and other debris were a constant hazard to the children's health and safety. I thought that a good temporary solution to the problem was simply to extend some form of netting over the top of the playground while we looked for a long-term solution. The daycare provider agreed. So I set about the task of finding the appropriate city agency that could make and install such a net. Without going into the elaborate and time-consuming details, suffice it to say that when I left the Manhattan borough president's office, no net had been made or installed over the playground area to protect the children from potential harm. My failure to obtain a tangible result in this seemingly minor task was only one of the many frustrations I encountered while working in city government.

Another important lesson I learned early on was that decisions made by elected officials are often made in the context of compromise, in which there are competing political interests. Hence, the critical issues center on the nature of the compromise and whose interests are more likely to be compromised in the process of negotiation. I was introduced to this reality during the Audubon Ballroom dispute.

The Audubon Ballroom is widely known, especially in the black community, because it is the site where Malcolm X was assassinated on February 21, 1965. The city owned the Audubon Ballroom, and the building had fallen into serious disrepair, having sat vacant for years. Two important upper Manhattan constituents were seeking control over the site—Columbia University and a coalition composed of Harlem activists, historical preservationists, and students. However, the dispute over the disposition of the Audubon Ballroom rested in the hands of the Board of Estimate to resolve.

Columbia University, the prestigious Ivy League college located in Harlem (although the college calls its surrounding community Morningside Heights), put forth a plan to build a multimillion-dollar biomedical research center on a four-block area in upper Manhattan that included the Audubon Ballroom site. [16] Opposing this plan was a broadbased coalition of New Yorkers who called for the preservation of the ballroom and the building's terra-cotta façade to memorialize the slain black leader. [17]

On the surface, this dispute was a land-use issue with competing views over the best use of that particular space for the public good. It was especially tense because in the borough of Manhattan, physical space is quite limited and real estate of any kind is considered to be a premium. Beneath the surface, however, the dispute embodied the long-standing racial tensions and resentment of some Harlem residents over Columbia University's continual attempts to turn the historical black community into "Manhattanville" by gobbling up available real estate. [18] That tension can be traced back to 1968, when the college wanted to expand its footprint in the community by building a gymnasium in the local Morningside Park. Such a building would have restricted community access to the facility and the park grounds. Columbia's attempt to take over the park became widely known in the Harlem community as "Gym Crow," a pun on Jim Crow segregation.

Prior to the Board of Estimate vote on the matter, Mayor Dinkins attempted to negotiate between the two parties. He proposed a compromise to the dispute, which called for preserving 40 percent of the ballroom and establishing the Malcolm X and Dr. Betty Shabazz (his wife) Memorial and Educational Center, along with maintaining some of the exterior façade of the building. The coalition rejected the compromise and turned to the Manhattan borough president's office, seeking support to save the Audubon Ballroom in its entirety.

A series of meetings was held at the office, which I attended. The Manhattan borough president's proposal called for saving more of the building's infrastructure than that proposed by the mayor and also committed $4 million of discretionary funds for capital improvements to the building. Even though the president offered more in terms of additional space and resources, the coalition was still dissatisfied with the compromise, but realizing that it was the best offer on the table, they begrudgingly agreed to support the borough president's proposal. Under this plan, Columbia University would still get what it wanted—an extensive biotechnical research facility in a densely populated community.

Ruth's proposal was widely criticized by the corporate community, politicians, and the local media.[19] Then something peculiar happened during the meeting of the Board of Estimate. Prior to the vote to be taken concerning the Audubon Ballroom compromise, another issue was decided. The Manhattan borough president decided to vote against that proposal, which called for appropriating $8.1 million in city funds to the Port Authority, which in turn would go toward funding Columbia's biotechnology project. As the *New York Times* reported, "The veto effectively dooms it [Columbia's plan] before any other elected official has a chance to consider it."[20] In vetoing the Port Authority appropriation, Columbia's plan was removed from the Board of Estimate's agenda. But all was not lost; all Columbia and its powerful political allies had to do was simply wait.

A year later, the Board of Estimate was dismantled under the revisions to the city charter. The revisions shifted the power relations among city agencies. Authority over budgetary and land-use policies for the city was largely shifted to the mayor's office and the city council. With that shift, the borough presidents' offices no longer played a major role in exercising influence on those decisions. Subsequently, Columbia University not only won approval for its initial plan to establish a biotechnical research center, but also expanded that plan to develop "Manhattanville" in West Harlem. "Manhattanville" included a business center, additional research laboratories, and facilities for students and professors; obviously, Columbia sought even more land to accomplish that expansion. The college threatened to use its political power to seek eminent domain over local residential buildings and small businesses in the area to acquire the needed space. Some Harlem residents continued to oppose Columbia's efforts to encroach on their neighborhood, but to limited effect.

Another major lesson that I learned while working at the borough president's office was that there is only one person whose opinion really counts when making decisions—the elected official's. Regardless of how innovative or creative an idea appears, ultimately the political officeholder decides its merit based on policy positions, political considerations, and public opinion risks. Outside political pressures, particularly from financial backers and, to a lesser extent, voting constituents, influence a politician's decisions on issues. Consequently, there are few, if any, opportunities to advance progressive thoughts and actions while working for a political office.

I was not directly responsible for the political deals and compromises made in the Manhattan borough president's office while I worked there, but nonetheless, I felt accountable when implementing her decisions. If you do not like the realities of working in a political office, then you quit. After a year of working in the Manhattan borough president's office, feeling as if I had accomplished very little, I decided to quit. I returned to a more familiar role, that of working outside of government as a political activist.

o o o

The Manhattan borough president's office is located directly across the street from the New York City mayor's office. Like, me, Mayor Dinkins was also having a difficult time adjusting to his new role, but for a completely different reason. His struggles centered on governing a racially divided city and especially on asserting leadership over the largest black community in the United States, Brooklyn.

A short three weeks after his inauguration, an altercation took place between a Korean store owner and a Haitian customer at a small fruit and vegetable market in the Flatbush section of Brooklyn. The seemingly minor incident escalated into a major racial confrontation that focused national media attention on the city.

The highly disputed incident occurred on January 18, 1990, at the Red Apple grocery store. Bong Jae Jong, a Korean immigrant, owned the market; Mrs. Jiselaine Felissaint, a Haitian immigrant, was shopping there for plantains, peppers, and limes. Beyond these basic facts, the stories of what happened that day diverge wildly. Here are some examples of what national and local news sources reported concerning the incident:

> Jong said that Felissaint tried to pay only $2 for fruit priced at $3. When asked for the difference, Felissaint allegedly threw a pepper at the cashier and then fell to the floor feigning injury. She was treated at a hospital and released. —*Philadelphia Inquirer*[21]

> Felissaint entered Family Red Apple and took plantains costing $2 and limes priced at $1 to the cashier. According to the store's owners, she paid only $2 and, when the cashier demanded the difference, Felissaint allegedly hurled a pepper at the cashier. She was told to depart but fell to the floor. Employees said other customers told her to remain on the floor until police officers arrived. —*Los Angeles Times*[22]

> Around 5:30 P.M. Mrs. Felissaint arrived at the store carrying a shopping bag that contained meat purchased elsewhere. She placed some plantains and peppers in one of the store's portable baskets, but seeing a line at the cash register, put the basket down and started to leave. Near the door she was stopped by Bong Ok Jang, the manager, who said he wanted to look in her shopping bag. Mrs. Felissaint said he would first have to call the police. Mr. Jang then grabbed her by the back of the neck and slapped her several times on the face before she fell to the floor. —*New York Times*[23]

> According to the protesters, the Koreans "disrespected an African sister," a Creole-speaking Haitian named Jiselaine Felissaint, who tired of waiting in the check-out line and headed for the door. When she refused the grocers' demand that she open her bag, they beat her savagely. The Koreans claim Felissaint paid two dollars for three dollars' worth of plantains and limes and when the cashier requested the dollar, she retorted, "You Chinese, Korean motherfucker. Go back to your country." The cashier said, "This is not your country, not my country, it's everybody's, right?" After an exchange of hot peppers and a tussle, the woman fell to the ground, claiming injury. —*New Republic*[24]

Whatever actually happened does not compare to what would follow that fateful day. Word quickly spread throughout the black community that a black woman had been accused of shoplifting and the store manager had beaten her. As a result, some members of the community called for a boycott of the market to protest the allegations of shoplifting. The Brooklyn borough president and district attorney arranged meetings with community leaders to settle the dispute, but mediation went nowhere. By May, the boycott had gained momentum and garnered significant media attention within the city. Also by May, the trial of Joseph Fama, the accused ringleader of the bat-wielding white mob that killed Yusef Hawkins in Brooklyn, was nearing an end. [25]

Tension was strong in the city, so Mayor Dinkins went on television appealing for calm and racial harmony. He vowed to do "whatever is necessary" to maintain order and said that he was "personally prepared to mediate" the dispute in Flatbush. His appeal fell on deaf ears. The day following his televised appearance, two separate but related protest marches were held by blacks in the troubled communities of Brooklyn—one in Flatbush, the site of the boycott, and the other in Bensonhurst, where Yusef Hawkins had been murdered. Both marches occurred without incident, but the marchers were quite vocal in expressing their outrage over the respective situations. As reported by the *New York Times*, many of the marchers called Mayor Dinkins a "Judas" and a "traitor." Expressing his dissatisfaction with the mayor's televised appeal for harmony, C. Vernon Mason, a lawyer and one of the leaders of the dual marches, told the *Times* that the mayor "is a lover of white people and the system. And last night he bashed black people. He ain't got no African left in him. He's got too many yarmulkes on his head." [26]

Black activists received some solace for their outrage when Joseph Fama was convicted of second-degree murder for the killing of Yusef Hawkins. He received a sentence of thirty-two years to life for the crime. Although this was welcome news in the black community, the boycott at the Red Apple market continued. Keeping the pressure up by holding daily picket lines, activists obtained their desired effect—the boycott was forcing Mr. Jong out of business. Mr. Jong told the *New York Times* that the market had grossed about $2,000 a day, but with the boycott and the picket lines curtailing sales, the daily receipts plummeted to ten to thirty dollars, even though many people in the Korean community rallied to support Mr. Jong's effort to stay afloat during the crisis. [27]

Although this situation was viewed as a test case to break black-sponsored boycotts against Korean merchants, it was by no means the first organized boycott against a Korean green market located in a black community. That occurred in Harlem in 1984; a second boycott was held in Jamaica, Queens, in 1986; and in 1988, a third boycott was called for in the Bedford-Stuyvesant section of Brooklyn.

The underlying reasons for the boycotts and the tension between Koreans and African Americans were varied. Part of the reason for the conflict could simply be attributed to communication. Mr. Jong, for example, told the *New York Times* through an interpreter that he and his family had arrived in the United States in 1983, and his English was poor. He said, "Sometimes, when I try to express myself in English, I come across as angry," and acknowledged yelling at Mrs. Felissaint.[28]

Another reason for the boycott may rest with the differences in culture, which led some blacks to view Korean merchants as rude and disrespectful to their customers. Jonathan Rieder, in an article titled "Trouble in Store," published in *New Republic*, noted that Koreans tend to shy away from direct eye contact, avoid smiling at customers, and often drop change on the counter rather than placing it in customers' hands; these actions are not disrespectful in Korea, but this style may appear as unwelcoming and discourteous to American customers. On the other hand, some Korean merchants held on to the stereotype that all blacks were potential criminals, with the specific presumption that they were all shoplifters.[29]

Economic consideration exacerbated these ideas; some black activists resented outsiders for profiting from the social disinvestment of economically vulnerable poor black communities. Sonny Carson, one of the leaders of the boycott and a major media protagonist, told the *New York Times* that "we are not going to tolerate continued assaults by people who don't live in our community, don't employ people in our community, don't spend in our community, and don't have our best interests at heart."[30]

The media added fuel to the boycotters' resentment when it portrayed—whether explicitly or implicitly—the situation as a conflict between hard-working Korean immigrants seeking to build their American dream and dishonest and lazy blacks unable to pull themselves up by their bootstraps. Debunking this racial stereotype of blacks, Sonny Carson told the *New York Times*: "People say the Koreans work hard, but they don't have a monopoly on working hard in

America. Nobody's worked harder than the blacks, and we didn't get paid for it."[31]

Discussing the political complexities of the issues raised by the boycott, Claire Jean Kim aptly noted in her article, "No Justice, No Peace!: The Politics of Black-Korean Conflict":

> Mainstream media coverage of the Red Apple Boycott criminalized the conflict, thereby obscuring its political dimensions. While a few journalists attributed the boycott to such innocuous causes as "cultural" differences or the language barrier, the vast majority depicted it as scapegoating—the irrational venting of frustrations upon an innocent group. Portraying Korean-American merchants as a "model minority" (hard-working, family-oriented, etc.) that was being scapegoated by elements of the "underclass" (morally deviant, behaviorally pathological, etc.), the media effectively denied the rationality, purpose, and political agency of the Red Apple Boycott's participants.[32]

Ralph Jeremiah, a resident and supporter of the boycott, noted the importance of history in shaping the "rationality, purpose, and political agency" of the protests when he told the New York Times, "If there were no boycotts or civil disobedience the mayor wouldn't be the first black mayor of New York. What about Rosa Parks or Martin Luther King? These issues are unpopular, but it has to be done."[33]

The boycott continued to drag on. As the months passed, the market was able to remain open only because the Korean Produce Association was subsidizing it. Mr. Bo Young Jung, president of the association, contributed $8,000 a month on behalf of the Korean merchants in an effort to maintain the fruit and vegetable inventory and to pay the store's personnel. Many in the Korean community were determined to keep the Red Apple market from closing. As Mr. Sik Ju Shin, also a greengrocer in Flatbush, told the New York Times through an interpreter, "Other black-supported boycotts have forced merchants to close. This must stop and it will stop here."[34]

The Koreans also held a protest rally at City Hall Park, which about two thousand protesters attended. Mayor Dinkins spoke at the rally. Initially he was greeted with boos, but after he promised to enforce a restraining order imposed by a court to keep picketers a set distance from the entrance of the market, the crowd cheered loudly.

Amid the tension, the mayor wanted to avoid any public perception that he was taking sides in the boycott dispute, so he tried to mediate through quiet negotiation. Many New Yorkers saw this approach as apparent inaction by the major to resolve the conflict.

With the constant media attention, the Red Apple market boycott was fast becoming a national symbol that reflected the simmering racial tensions in the country during the early 1990s. Many New Yorkers were growing tired of the ongoing negative media attention and the criticism of the city that was brought on by it. By September, eight months after the start of the boycott, it was clear that Mayor Dinkins was on the political hot seat. The media was clamoring for the mayor to take decisive action. Claire Jean Kim argues, "The media-led, ideological counter-mobilization against the boycott eventually compelled a reluctant Mayor Dinkins to take action against the protesters. . . . Mayor Dinkins was thought to be guilty of racial favoritism until he took concrete steps."[35] The steps he was forced to take on the racial tightrope indicated clear opposition to the boycotters' agenda.

Surrounded by media, the mayor went to the Red Apple market and spent $10.67 on produce. To ensure that the protesters complied with the court order to stay fifty feet away from the store, large numbers of police officers lined the street, and some were even positioned on neighboring rooftops. Dinkins's steps across the picket line marked the waning days of the Red Apple store boycott.

Those defiant steps would come back to haunt him, particularly affecting his constituency base. Having campaigned on the promise of healing a racially divided city, the significance of Dinkins's steps would have a defining impact on his political career. Wilbur Rich noted their importance by stating, "The Red Apple incident represented an opportunity for Dinkins to show his conciliatory skills. If he stumbled in this situation, then a future racial incident could sink his image."[36]

As the momentum of the boycott dwindled, another racial incident appeared that would not only sink the mayor's image but would also begin to unravel his political career.

❊ ❊ ❊

As Mayor Dinkins was settling into what appeared to be a continual racial drama, which was slowly breaking apart his "gorgeous mosaic," my attention was focused somewhere else. When I left the borough president's office I needed to find a job, but I also needed to reconnect to the activist community. I have always had a particular concern regarding the sociopolitical vulnerability of poor women and children. It seems to me that of the myriad issues challenging the black community, the hardships faced by women and children have often been the last ones added to the list of priorities on the political agendas of activists. In other words, the concerns of men and a need for concerted action on their behalf more often overshadowed any particular concerns of women and children. This was especially the case when it came to the issue of violence against women.

I began to notice what appeared to be an increase in violence against black women, especially at the hands of black men.[37] By 1991, other black women were homing in on the severity of the problem as well. This was largely because of national and international media exposure of the issue. The complexities of the problem were on full display during the televised confirmation hearing of Clarence Thomas, who was being considered for a seat on the US Supreme Court. Over a three-day period, male dominance, institutional arrangements, due process, cultural sentiments, public voice, and private suffering, all within the working of race, gender, and class relations, were exhibited as the issue of workplace violence moved to the forefront of the nation's attention. What happened was this:

> The Senate Judiciary Committee interrupted its confirmation hearing on Clarence Thomas's nomination to the Supreme Court to hold a special hearing on allegations of sexual harassment made against the nominee by Anita Hill. It was high drama, worthy of popcorn, and I was glued to my television set. I had never witnessed such a spectacle before, and at the heart of this television drama was a lone middle-class black woman attempting to convey to an international audience her experiences at the hands of a lone middle-class black man, who used his positional power to abuse her. After the testimony of the "pubic hair" on the coke can, a friend called from London to ask if we in this country had lost our collective minds.[38]

Nonetheless, I continued to watch this televised drama unfold as white men, white women, and black men sat as analysts before television cameras claiming and disclaiming Anita Hill's experience. They provided no historical context for black women's experience of violence, and I watched the audacity they displayed in their attempts to interpret and frame what I was watching while I wondered on which television channel the black women analysts were sequestered, because in channel surfing I could not seem to find their commentary.

I recognized the different sociopolitical layers and dimensions of this complex drama, but what struck me the most was what can happen to a black woman who dares to speak publicly about her private pain and the attacks on her personhood as a result of giving voice to her experience. I learned that there are important implications to a public fight and that a lone black woman is extremely vulnerable to additional violence. I was not the only one who noted this lesson; other black women were also noting its importance as well.

Initially, many in the civil rights community were either highly skeptical of or outright opposed to Clarence Thomas's nomination by republican president George H. W. Bush. Mainly, it was because even though Thomas enjoyed educational and professional opportunities that had been won through the civil rights struggles, he sought to deny those very same opportunities to other blacks. Thomas was a staunch black political conservative who disavowed the need for affirmative-action policies to redress past patterns and practices of discrimination. Giving voice to his skepticism, A. Leon Higginbotham Jr. penned a poignant letter to Clarence Thomas on his confirmation. In one part of the letter, Higginbotham says:

> During the last ten years, you have often described yourself as a black conservative. I must confess that, other than their own self-advancement, I am at a loss to understand what it is that the so-called black conservatives are so anxious to conserve. Now that you no longer have to be outspoken on their behalf, perhaps you will recognize that in the past it was the white "conservatives" who screamed "segregation now, segregation forever!" it was primarily the conservatives who attacked the Warren Court relentlessly because of Brown v. Board and who stood in the way of almost every measure to ensure gender and racial advancement.
>
> In my lifetime I have seen African-Americans denied the right to vote, the opportunities to a proper education, to work, and to live where they choose. I have seen and known racial segregation and discrimination. But I have also seen the decision in Brown rendered.

I have seen the first African-American sit on the Supreme Court. And I have seen brave and courageous people, black and white, give their lives for the civil rights cause.

You have found a door newly cracked open and you have escaped. I trust you shall not forget that many who preceded you and many who follow you have found, and will find, the door of equal opportunity slammed in their faces through no fault of their own.[39]

But during the special hearing on sexual harassment, political sentiments started to shift within the black community regarding Thomas's confirmation. But that shift was largely demarcated along gender divisions. Because he was an African American and, if approved, he would be the only black on the US Supreme Court—since Justice Thurgood Marshall—many within the community avoided public criticism of his nomination. However, when Thomas asserted his racial authenticity— "his birth in Jim Crow Georgia, his childhood spent as the grandson of a black sharecropper, his undeniably black phenotype degraded by racist ideals of beauty, and his gallant black struggle for achievement in racist America"[40]—and declared the special hearing on sexual harassment to be a "high-tech lynching for uppity blacks," this resonated with many, particularly black men. A gender schism deepened within the black community over the nomination. Even against their own political interests and in racial solidarity, some black men came out in support of Thomas's nomination. This was not the case for many black women, particularly feminists.

Frustrated and appalled by both the media intrepretations and some black men's reactions, Barbara Ransby, Deborah King, and Elsa Barkley created a manifesto titled "African American Women in Defense of Ourselves" that gave voice to the sentiments of many black women. Insisting on being heard, in "less than six weeks nearly 1,600 women joined an effort to buy their way into the discourse, contributing nearly $50,000 to pay for a (New York) *Times* ad, published November 17, 1991."[41] In part, the lengthy manifesto said:

> We are particularly outraged by the racist and sexist treatment of Professor Anita Hill, an African American Woman who was maligned and castigated for daring to speak publicly of her own experience of sexual abuse. The malicious defamation of Professor Hill insulted all

women of African descent and sent a dangerous message to any woman who might contemplate a sexual harassment complaint.

We speak here because we recognize that the media are now portraying the Black community as prepared to tolerate both the dismantling of affirmative action and the evil of sexual harassment in order to have any Black man on the Supreme Court. We want to make clear that the media have ignored or distorted many African American voices. We will not be silenced.

Many have erroneously portrayed the allegations against Clarence Thomas as an issue of either gender or race. As women of African descent, we understand sexual harassment as both. We further understand that Clarence Thomas outrageously manipulated the legacy of lynching in order to shelter himself from Anita Hill's allegations. To deflect attention away from the reality of sexual abuse in African American women's lives, he trivialized and misrepresented this painful part of African American people's history. This country, which has a long legacy of racism and sexism, has never taken the sexual abuse of black women seriously. . . . As Anita Hill's experience demonstrates, Black women who speak of these matters are not likely to be believed.

We pledge ourselves to continue to speak out in defense of one another, in defense of the African American community and against those who are hostile.

In defense of ourselves, in 1992 I organized a meeting of more than twenty black women, many of whom were violence against women activists, to discuss strategies for responding to the issue of black women's experiences of violence. Over a two-year period this group researched, analyzed, and developed a plan of action for establishing a nonprofit organization to respond to the particular needs and aspirations of black women. For ten years, I was the executive director of the Institute on Violence, Inc.

¤ ¤ ¤

Meanwhile, on the evening of August 19, 1991, another racial incident occurred in the city, and this time it would shatter Mayor Dinkins's image and sink his political career. There was a fatal traffic accident at the intersection of President Street and Utica Avenue, in the Crown Heights section of Brooklyn. A three-car motorcade was escorting Rabbi Menachem Schneerson, the grand rebbe of the Hasidic Jewish sect called the Chabad-Lubavitch, from his weekly visit to his wife's and father-in-law's graves. Meanwhile, seven-year-old Gavin Cato was playing with his seven-year-old Guyanese cousin Angela Cato on the sidewalk at this intersection. Two cars in the grand rebbe's motorcade passed safely through the intersection where the children were playing; the third car, however, sped up to avoid stopping as the traffic light turned red. It struck another car, which veered onto the sidewalk, hitting the children. Gavin was instantly killed, and Angela was seriously injured. Minutes later, the privately sponsored Jewish Hatzolah ambulance service arrived on the scene and took Yosef Lifish, the driver of the vehicle that caused the accident, to the hospital. The children waited for a city ambulance service to arrive.

About three hours later, in retaliation for the harm done to the children in the accident, a group of black teens killed Yankel Rosenbaum, a Hasidic Jewish doctoral student from Australia. Immediately following these highly incendiary incidents, a riot broke out in the Crown Heights community.

Crown Heights, located in central Brooklyn, is a community that is heavily populated by Caribbean Americans and Caribbean immigrants, both of African descent, and by African Americans. The first black residents of Crown Heights were freed black farmers and craftsmen, but over time, they were supplanted by white ethnic immigrants. In the 1950s, African Americans began to replace the white population, and they were joined by an influx of black Caribbeans. By the 1990s, the more than two hundred thousand residents were either first- or second-generation immigrants from the Caribbean, including people who trace their ethnicity and culture to such countries as Guyana, Haiti, Barbados, Jamaica, Grenada, and Trinidad. Carol B. Conaway, a political scientist, discusses the racial history of Caribbean Americans in this area in her article "Crown Heights: Politics and Press Coverage of the Race War That Wasn't." She notes:

> When Caribbean-Americans first arrived in the United States, their social and political experiences were structured by race. Their being categorized as "black" determined where they could and could not live, where they could and could not go, what type of job they could get, etc. [42]

Within this largely black community, a much smaller and very insular community existed—the Hasidic religious sect of the Chabad-Lubuvitch, which made up about 10 percent of the residents. This group fled the Holocaust of World War II with Rabbi Schneerson and established its international headquarters in the Crown Heights section of Brooklyn. The Lubavitchers are unique in their religious traditions and customs, even among other Hasidic sects. Conaway points out:

> Many of the Lubavitcher men wear beards, black hats, and black coats that are distinctive not only from the garb of gentiles, but also from that of other Jews. Married Lubavich women wear wigs or cover their hair, and are always clad in modest garb. Their families are usually large. . . . Lubavitchers worship in their own synagogues, separate from those of other Jews, and have their own schools and recreation, restaurants, and social life. Because they do not drive or ride on the Sabbath or on other holy days, most of the 10,000 to 16,000 Lubavitchers in Crown Heights live in an area of about 42 blocks concentrated around their headquarter on Eastern Parkway. [43]

Given the very stark cultural differences between the larger Caribbean and smaller Lubavitcher communities, the two groups rarely interacted with each other in any meaningful way. That lack of significant contact created distrust and suspicion between them. For blacks, their suspicion evolved around concerns that "the Lubavitchers had a disproportionate share of political clout and therefore received preferential treatment from city government." The Lubavitchers, for their part, "did not acknowledge racism in their community or favoritism from city government. They contended that their distinctiveness and reticence made them a highly vulnerable minority group in the neighborhood." Given their appearance and reticence, the Lubavitchers believed that they were vulnerable to black anti-Semitism and crime.

Conaway suggests that the distrust between the two groups was apparent in many areas of community life, but it was most obvious when it concerned the issue of whether or not law enforcement and police protection were conducted in an evenhanded manner within the two communities. Racial tensions between the blacks and the Lubavitchers were heightened by the creation of a Hasidic anticrime patrol:

The Lubavitchers instituted a civilian anti-crime patrol, contending it was necessary to ensure their safety in the community. They cited crime as their biggest fear and maintained that they were particularly vulnerable because they were easily identified. But Caribbean and African-Americans labeled the patrol "vigilantes" and believed that the patrol was anti-black.

The black community protested these patrols as soon as they began, contending that the patrols were meant to harass black men. They also pointed out that the patrols were all Jewish, in a community that was predominantly black. In retaliation, the black community started its own crime patrol, but it soon disbanded. The Lubavitchers then invited blacks to join their patrol, but none did. [44]

Obviously, deep-seated racial resentments were already simmering just beneath the surface by August 19, 1991—the night of the fatal traffic accident.

In the immediate aftermath of the accident, a crowd of blacks began to assemble in response to rumors circulating throughout the black community that the Hatzolah paramedics ignored the medical needs of Gavin and Angela in their rush to assist Yosef Lifish, leaving the injured black children to die on the street. That allegation struck a raw nerve with many blacks due to their perception that more concern was given to Jewish life than to black life.

In recounting what actually occurred, Wilbur Rich said: "The Hatzolah ambulance and the emergency service ambulance arrived almost simultaneously. Police asked the Hatzolah ambulance to remove the driver of the station wagon in the interest of preserving the peace as the crowd was becoming increasingly violent." [45]

Despite this, the violence started almost immediately. The situation quickly became a full-blown race riot. In its investigation of the riot, the Girgenti Commission noted that "for two-and-a-half hours bottles and rocks flew at the accident scene, with blacks and Hasidim arguing fiercely and shouting racial epithets at each other. As tensions rose, objects were thrown from nearby rooftops. At one point, gunshots were fired." [46] The violence quickly escalated from that point on—cars were smashed, overturned, and burned; stores were looted and vandalized; and the police were pelted with rocks and bottles. The anger and violence on the streets of Crown Heights raged on throughout the night, and Yankel Rosenbaum was indiscriminately stabbed by a group of roving black teens.

On learning of the situation, Mayor Dinkins went to Crown Heights. He first visited the hospital to see the Cato children and Rosenbaum. Gavin had already been pronounced dead, and Angela and Yankel were receiving emergency care. Angela survived her wounds, but Rosenbaum died some hours later. Doctors initially thought that he would survive the stabbing, but they had overlooked the severity of his stab wounds, and as a result of that, he died. Mayor Dinkins went from the hospital to the Seventy-First Precinct, where he met with police officers and black and Jewish community leaders. He immediately ordered his staff, led by Deputy Mayor Bill Lynch, to set up headquarters at a local school in order to begin outreach efforts to quiet the rumors and restore order in the community.

The next day, Deputy Mayor Lynch convened a meeting with black residents in an attempt to dispel the rumors and quell the violence. Contrary to his intent, however, the residents took control of the meeting and used it as a forum to express their anger and criticism over the lack of evenhandedness by city officials in dealing with their grievances against the Lubavitchers. Meanwhile, members of the Hasidic community were meeting with other city officials to express their outrage over the inadequacy of the police response to the violence. They demanded greater police protection from the violence targeted against the Lubavitcher community.

In spite of the mayor's attempts to address citizens' concerns and restore peace in the community, anger on both sides was raging, and the situation was clearly spiraling out of control.

During the early afternoon, a crowd (of blacks) gathered at President Street and Utica Avenue. At about 3:00 p.m., this group marched to the Seventy-First Precinct. At the same time, Hasidim demonstrated at Eastern Parkway and Kingston Avenue over the perceived lack of police protection. When the black marchers reached Kingston Avenue, the two groups clashed, throwing rocks and bottles at each other. The police, outnumbered, could not prevent the confrontation.

The march (blacks) continued to the precinct, where its leaders demanded the arrest of the Hasidic man whose car struck the Cato children and the suspension of a police officer who allegedly had shoved the boy's father. The police refused these demands, so the marchers demonstrated outside and returned to President and Utica. On the way back, there was another confrontation between blacks and Hasidim. Twelve police officers and a civilian were injured. Two people were arrested.[47]

By the third day following the accident, the situation was completely out of control. As the violence had intensified, the police showed how thoroughly unprepared they were to handle the crisis—police commanders had no strategies and gave no clear orders, and the number of police officers on the streets was inadequate to respond to the level of violence they encountered in Crown Heights.

A large group of about five hundred to six hundred blacks marched to the Lubavitcher headquarters, where some chanted anti-Semitic slogans and pelted the building with rocks and bottles. From there, the demonstrators marched down Eastern Parkway, where the police met them. But the police were unable to control the crowd, and they, too, were pelted with rocks and bottles. When Police Commissioner Brown arrived on the scene, his car came under attack. A rooftop sniper shot and wounded eight police officers who were on the scene. When Mayor Dinkins arrived at the school outreach headquarters, he was also met with violence. Wilbur Rich reports what happened when Dinkins tried to calm the angry black residents:

> Dinkins used a bullhorn, declaring, "I care about you. I care about you very desperately. I too want justice, and we will get justice but we will not get it with violence." However, Dinkins was greeted with boos and soon became a target for flying rocks and bottles as he tried to enter a building on President Street.[48]

Finally, amid the chaos and confusion, 1,800 police officers were dispatched and ordered to saturate the streets of Crown Heights. In no uncertain terms, the police were told to use the unlawful assembly law to disperse crowds at the first sign of trouble and to make arrests if there were any signs of a disturbance. Consequently, more arrests were made on Thursday than the total for the previous three days, and relative order was restored to the neighborhood.

The disturbance in Crown Heights had taken a tremendous physical and economic toll on the community. At least thirty-eight residents were hurt, and more than 150 police officers were injured. Looting and vandalism forced many businesses to temporarily close, and some went out of business altogether.

In the aftermath of the Crown Heights disturbance, Mayor Dinkins was governing an even more racially polarized city. As the 1994 mayoral election approached, criticism mounted over his administration's mismanagement and the mishandling of the riot.

The Republican challenger for mayor was again Rudolph Giuliani. This time, however, he did not remain silent on racially charged issues. To the contrary, in his attacks on the mayor, he attempted to discredit Dinkins in the eyes of the Jewish community. Giuliani boldly proclaimed that the mayor had allowed a "pogrom" to occur in Crown Heights. The term "pogrom" is a Russian word that means to wreak havoc or demolish violently, and it is often used to describe anti-Semitic violence against Jews. The United States Holocaust Memorial Museum characterizes the term with the following description: "The perpetrators of pogroms organized locally, sometimes with government and police encouragement. They raped and murdered their victims and looted their property."[49]

The violence that occurred in Crown Heights was unjustified, regardless of any rationale to the contrary. Yet it is highly debatable as to whether or not the disturbance constituted a pogrom against Jews in general. It was clearly targeted against a specific segment of the Hasidic community, who are Jewish, but it was limited to that community and did not include all Jews in the city of New York.

The mere use of the word "pogrom" was highly inflammatory, especially within the Jewish community, because it readily evoked the historical image of the systematic killing of Jews carried out by Nazi Germany during World War II. Hence, when Giuliani called the violence in Crown Heights a pogrom against Jews, it was a highly calculated political move that was designed to deepen the wedge between Mayor Dinkins and his Jewish supporters. Giuliani exploited the tensions that existed within the Jewish community over Dinkins's handling of the riot to his political advantage.

He also exploited the political tensions that existed between the police and the Dinkins administration by once again campaigning on a law-and-order platform.

The police and their powerful labor union were the perfect audience for his "get tough on crime and criminals" message. A year following the

Crown Heights riot, Giuliani spoke at a mass police rally held at City Hall Park, which was sponsored by the Patrolmen's Benevolent Association. More than ten thousand officers attended the rally to protest the mayor's refusal to approve semiautomatic pistols for police use; his creation of a mayoral commission to investigate charges of police corruption; and the all-civilian complaint review board that investigated police misconduct.

The *New York Times* reported that Giuliani "led the crowd in a rousing condemnation of Mayor Dinkins's treatment of police issues."[50] Following his condemnation, "something went badly awry." That "something" was a police riot. As the *New York Times* reported:

> Police department officials appeared unprepared for the size and unruliness of the crowd, which included supervisors as well as rank-and-file members. There were relatively few police barricades up and they were sparsely attended by uniformed officers who joined in the chants, raised their own fists in support or passively stood to one side. Almost no effort was made by the 300 officers on duty to keep protesters from breaking police barricades to rush the steps of City Hall. Alarmed officials inside City Hall, fearing that the building would be overrun, bolted the doors and summoned a half-dozen uniformed guards from the basement to act as a last line of defense.[51]

Although the police were prevented from overrunning City Hall, another group of protesters—about four thousand officers—started marching to the Brooklyn Bridge, where they blocked traffic and harassed commuters.

In a sharply worded internal report on the riot, police officials called the rally "unruly, mean-spirited and perhaps criminal." Giuliani, however, defended the rioting policemen. He told the *New York Times* that the police officers were being used "as scapegoats for political gains." He said, "The real question is, has the relatively minor occurrence of racial epithets, if they occurred at all, been made the major focus of this rally for political purposes?" And he charged Mayor Dinkins with using a "double standard" in his attempts to punish police officers, stating that "the Mayor has been more aggressive about punishing them for the protest than finding those who caused the violent disturbance in Crown Heights last year."[52]

✿ ✿ ✿

By the 1993 mayoral election, I was thoroughly disillusioned and exhausted by the Dinkins administration. Racial symbolism was simply not enough for sustaining my continued support. That symbolism was not accompanied by meaningful change. I had expected that Dinkins, as the first black mayor of the city, would care—as much as I did—about issues of social equity and justice. I had expected that he would be innovative and aggressive in responding to some of the more vexing sociopolitical problems confronting the city, such as the high unemployment rates, homelessness, drug abuse, HIV and AIDS, crime, and police brutality—all of which disproportionally affected black New Yorkers. Surely, I thought, Dinkins would respond to the needs and aspirations of his core constituents, especially if he expected to win reelection. I took enormous pride in the fact that Dinkins was the first black mayor of New York City, but by no means did this diminish my expectations that he would improve the quality of life, particularly for poor black New Yorkers.

In retrospect, I still do not find that my expectations of the Dinkins administration were unreasonable at the time. Admittedly, I did not take into consideration the limitations that he would face simply because he was the first black mayor—the challenges that he would encounter in asserting his mayoral authority in a highly diverse yet racially polarized city. But, more important, I did not consider who Dinkins was as a politician, or his political views on issues. On this last point, I have to take responsibility and acknowledge my own lack of political due diligence. Swept up in the euphoria and momentum of electing the first black mayor of the city, I had simply failed to see who Dinkins was as a politician. He was a "transactional leader" instead of a "transformational leader." Wilbur Rich notes that as a transactional leader, Dinkins was a "bargainer" and "negotiator" but was never a transformational leader:

> Dinkins won the 1989 election by promising to bring the various ethnic and racial communities together. Transformational leaders seek fundamental changes in the status quo and in doing so raise the aspiration of their followers. Dinkins may have raised the hopes of the black and Latino constituencies, but he never promised to change the city's economic arrangements.[53]

I am a transformational seeker. I am conscious of the fact that my vote will often wind up on the political trash heap of mainstream electoral politics, but this fact does not deter me from continuing to try, to use my vote, and to make a difference. I will vote, and I will continue to be engaged in the political process. I do so out of an obligation to try and right those things that, for me, are simply wrong.

Over the past fifty years, as a nation we have engaged in a delicate balancing act on the racial tightrope. There is no denying that enormous shifts in race and race relations have occurred over that period and that those shifts are largely due to the continuous struggle of blacks to transform democratic institutions and eliminate practices of racial exclusion. Their struggles do not lurk in the shadows but rather appear on the front line of those shifts and embody the contributions they have made to strengthen our democracy. But, as the noted legal scholar Derrick Bell reminds us, those shifts, albeit meaningful, "produce no more than temporary peaks of progress, short-lived victories that slide into irrelevance as racial patterns adapt in ways that maintain white dominance."[54]

Hence, as a nation, we continue to take steps on the racial tightrope. As Bell suggests, "Continued struggle can bring about unexpected benefits and gains that in themselves justify continued endeavor. The fight itself has meaning and should give us hope for the future."[55] In the absence of fundamental changes in the structure of race and race relations, we are left with the reality of a continual struggle toward human equity and justice. Yet each step that we take in that struggle has its own merit, for it embodies our humanity. So, even amid the political clutter, I will continue to be politically engaged by voting, with the expectation that new and progressive history will be made on our racial tightrope.

I will do so because—beneath the layers of ad makers, financiers, lobbyists, pollsters, and the party machinery that plays a prominent role in influencing electoral outcomes—lives are at stake. The decisions and actions of those who hold the reins of political power, even if they themselves are black, can compromise human dignity and human worth.

EPILOGUE

The Age of Obama

Of all the urban treasures in New York City, Central Park is my most cherished site. Each day, as I gaze on the park, it gives me a sense of pleasure and holds my fascination. I am ever engaged in the stark changes of the seasons—the auburn colors that burst forth with the arrival of fall, the unveiling of secrets that are revealed during the barren winter, the birth of new life that makes its presence known in spring, and then the dazzling array of summer activities in full exhibition. The park is marked by seasonal change, yet within its firm boundaries continuity is ever present. This is the irony of Central Park's beauty. Each season embodies its own essence of change while in the absence of fundamental change.

Developed between 1857 and 1873, as the first urban landscaped park in the nation, Central Park is an oasis in the heart of the concrete jungle that is Manhattan. A heavy price was paid for this beloved refuge.[1] The park was built out of the forced sacrifices of African Americans. Compelled to live on the margin of the city, in the 1820s free blacks moved to Seneca Village. It was called "Nigger Village" at the time. Diana diZerega Wall, Nan A. Rothschild, and Cynthia Copeland document what happened to this thriving black middle-class community—with its three churches, colored school, and property owners—when the city imposed eminent domain to create an urban haven on much of what is known today as Central Park. They say:

As New York City began to undergo the dramatic growth that accompanied its burgeoning economy after the completion of the Erie Canal, its border rapidly moved north. By the 1850s, with its limits approaching Seneca Village, the city developed plans for the creation of a major park. After a great deal of political wrangling it chose the area known today as Central Park for its location. Using the right of eminent domain, the city seized the land to make the park, evicted all its residents, and razed their homes. Seneca Village was destroyed.[2]

The creation of Central Park illustrates the fact that there is no facet of our history where the African American presence has not played a prominent role in shaping who we are—in creating our identity—as a nation.

The black experience has influenced what we, as a nation, value and disvalue. However, like the experience of those who lived in Seneca Village, the black experience is largely relegated to the shadows of history. Yet our experience lies at the very cusp of the sociopolitical cycle of change amid continuity that has engendered profound contradictions in the shaping and reshaping of our nation. Those contradictions also lie at the heart of, and equally important, undermine the very structural foundation of our democracy. That cycle of change amid continuity has encompassed progressive racial trends along with regressive racial tendencies, and the contradictions therein continue to inform our teetering steps on the racial tightrope. As in the past, the black experience continues to serve as a critical gauge in measuring the strengths and limitations of our democracy. Our future steps on the racial tightrope—whether progressive or regressive—will continue to shape our identity as a nation.

In chronicling some of my steps over the past fifty years, there is no denying that since the days of growing up under Jim Crow segregation in Thomasville, Georgia, I have experienced important progressive shifts not only in the meaning of race but also in the altering of race relations. Yet I continue to experience a regressive racial melodrama, played out fifty years hence. Is it simply because I hang on to the lessons of the past and have become accustomed to seeing the world through the prism of a racial lens? Yes, given my experiences, I readily admit that this is a real possibility. Others have often accused me of seeing the presence of race in every minute detail of a given situation, particularly when on the surface race does not appear to be an obvious factor. I do not consider myself to be myopic, however. As I gaze on the world, in my lens the importance of gender and class relations readily comes into sharp view also.

Regardless of how my personal experiences inform my worldview, I know that even if I were completely color-blind to the significance of race and race relations, there is another important reason they continue to have an abiding presence in all of our lives. Our social institutions maintain a rigid system of racial norms because they are absolutely critical to how we, as a nation, function in determining sociopolitical advantages and disadvantages. Based on racial differences, those norms are deeply embedded within us and are revealed in the routine activities of our daily lives, in the decisions we make and the action we take. Because we share a cultural heritage, "we also inevitably share many ideas, attitudes, and beliefs that attach significance to an individual's race," often to the extent that we "do not recognize the ways in which our cultural experience has influenced our beliefs about race or the occasions on which those beliefs affect our actions."[3]

Going about our daily lives, we usually take racial difference and the circumstances that created their existence for granted—so much so that we may fail to even recognize them, or when we do, uncritically treat them as commonplace. Large sociopolitical issues cut across our private lives and are ever present, regardless of what we may think or do in response to them. Race and our reactions to it is one of those large issues. We attempt to treat race as a blind spot, and this allows us to deny the very presence of racism. It's like having a meeting in New York City—where two million blacks reside—but having no blacks at the table, and no one at the gathering thinking that this is unacceptable because there was no intent to exclude participation.

Charles Lawrence explains how racism is "much more complex than either the conscious conspiracy of a power elite or the simple delusion of a few ignorant bigots." As he points out, we are better able to identify the more blatant forms of racism; but it is the more insidious forms of racism that are often unrecognizable, and in that ambiguous space, racism is treated as a normal occurrence. This happens because racism

> is a part of our common historical experience and, therefore, a part
> of our culture. It arises from the assumptions we have learned to

make about the world, ourselves, and others as well as from the patterns of our fundamental social activities. [4]

A new term for expressing old patterns of racist behavior is called microaggression. It seeks to explain how racial norms are embedded within us and are revealed as "common sense—a way of comprehending, explaining, and acting in the world." [5] As individuals, we do not have to take the time to ponder the meaning or significance of our racial assumptions—except maybe when issues of race and race relations blatantly appear in our faces—because they represent the racial status quo, what is normal, or the usual way of "comprehending, explaining, and acting in the world."

Even if we deny the presence of racial norms, this does not mean that they do not exist. To the contrary, such a denial only evokes and highlights the contradictions, especially when racial norms are challenged. It is like when a white acquaintance tells me, "I don't see race." Really. What, then, is she looking at, as she gazes on me? In challenging her words, I am accused of misconstruing her meaning because her intent was simply to convey that she does not see people in racial terms. Her response may be a true reflection of what she actually sees. Honestly, I do not know, because I have never had the luxury of being color-blind—denying the ugly realities that race and race relations have imposed on black life.

Nonetheless, I do know that racial norms are firmly rooted in our social institutions and are revealed in our daily activities. Those norms circulate throughout the sociopolitical cycle of change amid continuity that has evoked profound contradictions in how we, as a nation, have stepped on the racial tightrope. Our insistence on maintaining racial norms and the contradictory foundation on which they are built continue to influence the hazardous steps we take along the rope, even as we enter a new phase of race and race relations—the age of Obama.

✿ ✿ ✿

On the night of November 8, 2008, in Chicago's Grant Park, President-Elect Barack Hussein Obama stood soberly before a large and enthusiastic crowd of supporters. In his acceptance speech, he told the nation that "at this defining moment, change has come to America." Obama was partially correct in his assessment—change had indeed arrived, and we were entering a new era of race and race relations. However, as I said previously, it is quite difficult to fully determine the actual meaning and dimensions of change when you are in the midst of that change. This is particularly the situation when continuity is also an integral part of the changing scenario.

On that night, right before my eyes, this new era was formally introduced to the nation. Clearly, by any measure, the election of the first African American president was an obvious change from previous presidential elections. This historical moment could only have arrived because a racially diverse electorate shared Obama's dreams of a better tomorrow, by casting a decisive vote in favor of a black man. His election was partly due to the demographic shifts that we are currently experiencing as a nation. Increasingly, the racial composition of the overall population is becoming nonwhite. The significance of that shift cannot be overlooked, for it conveys an important political message— never again in our history will future presidents win elections based solely on the voting strength of a white electorate. In this age of Obama, this is indeed a significant change to the racial status quo.

The US census predicts that by the year 2050, the nation will be largely composed of a majority-minority population—together blacks, Latinos, Asians, Native Americans, and other nonwhite groups will make up a substantial portion of the voters in the country.[6] By all indications, this shift in racial demographics is owing to the impact of immigration and, most notably, the increasing political influence of Latino and Asian voters. These trends are accompanied by other significant demographic shifts, especially in the voting patterns of white women and the growing inclusion of younger voters in the electoral process.

All of this is occurring at a time when the Republican Party is experiencing a gradual decline in the voter participation rate among its core political constituency, older white middle-class males.[7] In comparison, the Democratic Party is growing more diverse, with increased participation rates by Latinos and Asians, and particularly African Americans, along with white women and young people. Some Republicans recognize that greater inclusion is absolutely essential to challenging the effects that demographic shifts pose to the long-term political viability of their party. Others, however, have become more conservative in their views and have resisted any meaningful change in the racial status quo of the party.

Shifting social demographics and their immediate as well as long-term political impact on the future of electoral politics is critical to any understanding of how we, as a nation, have arrived at the age of Obama. Yet those demographic shifts do not fully explain the tears of elation that trickled down the faces of many as a direct result of electing a black president to the highest political office in our nation.

◦ ◦ ◦

Another reason for electing the first black president is a bit more complicated than shifting demographics. It has more do with how we, as a nation, see ourselves at this moment in history and what a black president symbolizes in those perceptions. In becoming increasingly diverse, in spite of our wavering steps on the racial tightrope, we want desperately to put the ugly issues that are associated with race and race relations behind us. We want to simply move on, and a perfect symbol to verify that race and race relations no longer matter is embodied in the image of a black president. But symbolism, regardless of its importance, must not be confused with fundamental change, especially in the racial status quo.

On our tightrope, an altering of the racial status quo has never been vested solely in the hands of a charismatic political leader. As history has revealed, such a leader may be a catalyst or a drum major for change. Yet our collective fate does not hinge on the decisions and actions of a single, albeit powerful, person—especially when there are constraints or even self-imposed restrictions on the use of that power in response to racial disparities and grievances. Instead, fate rests in the decisions of people who, through their active political engagement, bring about change. This is one of the important lessons of our history—change in the racial status quo does not emanate from above and then trickle downward, regardless of who is in power; it flows upward from the demands of those who are at the bottom.

The election of a black president symbolized for many Americans that we, as a nation, had finally realized Dr. King's dream of a color-blind society—the issue of race and race relations could, at last, be put to rest—alongside the controversies over erecting a Washington monument to honor Reverend Martin Luther King Jr., the Smithsonian's new National Museum of African American History and Culture, and the placement of Harriet Tubman's statue in the National Statuary Hall of the US Capitol building. In the age of Obama, for many, race and race relations no longer seem to matter—they are the relics of history, and a black president surely attests to this new sociopolitical reality that we have entered.

The value of symbols over tangible results, however, is quite limited in its import when considering the continuity of racial obstacles that remain barriers to meeting black needs and achieving aspirations. In the age of Obama, does a black president have a particular obligation to African Americans, especially to those who continue to stand outside— marginalized and excluded from our democracy? Or is the racial symbolism of a single individual who has ascended to the pinnacle of political power simply enough during this ambiguous new era of race and race relations?

Frederick Douglass's legacy reminds us that power concedes nothing without a demand: it never did, and it never will. Failing to heed this warning has led many, particularly within the black community, to fall into a gray zone in this age of Obama. They are torn in their reactions to a black president. They do not want to provide additional political fodder to the extreme right wing by exerting racial grievances, thereby becoming somehow complicit in the conservative political assaults on presidential power. At the same time, by exerting demands on presidential power, they do not want their actions to appear racially divisive in a diverse democracy, which could be taken as being unpatriotic and even ungrateful, even though, similar to other constituents' demands, there are expectations that go along with the exchange of votes.

Many blacks are unsure of how to proceed in this ambiguous new era. They are trapped in the murky haze of the gray zone, which has led them to adopt the dangerous posture of simply standing still on the racial tightrope; as a result, they pretend to "ignore racial issues during Obama's presidency, to help ensure him smooth sailing and a triumphant presidency, no matter how bad things are for African Americans in the meantime."[8]

This political predicament that many are in is attributed to the importance of racial symbolism. Such symbolism at its best offers a positive self-affirmation and at its worst demonizes and demoralizes the soul. Symbols are important because they are infused with meaning, even if that meaning is open to different interpretations. Symbolism reaffirms what is possible, and for many African Americans the election of the first black president symbolized racial pride: it embodied the historical struggles they have endured, the steps taken toward racial equality and justice that have finally led to a place of belonging, where they are no longer forced to stand outside but are included in our country's democracy.

As a black man, Obama is the embodiment of racial symbolism. It is reflected in his personal history. He was born biracial—the offspring of a black African father and a white American mother—thereby assuming his parents' African and American nationalities. That identity, however, was devoid of the contextual and cultural heritage that shaped the black experience in this country. Further complicating the matter, Obama was raised largely in Hawaii, separated from the other forty-eight contiguous states, by his white maternal grandparents, and while growing up he went by the name Barry. All of this is to say that Obama had an ambiguous persona, as revealed by being neither racially black nor white, but a mixture of the two races.

However, as an adult, he chose to embrace his given name of Barack Hussein Obama and willingly accepted the legacy of the black experience in the United States, on which his African American identity was affirmed. Given the malleability of race, he could have just as easily asserted a biracial identity, thereby negating any semblance of a particular racial obligation. Due to this personal history, many African Americans were initially skeptical of Obama and did not view him as a viable black political symbol that embodied the African American struggle for racial equity and justice. What helped to validate his symbolic racial bona fides were the impressive presence of Michelle, his African American wife, and the bigotry of some whites toward his ascendance to power. Both of these factors provided important racial signals to many Americans that he was indeed black enough. But the meaning of his blackness and what it symbolized was interpreted in vastly different ways, yet it linked racial symbolism to governance.

As a black president, Obama embodies the inherent contradictions that lie within the cycle of change amid continuity. Describing Obama's unique position in this cycle, Philip Howard says that as president, Obama occupies the "central office of power in the United States as well as an oppressed location by virtue of his racial positioning within the American racial hierarchy that places Blacks at or near the bottom."[9] That contradictory positioning is a particularly tricky balancing act on the racial tightrope for a black president to maneuver in that a special litmus test—fashioned by racial norms—is imposed to determine his racial allegiance.

In choosing to become an African American, as affirmed by the black experience in the United States, Obama is not a president who just happens to be black. He clearly declared his racial allegiance, but to what effect?

The importance of racial symbolism that embodies the black presence speaks to the difficult reality of governing in the established discourse of presidential power. In assuming the reins of that power, as Howard aptly noted, a black president accepts the structural limitations of the office that are built on a system of "checks and balances," which restrict his ability to single-handedly see his policies through to fruition.[10] To accomplish that objective, he must garner and maintain a broad consensus for the policies he wants to pursue. This, in turn, requires that he position himself to govern as president of all the people by ensuring that he will maintain the existing state of affairs. Effective governance requires that his decisions and actions take into account the needs and aspirations of the common good, where blacks represent only one of the many constituents he has sworn to serve.

Governance, by exercising presidential power to guide the focus and direction of policy, is presumed to be color-blind. Under our system of governance, that blindness places a special burden on a black president. Attempts to address racial disparities—offering race-based remedies for blacks within the scope of presidential authority—risk the appearance of racial favoritism that privileges the interests of a particular group over others. That risk undermines the political legitimacy of presidential authority, the abuse of power, in that racial favoritism violates the principle of the common good but violates the status quo on which it is built. The inherent contradiction of this discourse is that the very essence of the status quo, in and of itself, is racial favoritism—predicated on the unacknowledged racial norms that maintain white privilege, and within that existing state of affairs the saliency of racial disparities are also maintained.

Within this reality, how does a black president attempt to meet the sociopolitical, if not moral, obligations to African Americans, especially to those who remain marginalized and outside? In our system of checks and balances, where racial norms are omnipresent, eyes are constantly watching to see whether a black president maintains the racial status quo or steps outside of the dominant discourse of that office. No racial litmus test has ever been imposed on any other president and, quite frankly, it was never needed, especially in regard to maintaining the racial status quo. How, then, does a black president proceed? By advancing racially neutral remedies that may encompass concerns within the African American community.

President Obama has used presidential authority to address issues of discrimination, most notably policies regarding sex, gender, and immigration. Arguably, those attempts are racially neutral in their presentation, where not only the targeted groups (women, gays and lesbians, and Latinos) benefit as an important constituent, but blacks as well. Even a seemingly color-blind policy agenda that addresses basic human needs such as adequate health care, housing, employment, education, and the like are surely beneficial, particularly to vulnerable blacks, in this racially neutral approach to governing. Their needs and aspirations are neither a focus of nor excluded from President Obama's policy agenda. The advantage that this approach offers is that within the ensuing policy debates over issues, race is not an obvious pretext for opposition; other rationales are provided.

In this new era of race and race relations, a color-blind approach to governing further marginalizes the needs and aspirations of blacks.[11] No obvious considerations are made; the particular circumstances of their lives and ensuing experiences are positioned as being just as valid as any other group's experience—subsequently, all needs and aspirations are seen and positioned as equivalent. As a result, the racial status quo remains unchallenged, but the racial hierarchy remains firmly intact. Unfortunately, in the age of Obama, what is given in the exchange for black votes is racial symbolism—speeches on race and expressions of dismay over racist violence. That symbolism epitomizes the cycle of change amid the absence of fundamental change.

I know that in this new era, the structural nature of racial norms will not be altered anytime soon. Yet progress can be made. In *Stride toward Freedom*, Martin Luther King Jr. reminds us, "Government action is not the whole answer to the present crisis but it is an important partial answer."[12] The other part of the answer rests in our demands to power, regardless of who is president.

We cannot stand still on the racial tightrope, because lives are at stake. Race and race relations are not solely a black problem to be solved by blacks alone. We, as a nation, have a vested interest, because "racialized communities provide the early warning signs of poison in the social atmosphere." We are breathing poisonous air today, but in this ambiguous new era—where the presence of racism is increasingly masked and coded—it can be difficult, particularly for many blacks, to detect the poisonous fumes that are circulating. As Derrick Bell notes: "Today, blacks experiencing rejection for a job, a home, a promotion, anguish over whether race or individual failing prompted their exclusion. Either conclusion breeds frustration and eventually despair. We call ourselves 'African Americans,' but despite centuries of struggle none of us—no matter our prestige or position—is more than a few steps away from a racially motivated exclusion, restriction, or affront."[13]

The circumstances of black life, particularly the poor, alert us all to not only the dangers but also the possibilities that our future holds. In stepping forward on our racial tightrope, we can no longer afford to become seduced by symbolism, no matter how powerful that symbolism appears in this ambiguous age of Obama. History has revealed that inequality and injustice created by racial norms can shift under presidential authority, but with the caveat that demands must be made to power. To avoid falling off the racial tightrope, by taking advantage of this new moment that history has provided, it is incumbent on us to make demands to power.

NOTES

INTRODUCTION

1. Barack Obama, keynote address at the 2004 Democratic National Convention, available at http://www.americanrhetoric.com/speeches/convention2004/barackobama2004dnc.htm.

2. Michael K. Brown et al., *Whitewashing Race: The Myth of a Color-Blind Society* (Berkeley: University of California Press, 2003), 1–12.

3. Barack Obama, *Dreams from My Father: A Story of Race and Inheritance* (New York: Broadway, 2004), vii.

4. Barack Obama, *The Audacity of Hope: Thoughts on Reclaiming the American Dream* (New York: Three Rivers Press, 2006), 11.

I. WHO AM I?

1. Some of the details of my family history are taken from interviews with older relatives from around the country. Although my great uncle, Henry Spearman, is deceased, he wrote his interpretation of Elvie's (and, to a much lesser extent, Caroline's) history in a journal titled *Looking Back*, which has been passed along to family members.

2. Andrew Young, *An Easy Burden: The Civil Rights Movement and the Transformation of America* (New York: Harper Collins, 1996), 82–83.

3. This account is based on several sources: interviews with former Pebble Hill employees, personal visits to the plantation, and the only book describing the day-to-day experiences of blacks at Pebble Hill Plantation, Titus Brown

and James Hadley, eds., *African-American Life on the Southern Hunting Plantation* (Charleston, SC: Arcadia, 2000).

2. WHO WERE WE?

1. Jan Nederveen Pieterse, *White on Black: Images of Africa and Blacks in Western Popular Culture* (New Haven, CT: Yale University Press, 1992), 167.

2. Scott McAleer, "A Study of Racial Violence in Thomas County, Georgia, 1930," *Georgia Historical Quarterly* 87, no. 1 (Spring): 48.

3. Ibid.

4. Ibid., 49.

5. McAleer (p. 50), in "A Study of Racial Violence," identified "as many as nine local blacks besides Willie Kirkland and Lacy Mitchell" who were lynched between 1899 and 1930. He also emphasized that lynching was only one form of racist violence and that the rape of black women occurred as well. In describing this "rape-lynch syndrome," he said: "The rapes of black women are seen as a visible adjunct to the lynching of black men. While the causes, effects and dynamics of these rapes might be just as amorphous and difficult to discern as those of lynching, the intentions of the rapists and the results on the black communities were similar"; they evoked fear and conformity.

6. Brown v. Board of Education of Topeka, 347 U.S. 483 (1954), available at http://www.nationalcenter.org/brown.html.

7. The county unit system in Georgia was established in 1917, when the Georgia legislature, dominated by the Democratic Party, passed the Neill Primary Act. This act formalized the existing system of allotting votes by county in party primary elections. In allotting votes by county, there was little regard for population difference, which minimized the impact that urban centers had on elections. This system remained in place until the early 1960s. Scott E. Buchanan, "County Unit System," *New Georgia Encyclopedia*, April 15, 2005, http://www.georgiaencyclopedia.org/nge/ArticlePrintable.jsp?id=h-1381.

8. Eugene Talmadge was a staunch white supremacist. He played an instrumental role in Georgia politics and served three terms as governor. In 1946, he won the Democratic primary for governor for the fourth time. He was assured victory in the general election because there was no Republican challenger. But Talmadge was seriously ill when he ran for a fourth term. So his backers, fearing that the governor might die before taking office, chose his son, Herman, to run as a secret write-in candidate. There was one problem with this plan for succession: "The new state constitution created the office of lieutenant governor, which would be filled for the first time in the 1946 election. The lieutenant governor would become chief executive if the governor died in

office. The constitution was not clear about whether the lieutenant governor-elect would succeed if the governor-elect died before he took the oath of office. Melvin Thompson, a member of the anti-Talmadge camp, was elected lieutenant governor in 1946." Eugene Talmadge died in December 1946. Subsequently, the "three governors controversy" arose, when Herman Talmadge, the write-in candidate, Melvin Thompson, the lieutenant governor-elect, and the outgoing governor, Ellis Arnall, all made a claim to the governor's office. The state legislature elected Herman Talmadge as governor, and he served 1948–1954. Inheriting his father's white supremacist posture, Herman Eugene Talmadge would also serve as US senator from Georgia from 1957 to 1981. Harold Paulk, "Eugene Talmadge: 1884–1946," *New Georgia Encyclopedia*, August 25, 2004, http://www.georgiaencyclopedia.org/articles/government-politics/eugene-talmadge-1884-1946.

9. Andrew Young, *An Easy Burden: The Civil Rights Movement and the Transformation of America* (New York: Harper Collins, 1996), 90–91.

10. Young recounts this incident in discussing attempts at black voter registration in Thomasville, Georgia. Andrew Young, interview by Jack Bass and Watter Devries, January 31, 1974, interview A-0080, transcript, Southern Oral History Program Collection 4007, http://docsouth.unc.edu/sohp/playback.html?base_file=A-0080.

11. Young, *An Easy Burden*, 94.

12. Ibid, 94–95.

13. Boynton v. Virginia, 364 U.S. 454 (1960), available at http://supreme.justia.com/cases/federal/us/364/454/case.html.

14. The *Thomasville Times-Enterprise* covered the Albany movement extensively, and its articles and editorials included protesters' activities, city, state, and federal response, and opinions. In addition, given the historical significance of the Albany movement to civil rights, what happened there is well documented by oral sources, and written accounts from several authors: Taylor Branch, *At Canaan's Edge: America in the King Years, 1965–68* (New York: Simon and Schuster, 2006); Taylor Branch, *Parting the Waters: America in the King Years 1954–63* (New York: Simon and Schuster, 2007); Aldon D. Morris, *Origins of the Civil Rights Movement* (New York: Simon and Schuster, 1986); and Howard Zinn, *The Radical Sixties*, vol. 2, *The Southern Mystique* (Cambridge, MA: South End Press, 1964).

15. Associated Press, "Sanders on King; Griffin on Foes," *Thomasville Times-Enterprise*, July 19, 1962.

16. Associated Press, "King Loses Plea to Cancel Charge," *Thomasville Times-Enterprise*, July 25, 1962.

17. Dr. William Anderson, interview by Blackside, Inc. on November 7, 1985, *Eyes on the Prize: America's Civil Rights Years (1954–1965)*, Washing-

ton University Libraries, Film and Media Archive, Henry Hampton Collection, available at http://digital.wustl.edu/cgi/t/text/text-idx?c=eop;cc=eop;rgn= main;view=text;idno=and0015.1042.003.

18. Young, *An Easy Burden*, 90.

19. Laughlin McDonald, *A Voting Rights Odyssey: Black Enfranchisement in Georgia* (Cambridge: Cambridge University Press, 2003).

20. Gray v. Sanders, 372 U.S. 368 (1963), available at http://supreme.justia. com/cases/federal/us/372/368/case.html.

21. Lassiter v. Northampton County Board of Elections, 360 U.S. 45 (1959), available at http://supreme.justia.com/cases/federal/us/360/45/case.html.

22. The 1958 Georgia literacy test is available at http://cdm.georgiaarchives. org:2011/cdm/compoundobject/collection/adhoc/id/552/rec/4.

23. Associated Press, "Georgia Negro Senator Seeks Eased Registration Law," *Thomasville Times-Enterprise*, May 15, 1964.

24. "Stop Segregating Vote, Local Realtor Requests," *Thomasville Times-Enterprise*, August 17, 1965.

25. John F. Kennedy, address on civil rights, June 11, 1963, transcript available at http://www.pbs.org/wgbh/americanexperience/features/primary-resources/jfk-civilrights/.

26. Betty G. Pierson, "Negroes Plan March Here; Ask Better Job Chances," *Thomasville Times-Enterprise*, April 29, 1965.

3. WHO ARE WE BECOMING?

1. A. Leon Higginbotham, *In the Matter of Color: Race and the American Legal Process; The Colonial Period* (New York: Oxford University Press, 1978), 258.

2. W. E. B. Du Bois, Black Reconstruction in America 1860–1880 (New York: Harcourt, Brace, 1935), 123.

3. Gunnar Myrdal, *An American Dilemma: The Negro Problem and Modern Democracy* (New York: Harper and Row, 1944), 887.

4. With assistance from local bureau agents, educational associations were established in the subdistricts of Thomasville, Bainbridge, Albany, Georgetown, Cuthbert, and Americus. In early 1866, the Freedmen Bureau established a "pay your own way" policy, which led to the founding of the Georgia Educational Association (initially organized as the Georgia Equal Rights Association). The Educational Association worked closely with the bureau and northern aid societies and became the model "to encourage the freedmen to organized effort in supporting their own schools & managing their own affairs." By the end of 1866, freedmen owned 57 schoolhouses and provided support

for 96 of the 127 schools in the state of Georgia. By the spring of 1867, freedmen contributions sustained some 104 schools and teachers and more than 3,000 students. During the same period, the bureau maintained some 44 schools and 50 teachers and close to 3,100 pupils. Northern aid societies provided support for 84 schools, 78 teachers, and more than 7,000 students. Freedmen also defrayed the expenses for 45 schools under the control of the Bureau and the aid societies. Records of the Field Offices for the State of Georgia, Bureau of Refugees, M1903, Freedmen, and Abandoned, 1865–1872 (Washington, DC: United States Congress and National Archives and Records Administration, 2003), 8.

5. Ga. Const. of 1868, art. VI (educational provision), available at http://georgiainfo.galileo.usg.edu/con1868.htm.

6. Plessy v. Ferguson, 163 U.S. 537 (1886), available at http://www.law.cornell.edu/supremecourt/text/163/537.

7. Calvin L. Brown, "The Adequate Program for Education in Georgia," *Journal of Education Finance* 3, no. 4 (Spring 1978): 402–11.

8. Unnamed and undated report (one page), received by the AMA in early 1885, American Missionary Association archives, Amistad Research Center at Tulane University, New Orleans, LA.

9. Rev. Pharr to AMA officials, undated (five pages), American Missionary Association archives, Amistad Research Center at Tulane University, New Orleans, LA.

10. Ibid.

11. Ibid.

12. Unnamed, undated report (one page), American Missionary Association archives, Amistad Research Center at Tulane University, New Orleans, LA.

13. Ralph McChesney, "Little Is Known of Early Education System in Thomas County," *Thomasville Times-Enterprise* August 18, 1965.

14. This history of black schools in Thomasville, Georgia, is taken from the account given at Jack Hadley Black History Museum, available at http://www.jackhadleyblackhistorymuseum.com/douglas.htm.

15. Ralph McChesney, "Dual Superintendency Tied in Early Local Schools," *Thomasville Times-Enterprise*, August 25, 1965.

16. Northcross v. Board of Education of Memphis, 333 F.2d 661 (6th Cir. 1964).

17. United States Commission on Civil Rights, *Survey of School Desegregation in the Southern and Border States 1965–1966* (Washington, DC: US Government Printing Office, 1966), 19–47.

18. Political ad in *Thomasville Times-Enterprise*, November 24, 1965.

19. "Court Action Needed Now, Lawyer Says," *Thomasville Times-Enterprise*, April, 1, 1966.

20. "Thomasville's Desegregation Plan Approved," *Thomasville Times-Enterprise*, June 4, 1965.

21. "88 Negroes Ask Admission to 6 White Schools Here," *Thomasville Times-Enterprise*, June 9, 1965.

22. "HEW Pushes Area Schools for Desegregation Step-Up," *Thomasville Times-Enterprise*, March 12, 1968.

23. "Get Guns and Retaliate, Carmichael Urges Negroes," *Thomasville Times-Enterprise*, April 5, 1968.

24. "Hundreds Attend Service Honoring Dr. King Here," *Thomasville Times-Enterprise*, April 8, 1968.

25. Alexander v. Holmes County Board of Education, 396 U.S. 1218 (1969). Available at http://caselaw.lp.findlaw.com/scripts/getcase.pl?court=us&vol=396&invol=1218.

26. Ibid.

27. "Integration Date Moved Up Here," *Thomasville Times-Enterprise*, January 28, 1970.

28. "School Board Okays Plan to Eliminate Dual System," *Thomasville Times-Enterprise*, January 28, 1970.

29. "Board Reveals Action," *Thomasville Times-Enterprise*, January 15, 1970.

30. "New THS Principal Issues Stiff Warning," *Thomasville Times-Enterprise*, April 3, 1970.

31. A series of letters to the editor, *Thomasville Times-Enterprise*, September 17, 1970, through September 26, 1970.

4. ARE WE A PART OF EACH OTHER?

1. David Vassar Taylor, *African Americans in Minnesota*, The People of Minnesota (St. Paul: Minnesota Historical Society Press, 2002), 32.

2. Jennifer A. Delton, *Making Minnesota Liberal: Civil Rights and the Transformation of the Democratic Party* (Minneapolis: University of Minnesota Press, 2002), 2.

3. Ibid.

4. Michael Omi and Howard Winant argued that, as distinct from race, ethnicity was largely based on culture and descent. "Culture in this formulation included such diverse factors as religion, language, customs, nationality, and political identification. Descent involved heredity and a sense of group origins, thus suggesting that ethnicity was socially primordial, if not biologically given, in character." Early ethnicity-based theories were concerned with issues of immigration and culture contact. Michael Omi and Howard Winant, *Racial*

Formation in the United States: From the 1960s to the 1990s, 2nd ed. (New York: Routledge, 1994), 15.

5. Charles Fremont, a physician in Minneapolis, who believed that the state should control the reproductive patterns of undesirables, founded the eugenics movement in Minnesota. The movement enjoyed popularity during the 1930s but died out during the 1940s, following World War II. See the details for Minnesota in Lutz Kaelber, "Eugenics: Compulsory Sterilization in 50 American States" (presentation at the Thirty-Seventh Annual Meeting of the Social Science History Association, Vancouver, BC, November 12, 2012), available at http://www.uvm.edu/~lkaelber/eugenics/MN/MN.html.

6. Delton, *Making Minnesota Liberal*, 46–47.

7. Timothy N. Thurber, *The Politics of Equality: Hubert H. Humphrey and the African American Freedom Struggle* (New York: Columbia University Press, 1999), 24.

8. Karen Brodkin Sacks described in particular how Jews became a part of American's white middle class. She attributed their and other white ethnic groups' social mobility to hard work and to federal programs such as GI benefits administered by the Veterans Administration and the Federal Housing Administration, which favored white veterans from World War II. Karen Brodkin Sacks, "How Did Jews Become White Folks?" in *Race*, ed. Steven Gregory and Roger Sanjek (New Brunswick, NJ: Rutgers University Press, 1996), 78–97.

9. Gunnar Myrdal, *An American Dilemma: The Negro Problem and Modern Democracy* (New York: Harper and Brothers, 1944).

10. Thurber, *Politics of Equality*, 46.

11. Ibid., 32.

12. Ibid., 47.

13. Delton, *Making Minnesota Liberal*, 103.

14. Hubert H. Humphrey, "Speech on Civil Rights," Philadephia, PA, July 14, 1948, transcript and Adobe Flash audio, 10:00, Minnesota Historical Society, http://www.mnhs.org/library/tips/history_topics/42humphreyspeech/transcript.htm.

15. "Wit and Wisdom of Hubert H. Humphrey," University of Minnesota, Humphrey School of Public Affairs, available at http://www.hhh.umn.edu/about/HHHquotes.html.

16. Zora Neale Hurston to Charlotte Osgood Mason, November 25, 1930, in *Zora Neale Hurston: A Life in Letters*, ed. Carla Kaplan (New York: Anchor, 2003), 194.

17. Jared E. Leighton, "A Small Revolution: The Role of a Black Power Revolt in Creating and Sustaining a Black Studies Department at the Univer-

sity of Minnesota (master's thesis, University of Nebraska, Lincoln, 2008), 3, http://digitalcommons.unl.edu/historydiss/49.

18. Ibid., 47.

19. Ibid., 56.

20. Ibid., 75.

21. D. A. Maughan Brown, "Myth and the Mau Mau," *Theoria: A Journal of Social and Political Theory*, no. 55 (October 1980): 59–61.

22. Helen Crowley, "Women's Studies: Between a Rock and a Hard Place or Just Another Cell in the Beehive?" *Feminist Review*, no. 61 (Spring 1999): 139.

23. bell hooks, "Feminism and Black Women's Studies," *Sage: A Scholarly Journal on Black Women* 6, no. 1 (Summer 1989): 56.

24. Brown v. Board of Education of Topeka, 347 U.S. 483 (1954), available at http://www.nationalcenter.org/brown.html.

25. Harold Orlans, "Affirmative Action in Higher Education," in "Affirmative Action Revisited," *Annals of the American Academy of Political and Social Science* 523 (September 1992): 144–58; James T. Minor, "Segregation Residual in Higher Education: A Tale of Two States," *American Educational Research Journal* 45, no. 4 (December 2008): 861–85; Barbara A. Woods, "Affirmative Action and Today's Black Woman Historian," *National Women's Studies Association Journal* 10, no. 3 (Autumn 1998): 160–67.

26. NAACP chairman Julian Bond, speaking at a symposium on Affirmative Action at the Minnesota State Capitol, St. Paul, MN, June 25, 1998, available at http://www.hubert-humphrey.com/06251998.hhh.

27. Regents of the University of California v. Alan Bakke, 438 U.S. 265 (1978), available at http://www.law.cornell.edu/supremecourt/text/438/265.

28. Linda Sanderson, "Each University Department to Adopt Affirmative Action Plan," *Minnesota Daily*, March 4, 1996.

29. Phil Carruthers, "HHH Institute to Retain State and Local Government Focus," *Minnesota Daily*, August 1, 1977.

5. ARE WE DIFFERENT YET THE SAME?

1. Beverly Xaviera Watkins, Robert E. Fullilove, and Mindy Thompson Fullilove, "Arms against Illness: Crack Cocaine and Drug Policy in the United States," *Health and Human Rights* 2, no. 4 (1998): 49–50.

2. Joe R. Feagin and Aaron Porter, "Affirmative Action and African Americans: Rhetoric and Practice," *Humboldt Journal of Social Relations* 21, no. 2 (1995): 81–103.

3. Tim Wise, "Is Sisterhood Conditional? White Women and the Rollback of Affirmative Action," *National Women's Studies Association Journal* 10, no. 3 (Autumn 1998): 1–26.

4. Dennis J. Downey, "Situating Social Attitudes toward Cultural Pluralism: Between Culture Wars and Contemporary Racism," *Social Problems* 47, no. 1 (February 2000): 90–111.

5. Pamela Johnston Conover, "The Mobilization of the New Right: A Test of Various Explanations," *Western Political Quarterly* 36, no. 4 (December 1983): 632–49.

6. Rebecca Klatch, "Coalition and Conflict among Women of the New Right," *Signs* 12, no. 4 (Summer 1988): 671.

7. Ibid., 676.

8. Joel Olson, "Whiteness and the Polarization of American Politics," *Political Research Quarterly* 61, no. 4 (December 2008): 71.

9. Andrew Rosenthal, "Lee Atwater's Southern Strategy Interview," *New York Times*, November 14, 2012.

10. Feagin, Joe R., *White Party, White Government: Race, Class, and U.S. Politics* (New York: Routledge, 2012), 82–83.

11. "The Election of 1976," *The American Experience*, WGBH/PBS, available at http://www.pbs.org/wgbh/americanexperience/features/general-article/carter-election1976/.

12. Barbara Jordan, keynote address, 1976 Democratic National Convention, New York, July 12, 1976, available at http://www.americanrhetoric.com/speeches/barbarajordan1976dnc.html.

13. Gail Garfield, *Through Our Eyes: African American Men's Experiences of Race, Gender, and Violence* (New Brunswick, NJ: Rutgers University Press, 2010), 189.

14. Anti-Drug Abuse Act of 1986, Pub. L. no. 99-570, 100 Stat. 3207 (1986), available at http://www.unodc.org/doc/enl/1986-30-E.pdf.

15. Michelle Alexander, *The New Jim Crow: Mass Incarceration in the Age of Colorblindness* (New York: New Press, 2010), 5.

16. David A. Sklansky, "Cocaine, Race, and Equal Protection," *Stanford Law Review* 47, no. 6 (July 1995): 1287–88.

17. Ibid., 1292.

18. Claudia Card, "Women, Evil, and Gray Zones," *Metaphilosophy* 31, no. 5 (2000): 512.

19. Ibid., 515.

20. Primo Levi, "The Gray Zone," in *Violence in War and Peace: An Anthology*, ed. Nancy Scheper-Hughes and Philippe I. Bourgois (Malden, MA: Blackwell, 2004), 89.

21. Kenneth B. Nunn, "Race, Crime and the Pool of Surplus Criminality: Or Why the 'War on Drugs' Was a 'War on Blacks,'" *Journal of Gender, Race, and Justice* 6, no. 2 (Fall 2002): 382. Available at http://scholarship.law.ufl.edu/cgi/viewcontent.cgi?article=1178&context=facultypub.

22. Patrick A. Langan, "Race of Prisoners Admitted to State and Federal Institutions, 1926–86," report NCJ-125618, US Department of Justice, Office of Justice Programs, Bureau of Justice Statistics, May 1991, 8.

23. Ibid.

24. Gloria J. Browne-Marshall, *Race. Law, and American Society: 1607 to Present* (New York: Routledge, 2007), 217.

6. WHO IS INCLUDED AND WHO BELONGS?

1. Voting Rights Act of 1965, Pub. L. No. 89-110, 79 Stat. 437 (1965), available at http://library.clerk.house.gov/reference-files/PPL_Voting RightsAct_1965.pdf.

2. "Election 2012: Voting Laws Roundup," Brennan Center for Justice at New York University School of Law, October 11, 2012, available at http://www.brennancenter.org/analysis/election-2012-voting-laws-roundup.

3. Shelby County, Alabama v. Holder, Attorney General et al., 557 U.S. 193 (2013). Available at http://www.law.cornell.edu/supremecourt/text/12-96.

4. Selwyn Raab, "State Judge Dismisses Indictment of Officer in the Bumpurs Killing," *New York Times*, October 29, 1984.

5. Ibid.

6. Robert J. Howe, "Fast over Thin Ice: Hate's in Season, and It's a Bumper Crop," *Pulphouse Magazine*, June 1992, available at http://www.rjhowe.net/fast_hate.html.

7. Robert D. McFadden, "Edward I. Koch, a Mayor as Brash, Shrewd and Colorful as the City He Led, Dies at 88," *New York Times*, February 1, 2013.

8. Elizabeth Kolbert, "Two Views on Dinkins: Conciliator or Hesitater?" *New York Times*, August 14, 1989.

9. Sam Roberts, "Park Rampage and Mayor Race: Fear and Politics," *New York Times*, May 1, 1989.

10. Chris Smith, "Central Park Revisited," *New York Magazine*, October, 21, 2002, 2. Available at http://nymag.com/nymetro/news/crimelaw/features/n_7836/.

11. Lisa W. Foderaro, "Angered by Attack, Trump Urges Return of the Death Penalty," *New York Times*, May 1, 1989.

12. Roberts, "Fear and Politics."

13. Smith, "Central Park Revisited," 1.

14. Wilbur C. Rich, *David Dinkins and New York City Politics: Race, Images, and the Media* (New York: State University of New York Press, 2007), 46.

15. Ibid., 49.

16. David W. Dunlap, "Columbia's Big Medical Center Plans Expansion," *New York Times*, March 29, 1992.

17. Ned Kaufman, "Heritage and the Cultural Politics of Preservation: Speaking of Places," *Places* 11, no. 3 (1998): 1–8, available at *eScholarship*, University of California, http://escholarship.org/uc/item/57j0g7jq.

18. Ed Pilkington, "Harlem Takes on University in Battle of Town versus Gown: Residents Object to Plans to Turn Black Neighborhood into 'Manhattanville,'" *Guardian*, November 19, 2007.

19. "Ms. Messinger's Obstructionism," *New York Times*, August 10, 1990.

20. Ibid.

21. Andrew Maykuth, "New York Boycott Settles in for the Long Haul," *Philadelphia Inquirer*, September 30, 1990.

22. John J. Goldman and Karen Tumulty, "Dinkins Tries to Break Black Boycott of Korean Stores: Race; New York Mayor Shops at Market to Show Support for Owners; Tensions Remain High Eight Months after Incident with Customer," *Los Angeles Times*, September 22, 1990.

23. M. A. Farber, "Black-Korean Who-Pushed-Whom Festers," *New York Times*, May 7, 1990.

24. Jonathan Rieder, "Trouble in Store," *New Republic*, July 2, 1990, 1–9, available at http://www.newrepublic.com/article/90877/brooklyn-boycott-racism-1990.

25. Jen Fiorentino, "Twenty-Three Years after a Notorious Murder, the Convicted Killer Speaks," *Brooklyn Ink*, December 10, 2012, available at http://thebrooklynink.com/2012/12/10/50766-convicted-killer-writes-to-reporter/.

26. Dennis Hevesi, "Black Protesters March in Brooklyn Communities," *New York Times*, May 13, 1990.

27. Farber, "Who-Pushed-Whom Festers."

28. April Goldman, "Other Korean Grocers Give to Those in Brooklyn Boycott," *New York Times*, May 14, 1990.

29. Rieder, "Trouble in Store."

30. Farber, "Who-Pushed-Whom Festers."

31. Ibid.

32. Claire Jean Kim, "'No Justice, No Peace!': The Politics of Black-Korean Conflict," *Trotter Review* 7, no. 2 (1993): 13.

33. Hevesi, "Black Protestors March."

34. Goldman, "Other Korean Grocers Give."

35. Kim, "No Justice, No Peace!" 13.

36. Rich, *David Dinkins*, 115.

37. In New York City, the black female population is around 15 percent of the total population. Between 1990 and 1994, the New York City Department of Health reported that 52 percent (or six hundred) of all female victims of homicide were black women. These figures do not include incidents of violence that did not end in death but may have resulted in permanent disability, hospitalization, emergency room visits, physician visits, and silent suffering. Taken from a report prepared by Susan A. Wilt, Susan M. Illman, and Maia Brody Field, "Female Homicide Victims in New York City 1990–1994" (report, New York City Department of Health, Injury Prevention Program, 1996).

38. Gail Garfield, *Knowing What We Know: African American Women's Experiences of Violence and Violation* (New Brunswick, NJ: Rutgers University Press, 2005), xvi–xvii.

39. A. Leon Higginbotham Jr., "An Open Letter to Justice Clarence Thomas from a Federal Judicial Colleague," in *Race-ing Justice, En-gendering Power*, ed. Toni Morrison (New York: Pantheon, 1992), 17–28.

40. Cornel West, "Black Leadership and the Pitfalls of Racial Reasoning," in *Race-ing Justice, En-gendering Power*, ed. Toni Morrison (New York: Pantheon, 1992), 391–92.

41. Kemberle Williams Crenshaw, "Black Women Still in Defense of Ourselves." *Nation*, October 24, 2011, available at http://www.thenation.com/article/163814/black-women-still-defense-ourselves#.

42. Carol B. Conaway, "Crown Heights: Politics and Press Coverage of the Race War That Wasn't," *Polity* 32, no. 1 (Autumn 1999): 98.

43. Ibid., 99.

44. Ibid., 102.

45. Rich, *David Dinkins*, 116.

46. Richard H. Girgenti, *A Report to the Governor on the Disturbances in Crown Heights*, vol. 1, *An Assessment of the City's Preparedness and Response to Civil Disorder* (Albany, NY: New York State Division of Criminal Justice Services, 1993), 4–5.

47. Ibid., 5–6.

48. Rich, *David Dinkins*, 117.

49. *Holocaust Encyclopedia Online*, s.v. "Pogroms," http://www.ushmm.org/wlc/en/article.php?ModuleId=10005183.

50. Catherine S. Manegold, "Rally Puts Police under New Scrutiny," *New York Times*, September 27, 1992.

51. Ibid.

52. George James, "Police Dept. Report Assails Officers in New York Rally," *New York Times*, September 29, 1992.

53. Rich, *David Dinkins*, 186.

54. Derrick Bell, "Racial Realism," in *Critical Race Theory: The Key Writings That Formed the Movement*, ed. Kimberlé Crenshaw et al. (New York: New Press, 1995), 306.

55. Ibid., 308.

EPILOGUE

1. Douglas Martin, "A Village Dies, a Park Is Born," *New York Times*, January 21, 1997.

2. Diana diZerega Wall, Nan A. Rothschild, and Cynthia Copeland, "Seneca Village and Little Africa: Two African American Communities in Antebellum New York City," *Historical Archaeology* 42, no. 1 (2008): 98.

3. Charles R. Lawrence III, "The Id, the Ego, and Equal Protection: Reckoning with Unconscious Racism," *Stanford Law Review* 39, no. 2 (January 1987): 322.

4. Ibid., 330.

5. Michael Omi and Howard Winant, *Racial Formation in the United States: From the 1960s to the 1990s*, 2nd ed. (New York: Routledge, 1994), 60.

6. US Census Bureau, "Projections Show a Slower Growing, Old, More Diverse Nation a Half Century from Now," news release CB12-243, December 12, 2012, https://www.census.gov/newsroom/releases/archives/population/cb12-243.html.

7. Sam Tanenhaus, "The Original Sin: Why the GOP Is and Will Continue to Be the Party of White People," *New Republic*, February 10, 2013, 1–13, available at http://www.newrepublic.com/article/112365/why-republicans-are-party-white-people.

8. Michelle Alexander, *The New Jim Crow: Mass Incarceration in the Age of Colorblindness* (New York: New Press, 2010), 254.

9. Philip S. S. Howard, "Turning Out the Center: Racial Politics and African Agency in the Obama Era," *Journal of Black Studies* 40, no. 3 (January 2010): 382.

10. Ibid., 384.

11. Eduardo Bonilla-Silva and David Dietrich, "The Sweet Enchantment of Color-Blind Racism in Obamerica," *Annals of the American Academy of Political and Social Science* 634, no. 1 (March 2011): 190–206.

12. Martin Luther King Jr., *Stride toward Freedom: The Montgomery Story* (New York: Harper and Brothers, 1958), 198.

13. Derrick Bell, "Racial Realism," in *Critical Race Theory: The Key Writings That Formed the Movement*, ed. Kimberlé Crenshaw et al. (New York: New Press, 1995), 306.

BIBLIOGRAPHY

African American Women In Defense of Ourselves. 1991 Manifesto. Available at http://racialicious.tumblr.com/post/43158287342/we-are-particularly-outraged-by-the-racist-and.

Alexander, Michelle. *The New Jim Crow: Mass Incarceration in the Age of Colorblindness.* New York: New Press, 2010.

Alexander v. Holmes County Board of Education, 396 U.S. 1218 (1969). Available at http://caselaw.lp.findlaw.com/scripts/getcase.pl?court=us&vol=396&invol=1218.

American Missionary Association. Unnamed, undated documents. Amistad Research Center at Tulane University, New Orleans, Louisiana.

Anderson, William. Interview by Blackside, Inc. on November 7, 1985. *Eyes on the Prize: America's Civil Rights Years (1954–1965).* Washington University Libraries Film and Media Archive, Henry Hampton Collection. Available at http://digital.wustl.edu/cgi/t/text/text-idx?c=eop;cc=eop;rgn=main;view=text;idno=and0015.1042.003.

Arden, Caroline. *Getting the Donkey out of the Ditch: The Democratic Party in Search of Itself.* New York: Greenwood, 1988.

Associated Press. "Georgia Negro Senator Seeks Eased Registration Law." *Thomasville Times-Enterprise,* May 15, 1964.

———. "King Loses Plea to Cancel Charge." *Thomasville Times-Enterprise,* July 25, 1962.

———. "Sanders on King; Griffin on Foes." *Thomasville Times-Enterprise,* July 19, 1963.

Atwater, Deborah F. "Senator Barack Obama: The Rhetoric of Hope and the American Dream." *Journal of Black Studies* 38, no. 2 (November 2007): 121–29.

Baldwin, Bridgette. "Colorblind Diversity: The Changing Significance of Race in the Post-Bakke Era." *Albany Law Review* 72, no. 4 (2009): 863.

Bell, Derrick. *And We Are Not Saved: The Elusive Quest for Racial Justice.* New York: Basic, 1987.

———. "Racial Realism." In *Critical Race Theory: The Key Writings That Formed the Movement,* edited by Kimberlé Crenshaw, Neil Gotanda, Gary Peller, and Kendall Thomas, 302–12. New York: New Press, 1995.

Biskupic, Joan. "On Race, a Court Transformed." *Washington Post,* December 15, 1997.

Blackmon, Douglas A. *Slavery by Another Name: The Re-Enslavement of Black Americans from the Civil War to World War II.* New York: Doubleday, 2008.

Blight, David W. "Voter Suppression, Then and Now." *New York Times,* September 6, 2012.

Blow, Charles M. "Barack and Trayvon." *New York Times,* July 19, 2013.

Bond, Julian. Speech at symposium on Affirmative Action at the Minnesota State Capitol, St. Paul, MN, June 25, 1998. Available at http://www.hubert-humphrey.com/06251998.hhh.

Bonilla-Silva, Eduardo, and David Dietrich. "The Sweet Enchantment of Color-Blind Racism in Obamerica." *Annals of the American Academy of Political and Social Science* 634, no. 1 (March 2011): 190–206.

Boynton v. Virginia. 364 U.S. 454. 1960. Available at http://supeme.justia.com/cases/federal/us/364/454/case.html.

Branch, Taylor. *At Canaan's Edge: America in the King Years, 1965–68*. New York: Simon and Schuster, 2006.

———. *Parting the Waters: America in the King Years 1954–63*. New York: Simon and Schuster, 2007.

Brennan Center for Justice at New York University School of Law. "Election 2012: Voting Laws Roundup." October 11, 2012. Available at http://www.brennancenter.org/analysis/election-2012-voting-laws-roundup.

Brown, Calvin L. "The Adequate Program for Education in Georgia." *Journal of Education Finance* 3, no. 4 (Spring 1978): 402–11.

Brown, D. A. Maughan. "Myth and the Mau Mau." *Theoria: A Journal of Social and Political Theory*, no. 55 (October 1980): 59–85.

Brown, Michael K., Martin Carnoy, Elliott Currie, Troy Duster, David B. Oppenheimer, Marjorie M. Shultz, and David Wellman. *Whitewashing Race: The Myth of a Color-Blind Society*. Berkeley: University of California Press, 2003.

Brown, Titus, and James Hadley. *African-American Life on the Southern Hunting Plantation*. Charleston, SC: Arcadia, 2000.

Brown v. Board of Education of Topeka. 347 U.S. 483. 1954. Available at http://www.nationalcenter.org/brown.html.

Browne-Marshall, Gloria J. *Race, Law, and American Society: 1607 to Present*. New York: Routledge, 2007.

Buchanan, Scott E. "County Unit System." *New Georgia Encyclopedia*, April 15, 2005. http://www.georgiaencyclopedia.org/nge/ArticlePrintable.jsp?id=h-1381.

Calmes, Jackie, and Helene Cooper. "A Personal Note as Obama Speaks on Death of Boy." *New York Times*, March 23, 2012.

Card, Claudia. "Women, Evil, and Gray Zones." *Metaphilosophy* 31, no. 5 (2000): 509–28.

Carruthers, Phil. "HHH Institute to Retain State and Local Government Focus." *Minnesota Daily*, August 1, 1977.

Chalfen, Michael. "The Way Out May Lead In: The Albany Movement beyond Martin Luther King, Jr." *Georgia Historical Quarterly* 79, no. 3 (Fall 1995): 560–98.

Coates, Ta-Nehisi. "The Good, Racist People." *New York Times*, March 6, 2013.

Cobb, William Jelani. *The Substance of Hope: Barack Obama and the Paradox of Progress*. New York. Walker, 2010.

Colburn, David R., and Jeffrey S. Adler. *African American Mayors: Race, Politics, and the American City*. Chicago: University of Illinois Press, 2001.

Conaway, Carol B. "Crown Heights: Politics and Press Coverage of the Race War That Wasn't." *Polity* 32, no. 1 (Autumn 1999): 93–118.

Conover, Pamela Johnston. "The Mobilization of the New Right: A Test of Various Explanations." *Western Political Quarterly* 36, no. 4 (December 1983): 632–49.

Crowley, Helen. "Women's Studies: Between a Rock and a Hard Place or Just Another Cell in the Beehive?" *Feminist Review*, no. 61 (Spring 1999): 131–50.

Crenshaw, Kimberlé Williams. "Black Women Still in Defense of Ourselves." *Nation*, October 24, 2011. Available at http://www.thenation.com/article/163814/black-women-still-defense-ourselves#.

Davis, Timothy, Kevin R. Johnson, and George A. Martinez, eds. *A Reader on Race, Civil Rights, and American Law: A Multiracial Approach*. Durham, NC: Carolina Academic Press, 2001.

Davis v. Thomas County, Georgia, et al. 380 F. 2d 93 (1967).

Dawson, Michael. *Not in Our Lifetimes: The Future of Black Politics*. Chicago: University of Chicago Press, 2011.

Delton, Jennifer A. *Making Minnesota Liberal: Civil Rights and the Transformation of the Democratic Party*. Minneapolis: University of Minnesota Press, 2002.

Desmond, Matthew, and Mustafa Emirbayer, eds. *Racial Domination, Racial Progress: The Sociology of Race in America*. New York: McGraw-Hill, 2010.

Dowd, Maureen. "On Washington: The Cult of Lee Atwater." *New York Times*, November 21, 1993.

Downey, Dennis J. "Situating Social Attitudes toward Cultural Pluralism: Between Culture Wars and Contemporary Racism." *Social Problems* 47, no. 1 (2000): 90–111.

Du Bois, W. E. B. *Black Reconstruction in America 1860–1880*. New York: Harcourt, Brace, 1935.

Dunlap, David W. "Columbia's Big Medical Center Plans Expansion." *New York Times*, March 29, 1992.

Edgell, Penny, and Eric Tranby. "Shared Visions? Diversity and Cultural Membership in American Life." *Social Problems* 57, no. 2 (May 2010): 175–204.

Eibach, Richard P. "Change We Can Believe In? Barack Obama's Framing Strategies for Bridging Racial Divisions." *Du Bois Review* 6, no. 1 (2009): 137–51.

Entman, Robert M., and Andrew Rojecki. *The Black Image in the White Mind: Media and Race in America*. Chicago: University of Chicago Press, 2000.

Farber, M. A. "Black-Korean Who-Pushed-Whom Festers." *New York Times*, May 7, 1990.

Feagin, Joe R. *Racist America: Roots, Current Realities, and Future Reparations*. New York: Routledge, 2000.

———. *White Party, White Government: Race, Class, and U.S. Politics*. New York: Routledge, 2012.

Feagin, Joe R., and Aaron Porter. "Affirmative Action and African Americans: Rhetoric and Practice." *Humboldt Journal of Social Relations* 21, no. 2 (1995): 81–103.

Ferguson, Thomas, and Joel Rogers. *Right Turn: The Decline of the Democrats and the Future of American Politics*. New York. Hill and Wang, 1986.

Fiorentino, Jen. "Twenty-Three Years after a Notorious Murder, the Convicted Killer Speaks." *Brooklyn Ink*, December 10, 2012. Available at http://thebrooklynink.com/2012/12/10/50766-convicted-killer-writes-to-reporter.

Foderaro, Lisa W. "Angered by Attack, Trump Urges Return of the Death Penalty." *New York Times*, May 1, 1989.

Garfield, Gail. *Knowing What We Know: African American Women's Experiences of Violence and Violation*. New Brunswick, NJ: Rutgers University Press, 2005.

———. *Through Our Eyes: African American Men's Experiences of Race, Gender, and Violence*. New Brunswick, NJ: Rutgers University Press, 2010.

Georgia Literacy Test, 1958. Available at http://cdm.georgiaarchives.org:2011/cdm/compoundobject/collection/adhoc/id/552/rec/4.

Georgia State Constitution of 1868. Article VI (educational provision). Available at http://georgiainfo.galileo.usg.edu/con1868.htm.

Girgenti, Richard H. *A Report to the Governor on the Disturbances in Crown Heights*. Vol. 1, *An Assessment of the City's Preparedness and Response to Civil Disorder*. Albany: New York State Division of Criminal Justice Services, 1993.

Glaberson, William. "The Crown Heights Report: Covering the Unrest; Press Had Blind Spots, Too." *New York Times*, July 22, 1993.

Goldman, April. "Other Korean Grocers Give to Those in Brooklyn Boycott." *New York Times*, May 14, 1990.

Goldman, John J., and Karen Tumulty. "Dinkins Tries to Break Black Boycott of Korean Stores: Race; New York Mayor Shops at Market to Show Support for Owners; Tensions Remain High Eight Months after Incident with Customer." *Los Angeles Times*, September 22, 1990.

Goldschmidt, Henry. *Race and Religion among the Chosen People of Crown Heights*. New Brunswick, NJ: Rutgers University Press, 2006.

Gotsch, Kara. "After the War on Drugs: Fair Sentencing Act and the Unfinished Drug Policy Reform Agenda." Issue brief, American Constitution Society for Law and Policy, December 2011.

Gray v. Sanders. 372 U.S. 368. 1963. Available at http://supreme.justia.com/cases/federal/us/372/368/case.html.

Gregory, Steven, and Roger Sanjek, eds. *Race*. New Brunswick, NJ: Rutgers University Press, 1996.

Guinier, Lani. *The Tyranny of the Majority: Fundamental Fairness in Representative Democracy*. New York: Free Press, 1994.

Guinier, Lani, and Gerald Torres. *The Miner's Canary: Enlisting Race, Resisting Power, Transforming Democracy*. Cambridge, MA: Harvard University Press, 2002.

Habermas, Jürgen. *Legitimation Crisis*. Boston: Beacon, 1973.

Hartmann, Douglass, and Joseph Gerteis. "Dealing with Diversity: Mapping Multiculturalism in Sociological Terms." *Sociological Theory* 23, no. 2 (2005): 218–40.

Hevesi, Dennis. "Black Protesters March in Brooklyn Communities." *New York Times*, May 13, 1990.

Higginbotham, A. Leon, Jr. "An Open Letter to Justice Clarence Thomas from a Federal Judicial Colleague." In *Race-ing Justice, En-gendering Power*, edited by Toni Morrison, 17–28. New York: Pantheon, 1992.

———. *In the Matter of Color: Race and the American Legal Process: The Colonial Period*. New York: Oxford University Press, 1978.

Higginbotham, Elizabeth. *Too Much to Ask: Black Women in the Era of Integration*. Chapel Hill: The University of North Carolina Press, 2001.

Honneth, Axel. *The Fragmented World of the Social: Essays in Social and Political Philosophy*. Edited by Charles W. Wright. New York: State University of New York Press, 1995.

hooks, bell. "Feminism and Black Women's Studies." *Sage: A Scholarly Journal on Black Women* 6, no. 1 (Summer 1989): 54–56.

Howard, Philip S. S. "Turning Out the Center: Racial Politics and African Agency in the Obama Era." *Journal of Black Studies* 40, no. 3 (January 2010): 380–94.

Howe, Robert J. "Fast over Thin Ice: Hate's in Season, and It's a Bumper Crop." *Pulphouse Magazine*, June 1992. Available at http://www.rjhowe.net/fast_hate.html.

Human Rights Watch. "United States: Stark Race Disparities in Drug Incarceration." June 8, 2000. Available at http://www.hrw.org/news/2000/06/07/united-states-stark-race-disparities-drug-incarceration.

Humphrey, Hubert H. "Speech on Civil Rights," Philadephia, PA, July 14, 1948. Transcript and Adobe Flash audio. 10:00. Minnesota Historical Society. Available at http://www.mnhs.org/library/tips/history_topics/42humphreyspeech/transcript.htm.

Hurston, Zora Neale. Letter to Charlotte Osgood Mason, November 25, 1930. In *Zora Neale Hurston: A Life in Letters*, edited by Carla Kaplan. New York: Anchor, 2003.

James, George. "Police Dept. Report Assails Officers in New York Rally." *New York Times*, September 29, 1992.

Jeffries, Michael P. *Paint the White House Black: Barack Obama and the Meaning of Race in America*. Stanford, CA: Stanford University Press, 2013.

Jensen, Richard. "The Culture Wars, 1965–1995: A Historian's Map." *Journal of Social History* 29 (1995): 17–37.

Jordan, Barbara. Keynote address, 1976 Democratic National Convention, New York, July 12, 1976. Available at http://www.americanrhetoric.com/speeches/barbarajordan1976dnc.html.

Kaelber, Lutz. "Eugenics: Compulsory Sterilization in 50 American States." Presentation at the Thirty-Seventh Annual Meeting of the Social Science History Association meeting, Vancouver, BC, November 12, 2012. Available at http://www.uvm.edu/~lkaelber/eugenics/MN/MN.html.

Kaufman, Ned. "Heritage and the Cultural Politics of Preservation: Speaking of Places." *Places* 11, no. 3 (1998): 1–8. Available at *eScholarship*, University of California, http://escholarship.org/uc/item/57j0g7jq.

Kennedy, John F. Address on civil rights. June 11, 1963. Transcript available at http://www.pbs.org/wgbh/americanexperience/features/primary-resources/jfk-civilrights.

Kennedy, Randall. *The Persistence of the Color Line: Racial Politics and the Obama Presidency*. New York: Pantheon, 2011.

Kerr, Peter. "War on Drugs Shifting Focus to Street Deals." *New York Times*, April 13, 1987.

Kim, Claire Jean. "'No Justice, No Peace!': The Politics of Black-Korean Conflict." *Trotter Review* 7, no. 2 (1993): 12–13.

King, Martin Luther, Jr. *Stride toward Freedom: The Montgomery Story.* New York: Harper and Brothers, 1958.

Klatch, Rebecca. "Coalition and Conflict among Women of the New Right." *Signs* 13, no. 4 (Summer 1988): 671–94.

Kluger, Richard. *Simple Justice: The History of* Brown v. Board of Education *and Black America's Struggle for Equality.* New York: Vintage, 1975.

Kolbert, Elizabeth. "Two Views on Dinkins: Conciliator or Hesitater?" *New York Times,* August 14, 1989.

Koven, Steven G. "Fighting the Drug Wars: Rhetoric and Reality." *Public Administration Review* 49, no. 6 (1989): 580–83.

Langan, Patrick A. "Race of Prisoners Admitted to State and Federal Institutions, 1926–86." Report NCJ-125618. US Department of Justice Office of Justice Programs Bureau of Justice Statistics, May 1991.

Lassiter v. Northampton County Board of Elections. 360 U.S. 45. 1959. Available at http://supreme.justia.com/cases/federal/us/360/45/case.html.

Lawrence, Charles R., III. "The Id, the Ego, and Equal Protection: Reckoning with Unconscious Racism." *Stanford Law Review* 39, no. 317 (January 1987): 317–88.

Leighton, Jared E. "A Small Revolution: The Role of a Black Power Revolt in Creating and Sustaining a Black Studies Department at the University of Minnesota." Master's thesis, University of Nebraska, Lincoln, 2008. http://digitalcommons.unl.edu/historydiss/49.

Levi, Primo. 2004. "The Gray Zone." In *Violence in War and Peace: An Anthology,* edited by Nancy Scheper-Hughes and Philippe I. Bourgois, 83–90. Malden, MA: Blackwell.

Lewis, Anthony. "The Legality of Racial Quotas." *New York Times,* March 3, 1974.

Lindaman, Kara, and Donald P. Haider-Markel. "Issue Evolution, Political Parties, and Culture Wars." *Political Research Quarterly* 55, no. 1 (March 2002): 91–110.

Liptak, Adam. "Supreme Court Invalidates Key Part of Voting Rights Act." *New York Times,* June 25, 2013.

Manegold, Catherine S. "Rally Puts Police under New Scrutiny." *New York Times,* September 27, 1992.

Marable, Manning. *Black Leadership.* New York: Columbia University Press, 1998.

Martin, Douglas. "A Village Dies, a Park Is Born." *New York Times,* January 21, 1997.

Martin, Frank. D., III. "Race Relations in Thomasville a Two-Way Street." *Thomasville Times-Enterprise,* August 9, 1968.

Mauer, Marc, and Ryan S. King. "A 25-Year Quagmire: The War on Drugs and Its Impact on American Society." Report, Sentencing Project, September 2007.

Maykuth, Andrew. "New York Boycott Settles in for the Long Haul." *Philadelphia Inquirer,* September 30, 1990.

McAleer, Scott. "A Study of Racial Violence in Thomas County, Georgia, 1930." *Georgia Historical Quarterly* 87, no. 1 (Spring 2003): 48–87.

McChesney, Ralph. "Dual Superintendency Tied in Early Local Schools." *Thomasville Times-Enterprise,* August 25, 1965.

———. "Little Is Known of Early Education System in Thomas County." *Thomasville Times-Enterprise,* August 18, 1965.

McDonald, Laughlin. *A Voting Rights Odyssey: Black Enfranchisement in Georgia.* Cambridge: Cambridge University Press, 2003.

McFadden, Robert D. "Edward I. Koch, a Mayor as Brash, Shrewd and Colorful as the City He Led, Dies at 88." *New York Times,* February 1, 2013.

Meagher, Richard J. "Remembering the New Right: Political Strategy and the Building of the GOP Coalition," *Public Eye,* Summer 2009.

Menand, Louis. "The Color of Law." *New Yorker,* July 8, 2013.

Metzler, Christopher. "Barack Obama's Faustian Bargain and the Fight for America's Racial Soul." *Journal of Black Studies* 40, no. 3 (January 2010): 395–410.

Minor, James T. "Segregation Residual in Higher Education: A Tale of Two States." *American Educational Research Journal* 45, no. 4 (December 2008): 861–85.

Mitchell, Katharyn. "Educating the National Citizen in Neoliberal Times: From the Multicultural Self to the Strategic Cosmopolitan." *Transactions of the Institute of British Geographers*, n.s., 28, no 4 (2003): 387–403.

Morris, Aldon D. *Origins of the Civil Rights Movement*. New York: Simon and Schuster, 1986.

Morrison, Toni, ed. *Race-ing Justice, En-gendering Power: Essays on Anita Hill, Clarence Thomas, and the Construction of Social Reality*. New York: Pantheon, 1992.

Myrdal, Gunnar. *An American Dilemma: The Negro Problem and Modern Democracy*. New York: Harper and Brothers, 1944.

Nelson, Janai S. "Defining Race: The Obama Phenomenon and the Voting Rights Act," *Albany Law Review* 72, no. 4 (2009): 899–907.

Nelson, William E., Jr. "Black Mayors as Urban Managers." *Annals of the American Academy of Political and Social Science* 439 (1978): 53–67.

New York Times. "Bus Riders Press to North Florida; Meet Little Trouble as They Also Test South Georgia." June 16, 1961.

———. "Ms. Messinger's Obstructionism." August 10, 1990.

———. "President Obama's Anguish." July 19, 2013.

Northcross v. Board of Education of Memphis. 333 F.2d 661. 6th Cir. 1964.

Nunn, Kenneth B. "Race, Crime and the Pool of Surplus Criminality: Or Why the 'War on Drugs' Was a 'War on Blacks.'" *Gender, Race, and Justice* 6, no. 2 (Fall 2002): 381–445.

Obama, Barack. *The Audacity of Hope: Thoughts on Reclaiming the American Dream*. New York: Three Rivers Press, 2006.

———. *Dreams from My Father: A Story of Race and Inheritance*. New York: Broadway, 2004.

———. Keynote address, 2004 Democratic National Convention. Boston, MA, July 27, 2004. Available at http://www.americanrhetoric.com/speeches/convention2004/barackobama2004dnc.htm.

———. "We the people, in order to form a more perfect union" speech. Philadelphia, PA, March 18, 2008. Transcript available at *Politico*, http://www.politico.com/news/stories/0308/9100.html.

Olson, Joel. "Whiteness and the Polarization of American Politics." *Political Research Quarterly* 61, no. 4 (December 2008): 704–18.

Omi, Michael, and Howard Winant. *Racial Formation in the United States: From the 1960s to the 1990s*. 2nd ed. New York: Routledge, 1994.

Oreskes, Michael. "Lee Atwater, Master of Tactics for Bush and G.O.P, Dies at 40." *New York Times*, March 30, 1991.

Orlans, Harold. "Affirmative Action in Higher Education." Special issue "Affirmative Action Revisited." *Annals of the American Academy of Political and Social Science* 523 (September 1992): 144–58.

Patterson, Orlando. *The Ordeal of Integration: Progress and Resentment in America's Racial Crisis*. Washington, DC: Civitas Counterpoint, 1997.

Paulk, Harold. "Eugene Talmadge: 1884–1946." *New Georgia Encyclopedia*, August 25, 2004. http://www.georgiaencyclopedia.org/articles/government-politics/eugene-talmadge-1884-1946.

Perkinson, Robert. "American Race Relations in the Age of Obama." Unpublished paper presented at Ewha BK International Conference, Seoul, Korea, November 19, 2008.

Perlstein, Rick. "America's Forgotten Liberal," *New York Times*, May 26, 2011.

———. "Exclusive: Lee Atwater's Infamous 1981 Interview on the Southern Strategy." *Nation*, November 13, 2012.

Pettit, Backy, and Bruce Western. "Mass Imprisonment and the Life Course: Race and Class Inequality in U.S. Incarceration." *American Sociological Review* 69, no. 2 (2004): 151–69.

Pew Research Social and Demographic Trends. "Social and Demographic Trends: King's Dream Remains an Elusive Goal; Many Americans see Racial Disparities." August 22, 2013. Available at http://www.pewsocialtrends.org/2013/08/22/kings-dream-remains-an-elusive-goal-many-americans-see-racial-disparities.

Rev. Pharr to AMA Officials. Undated letter (five pages). American Missionary Association archives, Amistad Research Center at Tulane University, New Orleans, LA.

Pierson, Betty G. "Negroes Plan March Here; Ask Better Job Chances." *Thomasville Times-Enterprise*, April 29, 1965.

Pieterse, Jan Nederveen. *White on Black: Images of Africa and Blacks in Western Popular Culture*. New Haven, CT: Yale University Press, 1992.

Pilkington, Ed. "Harlem Takes on University in Battle of Town versus Gown: Residents Object to Plans to Turn Black Neighborhood into 'Manhattanville.'" *Guardian*, November 19, 2007.

Plessy v. Ferguson. 163 U.S. 537. 1886. Available at http://www.law.cornell.edu/supremecourt/text/163/537.

Powell, Michael. "In a Volatile City, a Stern Line on Race and Politics." *New York Times*, July 22, 2007.

Raab, Selwyn. "State Judge Dismisses Indictment of Officer in the Bumpurs Killing." *New York Times*, October 29, 1984.

Records of the Field Offices for the State of Georgia, M1903, Bureau of Refugees, Freedmen, and Abandoned, 1865–1872. United States Congress and National Archives and Records Administration, Washington, DC.

Regents of the University of California v. Alan Bakke. 438 U.S. 265. 1978. Available at http://www.law.cornell.edu/supremecourt/text/438/265.

Rich, Wilbur C. *David Dinkins and New York City Politics: Race, Images, and the Media*. New York: State University of New York Press, 2007.

Richie, Beth. *Arrested Justice: Black Women Violence and America's Prison Nation*. New York: New York University Press, 2012.

Rieder, Jonathan. "Trouble in Store." *New Republic*, July 2, 1990. Available at http://thebrooklynink.com/2012/12/10/50766-convicted-killer-writes-to-reporter.

Roberts, Sam. "Park Rampage and Mayor Race: Fear and Politics." *New York Times*, May 1, 1989.

Robinson, Eugene. *Disintegration: The Splintering of Black America*. New York: Anchor, 2010.

Rolison, Garry L., Kristin A. Bates, Mary Jo Poole, and Michelle Jacob. "Prisoners of War: Black Female Incarceration at the End of the 1980s." *Social Justice* 29, no. 1/2 (2002): 131–43.

Rosenthal, Andrew. "Lee Atwater's Southern Strategy Interview." *New York Times*, November 14, 2012.

Sacks, Karen Brodkin. "How Did Jews Become White Folks?" In *Race*, edited by Steven Gregory and Roger Sanjek, 78–97. New Brunswick, NJ: Rutgers University Press, 1996.

Sanderson, Linda. "Each University Department to Adopt Affirmative Action Plan." *Minnesota Daily*, March 4, 1996.

Shay, Alison. "Remembering the Albany Movement." November 17, 2012. Available at *Publishing the Long Civil Rights Movement*, https://lcrm.lib.unc.edu/blog/index.php/2012/11/17/remembering-the-albany-movement.

Shelby County, Alabama v. Holder, Attorney General et al. 557 US 193. 2013. Available at http://www.law.cornell.edu/supremecourt/text/12-96.

Sklansky, David A. "Cocaine, Race, and Equal Protection." *Stanford Law Review* 47, no. 6 (July 1995): 1283–1322.

Smith, Chris. "Central Park Revisited." *New York Magazine*, October 21, 2002. Available at http://nymag.com/nymetro/news/crimelaw/features/n_7836.

Smithers, Gregory D. "Barack Obama and Race in the United States: A History of the Future." *Australasian Journal of American Studies* 28, no. 1 (July 2009): 1–16.

Steinberg, Stephen. *Turning Back: The Retreat from Racial Justice in American Thought and Policy*. Boston: Beacon, 1995.

Stevenson, Bryan. "Drug Policy, Criminal Justice and Mass Imprisonment." Working Paper, Global Commission on Drug Policies, Rio de Janeiro, Brazil, January 2011.

Sundquist, Christian. "On Race Theory and Norms," *Albany Law Review* 72, no. 4 (2009): 953–60.

Tanenhaus, Sam. "The Original Sin: Why the GOP Is and Will Continue to Be the Party of White People." *New Republic*, February 10, 2013. Available at http://www.newrepublic.com/article/112365/why-republicans-are-party-white-people.

Taylor, David Vassar. *African Americans in Minnesota.* The People of Minnesota. St. Paul: Minnesota Historical Society Press, 2002.

Thomas, R. Roosevelt, Jr. "Affirmative Action: From the Perspective of Diversity." *Phylon* 49, no. 3/4 (Autumn–Winter2001): 99–136.

Thomasville Branch of NAACP v. Thomas City, Georgia. 571 F.2d 257. 1968.

Thomasville Times-Enterprise. "9,212 Voters Eligible for Voting in Primary." July 21, 1960.

———. "Time for the South to Think." September 7, 1960.

———. "School Control at Stake." September 14, 1960.

———. "Worth Remembering." October 29, 1960.

———. "Integration Controversy." January 11, 1961.

———. "History Repeating Itself." January 18, 1961.

———. "King on Law Violations." February 17, 1961.

———. "Georgians Not Yet Ready to Quit Segregation Fight." April 26, 1961.

———. "The Desegregation Drive." May 10, 1961.

———. "White Freedom Riders." May 27, 1961.

———. "Is Segregation Immoral?" June 6, 1961.

———. "Freedom Riders Start Three-Pronged Attack: One Group Heads for Tallahassee." June 14, 1961.

———. "Negro Demonstration Jails 156 in Albany." December 13, 1961.

———. "Albany to Try 735 Negroes, with King First on Docket." February 6, 1962.

———. "Ignorant and Uninformed." February 8, 1962.

———. "Albany Postpones 735 Negroes Trials." February 20, 1962.

———. "Register Now for Voting." February 27, 1962.

———. "Negro News Notes." March 9, 1962.

———. "Why Not 2 States in Ga.?" April 9, 1962.

———. "Albany Negro Action Halted: Court Order Bars Pickets, Mass Marching." July 21, 1962.

———. "Sanders on King; Griffin on Foes." July 26, 1962.

———. "Albany Impasse Cited by Kelly." August 2, 1962.

———. "The South Is under Attack." August 3, 1962.

———. "A Discriminating World." June 29, 1963.

———. "The Klan Plans Action." July 12, 1963.

———. "Whites May Demonstrate." August 28, 1963.

———. "An Inconsistency." November 2, 1963.

———. "JFK, Warm Human Man." November 23, 1963.

———. "Can There Be Unity?" November 30, 1963.

———. "Steam-Roller Rolling." February 6, 1964.

———. "The Civil Rights Act of '64, What It Means to You." March 19, 1964.

———. "125 Thomasville Students Become Registered Voters." April 20, 1964.

———. "Pastor Here Sails into Rights Bill." June 17, 1964.

———. "Future Impact of Harsh Rights Bill Impossible to Foretell." July 2, 1964.

———. Public announcement, "New Law & Your City." July 2, 1964.

———. "Action and Reaction." July 14, 1964.

———. "Integrated Voting Here." September 12, 1964.

———. "Race Mixing in Schools." January 11, 1965.

———. "Moultrie Bare School Mix Plans." February 5, 1965.

———. "Negro Students Stage March on School Office at Moultrie." February 8, 1965.

———. "Negro Students Arrested after Protest March." February 8, 1965.

———. "Moultrie Listens to Negro Gripes." February 10, 1965.

———. "100 More Negroes Seized at Moultrie." February 17, 1965.

———. "Hearing Slated in Thomasville for February 25th." February 18, 1965.

———. "Court Here Asked to Shut Negro School at Moultrie." February 25, 1965.

———. "Flaming Liquid Is Tossed into Two Buildings." March 3, 1965.

————. "Negro Plan March Here; Ask Better Job Chances." April 29, 1965.

————. "Walk Will Be Quiet, Negro Minister Vows." May 13, 1965.

————. "Desegregation Set for All Grades Here." May 13, 1965.

————. "With Dignity." May 17, 1965.

————. "School Desegregation." May 20, 1965.

————. "Thomasville's Desegregation Plan Approved." June 4, 1965.

————. "Negro Doing Good Job Here as Policemen, Stegall Reports." June 4, 1965.

————. "88 Negroes Ask Admission to 6 White Schools Here." June 9, 1965.

————. "Negroes Here to Attend Albany Rally." August 12, 1965.

————. "Stop Segregating Vote, Local Realtor Requests." August 17, 1965.

————. "Little Is Known of Early Education System in Thomas County." August 18, 1965.

————. "McDaniel Won Confidence of All." August 23, 1965.

————. "First Day Goes Smoothly as City Schools Reopen." August 30, 1965.

————. "Two Negroes Enter Race for City, School Posts." November 2, 1965.

————. Political ad. November 24, 1965.

————. "Early City Vote Unusually Heavy." December 7, 1965.

————. "Why So Many 'Voids' in Tuesday's Vote?" December 8, 1965.

————. "Court Action Needed Now, Lawyer Says." April 1, 1966.

————. "Board of Education for the City of Thomasville, Georgia, Notice of School Desegregation Plan under Title VI of the Civil Rights Act of 1964." April 1, 1966.

————. "Will Thomasville City Schools Remain First Class?" March 27, 1967.

————. "Notice of School Desegregation Plan." March 29, 1967.

————. "Time to Be Concerned." August 14, 1967.

————. "Back to School For 4,000 Here." August 28, 1967.

————. "School Problems Still Vexing and Perplexing." December 20, 1967.

————. "HEW Pushes Area Schools for Desegregation Step-Up." March 12, 1968.

————. "A Tribute to Dr. King." April 5, 1968.

————. "Get Guns and Retaliate, Carmichael Urges Negroes." April 5, 1968.

————. "Hundreds Attend Service Honoring Dr. King Here." April 8, 1968.

————. "School Plan to Merge Thomasville and Douglass." October 1, 1968.

————. "School and Urban Renewal Projects Need Close Study." October 8, 1968.

————. "School Supt. Speaks to Rotary Club on Proposed New High School." November 22, 1968.

————. "Tentative Date Set for Referendum on School Issue." December 11, 1968.

————. "Must 'Mix or Abandon' School Says Court." December 18, 1968.

————. "New School Building Complex Poses Problems." December 20, 1968.

————. "Vote Your Opinion on School Finance Plan." March 5, 1969.

————. "Conversation Centers on How to Finance New School." March 7, 1969.

————. "School Problems Endless." March 14, 1969.

————. "Calling a Spade a Spade." March 20, 1969.

————. "McDaniel Outlines Problems." June 14, 1969.

————. "Initial Planning Underway for New High School Here." July 2, 1969.

————. "9,100 Students Return to Classrooms Here." August 29, 1969.

————. "School Planning Session 'Charrette' Scheduled for Local Citizens." September 22, 1969.

————. "Charrette Begins Here on Monday." September 27, 1969.

————. "Turnout Large for Charrette." September 30, 1969.

————. "Charrette Is a Misnomer to Many." October 4, 1969.

————. "Site Selected for New School." October 28, 1969.

————. "Supreme Court Order Immediate Desegregation." October 30, 1969.

————. "Selecting School Site Not the Only Problem." October 30, 1969.

————. "Some Don't Want to Sell." November 14, 1969.

————. "Homeowners Opposing Selected Site for School." November 14, 1969.

————. "Thomasville School Board Confused by HEW Letter." November 25, 1969.

————. "Group of Citizens Challenge Plan for New High School." November 25, 1969.

———. "School Desegregation Problem Dumped on State: Court Orders Georgia to Enforce HEW Rules." December 18, 1969.

———. "This Matter of Education." December 22, 1969.

———. "Wilson Urges Schools to Meet Tough Ruling." December 27, 1969.

———. "School Board Okays Plan to Eliminate Dual System." December 27, 1969.

———. "Board Reveals Action." January 15, 1970.

———. "When Immovable Object Meets Irresistible Force." January 16, 1970.

———. "Integration Date Moved Up Here." January 28, 1970.

———. "A Time of Controversy and General Frustration." January 28, 1970.

———. "Who Is Running the Desegregation Program?" January 29, 1970.

———. "Nixon, Hot and Cold on Integration, Busing." February 14, 1970.

———. "City Headed for School Showdown: 3 Bound for Washington for Showdown with HEW." February 24, 1970.

———. "Board Reveals Action: Freedom of Choice Plan Approved by School Board." March 2, 1970.

———. "The School Situation Here." March 3, 1970.

———. "2 Top School Administrators Leaving." March 11, 1970.

———. "Teachers Plan Firm Discipline with Human Touch." March 19, 1970.

———. "Public School Education Not at the Cross-Roads." March 24, 1970.

———. "Nixon Outlines Views on School Desegregation." March 26, 1970.

———. "New THS Principal Issues Stiff Warning." April 3, 1970.

———. "$582,300 Grant for New High School Site." June 30, 1970.

———. "Integrated Schools Begin Classes Here: Opening Day Goes Smoothly Principals Say." August 31, 1970.

———. "Black Students Hold THS Walkout, List Demands." September 15, 1970.

———. "An Editorial." September 17, 1970.

———. Letters to the editor. September 19, 1970–September 26, 1970.

———. "Student Discipline Probed Here." December 3, 1970.

———. "Save Our Public School and End Racial Strife." December 5, 1970.

———. "HEW Charges City with Non-compliance." December 9, 1970.

———. "HEW Demands Labeled Unreasonable by Wilson." December 9, 1970.

———. "City Administrators, Teachers to Tell Other-Side." January 7, 1971.

———. "Discipline Problem Cited." March 6, 1971.

———. "School Problems the Big Worry." March 17, 1971.

Thurber, Timothy N. *The Politics of Equality: Hubert H. Humphrey and the African American Freedom Struggle.* New York: Columbia University Press, 1999.

United States Census Bureau. "Projections Show a Slower Growing, Old, More Diverse Nation a Half Century from Now." News release CB12-243, December 12, 2012. https://www.census.gov/newsroom/releases/archives/population/cb12-243.html.

United States Commission on Civil Rights. *Federal Rights under School Desegregation Law.* Washington, DC: Commission on Civil Rights Clearinghouse, June 1966.

———. *Survey of School Desegregation in the Southern and Border States 1965–1966.* Washington, DC: Government Printing Office, 1966.

University of Minnesota, Humphrey School of Public Affairs. "Wit and Wisdom of Hubert H. Humphrey." http://www.hhh.umn.edu/about/HHHquotes.html.

Voting Rights Act of 1965. Pub. L. No. 89-110, 79 Stat. 437 (1965). Available at http://library.clerk.house.gov/reference-files/PPL_VotingRightsAct_1965.pdf.

Wall, Diana diZerega, Nan A. Rothschild, and Cynthia Copeland. "Seneca Village and Little Africa: Two African American Communities in Antebellum New York City." *Historical Archaeology* 42, no. 1 (2008): 97–107.

Watkins, Beverly Xaviera, Robert E. Fullilove, and Mindy Thompson Fullilove. "Arms against Illness: Crack Cocaine and Drug Policy in the United States." *Health and Human Rights* 2, no. 4 (1998): 42–58.

Wellington, Darryl Lorenzo. "Barack Obama in the Public Imagination," *Dissent* 55, no. 4 (Fall 2008): 27–33.

West, Cornel. "Black Leadership and the Pitfalls of Racial Reasoning." In *Race-ing Justice, En-gendering Power: Essays on Anita Hill, Clarence Thomas, and the Construction of Social Reality*, edited by Toni Morrison (New York: Pantheon, 1992), 391—92.

———. *Democracy Matters: Winning the Fight against Imperialism*. New York:Penguin, 2005.

WGBH/PBS. "The Election of 1976." *The American Experience*. Available at http://www.pbs.org/wgbh/americanexperience/features/general-article/carter-election1976.

White, John Kenneth. Review of Caroline Arden, *Getting the Donkey out of the Ditch: The Democratic Party in Search of Itself*. *Polity* 21, no. 3 (Spring 1989): 619–29.

Wilkerson, Isabel. *The Warmth of Other Suns: The Epic Story of America's Great Migration*. New York: Random House, 2010.

Wingfield, Adia Harvey, and Joe R. Feagin. *Yes We Can? White Racial Framing and the Obama Presidency*. New York: Routledge, 2013.

Wise, Tim. 1998. "Is Sisterhood Conditional? White Women and the Rollback of Affirmative Action." *National Women's Studies Association Journal* 10, no. 3 (1998): 1–26.

Woods, Barbara A. "Affirmative Action and Today's Black Woman Historian." *National Women's Studies Association Journal* 10, no. 3 (Autumn 1998): 160–67.

Young, Andrew. *An Easy Burden: The Civil Rights Movement and the Transformation of America*. New York: Harper Collins, 1996.

———. Interview by Jack Bass and Watter Devries, January 31, 1974. Interview A-0080. Southern Oral History Program Collection 4007. http://docsouth.unc.edu/sohp/playback.html?base_file=A-0080.

Zinn, Howard. *The Radical Sixties*. Vol. 2, *The Southern Mystique*. Cambridge, MA: South End, 1964.

INDEX